EPIC WIN
FOR ANONYMOUS:
HOW 4CHAN'S ARMY
CONQUERED THE WEB

EPIC WIN FOR ANONYMOUS:

HOW 4CHAN'S ARMY
CONQUERED THE WEB

COLE STRYKER

OVERLOOK DUCKWORTH
New York • London

This edition first published in hardcover in the United States
and the United Kingdom in 2011 by Overlook Duckworth

NEW YORK:
The Overlook Press
Peter Mayer Publishers, Inc.
141 Wooster Street
New York, NY 10012
www.overlookpress.com
For bulk and special sales, please contact sales@overlookny.com

LONDON:
Gerald Duckworth Publishers Ltd.
90-93 Cowcross Street
London EC1M 6BF
www.ducknet.co.uk
info@duckworth-publishers.co.uk

Cataloging-in-Publication Data is available from the Library of Congress

Typeset by Jackson Typesetting Co.
Manufactured in the United States of America

FIRST EDITION

10 9 8 7 6 5 4 3 2 1

ISBN 978-1-59020-710-9 (US)
ISBN 978-0-7156-4283-2 (UK)

For Charles and Janet Stryker, who once told me, "You're not going to get very far in this world without knowing how to work a computer," and then gave me one.

Contents

Contents

EPIC WIN

Introduction

THIS IS THE story of the most interesting place on the Internet: an imageboard called 4chan, where you're as likely to find a hundred photos of adorable kittens as a gallery of gruesome autopsy photos.

It's a seedy, unpredictable place, where people have complete freedom to experiment; to try on new ideas, alternate identities. 4chan allows its users to say and do almost whatever they can think of without fear of shame or retribution.

There are many individual boards that make up 4chan, and the strangest one is called */b/*, or *Random*. This is the "hivemind" of the site, where nearly anything the human mind is capable of conceiving is on display, for better or for worse. Some have called it the Asshole of the Internet, but a few million call it home.

/b/ is particularly special because the board has almost no rules. However, its nameless users, who call themselves */b/tards*, have created a semiserious list of metarules, the first and second of which are cribbed directly from Chuck Palahniuk's book *Fight Club*:

Rule 1: You do not talk about /b/.
Rule 2: You DO NOT talk about /b/.

The stated intent of these rules is to keep outsiders out. Longtime /b/tards detest new users more than anything, referring to them as "cancer" and go to great lengths to make their dialogue and community culture as unapproachable as possible. In writing this book, I've committed the most egregious violation of these rules in the short history of /b/, opening myself up to everything from prank calls to death threats. I'm no longer just another member of *"anonymous"*—the vast group of 4chan users.

When I first started telling friends about the project, they'd universally respond:

"You're writing a book about 4chan? Ha! Good luck with *that!*"

OK, so we've established that 4chan is, to borrow a phrase from a well-known Jedi, a hive of scum and villainy. It's a playground for weirdos, but why does it matter? I've talked to everyone from academics and advertisers to hackers in order to find out. I got my hands dirty talking with the /b/tards themselves, along with the people they love and those they love to hate. I approached 4chan not just as an observer, but as a participant, an antagonist, and an ombudsman.

I discovered that 4chan is a mysterious, misunderstood imageboard defined by anonymity and anarchy that influences the way you behave on the web, whether you realize it or not.

Introduction

It stands in contrast to a web that seems to be moving inexorably toward personal responsibility and a constant identity across all platforms that define the browsing experience. I can't read a movie review online anymore without seeing my friends' Facebook commentary alongside it. And somehow Google knows that I'm really attracted to Nicki Minaj. On proprietary platforms like Facebook, one's every move is documented. Some argue that this social accountability keeps us responsible. Others say it's another way to sell products. Either way, it's becoming more like real-life.

But didn't the Internet promise us an escape from real life? Wasn't that one of the reasons so many of us were drawn to it in the first place? 4chan is one of the few places that encourages the anarchy found in the early days of the web.

And while 4chan is known for hosting everything from innocuous cat photos to child pornography, it's also a place where would-be activists can gather to express social dissent. It's a forum where a lonely nerd can ask for help meeting girls. And where a closeted homosexual can vent about his abusive, homophobic parents.

The fear-mongering mainstream media tends to portray 4chan as a breeding ground for sociopathic superhackers and cyberterrorists. This is the case, yes, but it's a small part of the story. I wrote this book because I wanted to set the record straight. Namelessness matters. Freedom matters. And 4chan embodies those two ideals more concretely than anyplace else on the Internet.

If you've ever wondered, while browsing the web, "Why is this weird thing popular? Who cares about this stuff? How does this thing have so many views? Why do people waste their time

13

with this? Where did it come from and where is it all going?" then read on.

This isn't so much a book about how technology is changing society as it is the story of how technology expanded the scale of human creativity and social interaction that already existed and was just waiting for the right platform. When that platform came along, creative participatory culture went global—and just like that things were never the same. This isn't just a book about 4chan. It's a book about you.

4chan is a multimedia experience, and there's only so much information that can be conveyed on the printed page. I highly encourage the reader to read this book near a computer so you can look up pertinent information as you go. If you're having trouble wrapping your head around a specific concept, online resources like Google, Wikipedia and Know Your Meme will help fill in the blanks.

A final warning:

Because 4chan thrives on its lack of rules, it hosts content that ranges from harmless to downright terrifying. Violent fetish pornography, racist/sexist rants, and gory photography are just a few of the more unsettling items that litter the pages of /b/.

Dear reader, under no circumstances should you see this book as an invitation to hop onto 4chan to see what all the fuss is about. If you must, at least prepare by reading my third chapter so you'll know exactly what you're getting into. There are ways to browse 4chan while avoiding most of the nasty bits, and you should be aware of them.

Seriously. There are some things you can't unsee.

Chapter 1

Memes: Shared Nuggets of Cultural Currency

"**D**UDE, YOU'VE GOTTA see this."

The sound of machine gun fire filled my freshman dorm. Walking down the hallway, I'd hear the explosion of grenades and machine gun spray muffling anguished shrieks of the dying. This went on literally all day and night. It was 2002, and the bros on my hall were taking full advantage of our campus's T1 Internet connection by playing a run-and-gun PC shooter game called *Counter-Strike* till dawn.

For many of us, it was our first exposure to high-speed Internet. Previously we had to share 56k connections with siblings. It would take minutes to download a basic webpage. I remember setting up a string of downloads before bed each night and letting my computer run till morning. If AOL deigned to not kick me off the connection, I'd have four or five new songs in the morning. In college, I could accomplish the same in minutes. Webpages with streaming video loaded instantaneously. For the first time, the Internet moved as fast as my imagination. The guys on my hall spent most of their days taking advantage of this garden of earthly delights in hundreds of ways, some more illicit than others.

I vividly remember some gawky kid running into my room, doubled over in laughter.

"Dude, you've gotta see this."

"What?"

"I can't explain. Just google 'gonads and strife.'"

I heard the pinging of instant messages being sent back and forth throughout the hall. Laughter bubbled up all around me. And the sound of a chipmunk-like voice filled the air.

"Gonads and Strife" was a crude Flash animation that featured a monkey in a suit, a hyperactive squirrel, Stephen Hawking, R2-D2, and a spinning anatomic figure of a penis soaring through a lightning-filled sky. It was profane, catchy, and defied explanation. It spread through campus like wildfire. Like a virus, actually.

I can't explain why Gonads and Strife is funny. You pretty much had to have been male college freshman to appreciate it. For a moment there, before YouTube and the rise of user-driven content aggregators like Digg and Reddit, intensely creative folks uploaded their work to the web, and finding it felt like being in on something special. Gonads and Strife was far from the first meme I experienced, but it was the first time I'd seen anything "go viral," although my friends didn't have a name for it yet.

I can think of a dozen more flash animations that eventually surpassed it in popularity, but in my little world, Gonads and Strife was genius. We scratched our heads, "How did someone even conceive of this? I've never seen anything like it." It wasn't long before I was running into someone else's room, saying, "Dude, you've gotta see this."

A History of Memes

In the decade since, barely a day has gone by that I haven't gleefully shared something from the Internet with a friend. The Internet is home to gigs upon gigs of content that compel viewers to share, participate, augment, parody, and otherwise own it. Today we call these bits of cultural currency *memes*. In order to understand why 4chan matters, we first have to understand memes.

Of course, memes were not born on the Internet. They've been driving the human sociocultural experience since before we scribbled on cave walls. Memes seek to replicate themselves laterally—the ideological or cultural equivalent of a gene, naturally arising from human interaction.

Ask evolutionary biologist Richard Dawkins what a meme is and he'll tell you this:

> Examples of memes are tunes, ideas, catch-phrases, clothes fashions, ways of making pots or of building arches. Just as genes propagate themselves in the gene pool by leaping from body to body via sperms or eggs, so memes propagate themselves in the meme pool by leaping from brain to brain via a process which, in the broad sense, can be called imitation.

This is an excerpt from Dawkins's groundbreaking book, *The Selfish Gene*, published in 1976. Dawkins didn't originally come up with the idea of a meme, but he was the first one to use the word, and thus to inadvertently kick-start a new branch of anthropology called *memetics*, a catchall term for the study of human social evolution as opposed to biological evolution (i.e., genetics).

> I think that a new kind of replicator has recently emerged on this very planet. It is staring us in the face. It is still in its infancy, still drifting clumsily about in its primeval soup, but already it is achieving evolutionary change at a rate that leaves the old gene panting far behind.
>
> The new soup is the soup of human culture. We need a name for the new replicator, a noun that conveys the idea of a unit of cultural transmission, or a unit of imitation. 'Mimeme' comes from a suitable Greek root, but I want a monosyllable that sounds a bit like 'gene.' I hope my classicist friends will forgive me if I abbreviate mimeme to meme. If it is any consolation, it could alternatively be thought of as being related to 'memory,' or to the French word 'même.' It should be pronounced to rhyme with 'cream.'

So, for Dawkins, religion is a meme. Art is a meme. Every form of human social expression is memetic. We are surrounded by memes, ranging from every family tradition we hold dear to the comics in today's funny papers. Some memes are widespread, like progressivism. Others are specific and intimate, like the unique baby talk between mother and child.

Everything we do and say is an imitation, to some degree, of the things we've seen those around us do. In a matter of speaking, memes seek to replicate themselves. Of course, neither Dawkins nor I would argue that memes are sentient beings capable of "seeking" anything. Memes are simply mental expressions that behave like genes. But memes have several things in common with biological life-forms. That's why we often refer to memes as "going viral." They spread from person to person the way a virus does. Most of the time, we don't even realize we are spreading them, the same way a beast plays host to an intestinal parasite.

Memes can be ideologies, trends, fads, gossip, jokes, music, fashion, or adages—any concept that can be shared from one person to another. They're distinct and repeatable, and they live and die by natural selection in the same way that biological entities do. If a meme fails to spread, it's dead.

In the notes in Dawkins's 1989 reprint of *The Selfish Gene*, he admits that the word *meme* had become something of a strong meme in itself. In fact, his brief discussion of memes was only meant to serve a larger purpose: to establish that complex ecological systems arise from entities that seek to replicate.

> I believe that, given the right conditions, replicators automatically band together to create systems, or machines, that carry them around and work to favour their continued replication. The first ten chapters of *The Selfish Gene* had concentrated exclusively on one kind of replicator, the gene. In discussing memes in the final chapter I was trying to make the case for replicators in general, and to show that genes were not the only members of that important class.

Although Dawkins had no intention of creating a grand unified theory for human culture (he eventually distanced himself from the term), a slew of memeticists picked up where he left off, attempting to use memes to explain all human behavior. Countless heady discussions followed, influencing fields like cultural anthropology, sociology, and psychology, all dedicated to expanding Dawkins's theory of self-replicating units of cultural transmission.

Internet Memes

So how did we get from a broad, classical definition of a meme to an animated GIF of a dancing baby (or flying gonads)? Why has the term *meme* become so closely associated with web-borne viral content over the last ten years? Why, when we hear the word, do we think of something like the dancing baby rather than, say, Buddhism?

The Internet allows memes to spread more rapidly than any previous medium in human history. We now live in a world where any idea can be expressed instantly to nearly anyone on the globe, and millions of people take advantage of this capability every day, unconsciously spreading memes with every link shared, every video uploaded, every blog post written. Never before has the ratio of senders of memes to receivers of memes been so high.

Millions of memes are constantly fighting for your attention, for a chance to replicate. Meme populations grow and shrink in the "meme pool," as public awareness expands and contracts. The structure of the web has been built around ensuring that the strongest memes made up of the most compelling, "sticky" content rise to the top. We see this principle in action in content aggregators like Reddit and Digg, which often collectively scrape content from, you guessed it, 4chan. This process is a part of a phenomenon I call the Meme Life Cycle, which I'll explain later.

Since the Internet has made it so easy for memes to spread, it's become inextricably linked with how most people understand memes. Ask a fifteen-year-old what a meme is and he or she will probably say something along the lines of, "Have you ever seen lolcats? What about Antoine Dodson? Double Rainbow?" They'll rattle off Internet ephemera until you recognize something.

That's because today the word *meme* is shorthand for "A piece of content (e.g., a video, story, song, website, prank, trend, etc.) that achieved popularity primarily through word of mouth on the web."

When Internet phenomena such as viral videos, email-forwarded hoaxes, and web microcelebrities began to appear, journalists co-opted the term. As early as 1998, the word has been used to refer to bits of popular culture that are considered to be "from the Internet." But what does that mean, exactly? It's difficult to say, especially since the world of the web and the rest of popular culture are becoming increasingly intertwined.

It's difficult to pinpoint a precise time when the word *meme* started to refer to bits of Internet-borne cultural iconography, like lolcats. I'd guess that Richard Dawkins would scoff at the bastardization of his term, especially since he distanced himself from it before the Internet ever co-opted it. We know that memes are propagated through social networks. This form of transmission is distinctly different from that of genes. You can't share your genes with your pals. Because the Internet so tangibly manifests those social networks, the word *meme* became a convenient term to describe specific bits of information that are shared on those networks.

In 1998, Joshua Schachter, who later went on to sell social

bookmarking platform del.icio.us to Google, started Memepool, a multiauthor blog that contained links to interesting and offbeat content on the web. It was part of a growing network of blogs like Boing Boing, Waxy, and Laughing Squid, who made up a vibrant culture of sharing cool Internet content. Memepool tracked stuff that was going viral. At the time, news outlets that profiled Memepool naturally referred to memes when describing the site's subject matter.

In the mid-2000s, Jonah Peretti, who went on to found The Huffington Post and meme-tracker-of-note Buzzfeed, and Peretti's colleagues at Eyebeam, a not-for-profit art and technology research center, put together a research group called Contagious Media. The group was dedicated to performing culture-jammy "viral experiments" to demonstrate how information is passed around on the web. The project launched such viral phenomena as Black People Love Us (a satirical site about a dorky white couple's attempts to be accepted by the black community) and the "Nike sweatshop" email (a customer service exchange between Peretti and a Nike employee that resulted from Peretti trying to order a pair of customized shoes emblazoned with the word "sweatshop"). They held festivals and competitions based around this idea of contagious media.

Kenyatta Cheese, co-creator of Know Your Meme and former Eyebeamer, explains,

> Jonah Peretti put together a Contagious Media Festival that was basically asking, "What is the science and culture behind the viral Internet?" As we collectively started taking the work of connecting viral media and connecting it back to the older theory of Dawkins, the word *meme* became the go-to term to describe viral content.

Somewhere between the late 1990s and the mid-2000s, the word *meme* became synonymous with weird, cool, and silly web stuff, and most people remain unaware of its original meaning in the field of evolutionary biology. I hope Richard Dawkins can at least get a kick out of how the word's definition has spread and evolved, memetically. In a 2010 interview with NPR, Dawkins said, "Well, I was pretty computer-literate for the time, but neither I nor anybody else, I think, had any very clear idea of what this enormous flowering that would become the Internet. It's become the perfect ecology for memes. I mean, the Internet is now one, great, memetic ecosystem."

Pre-Internet Memes

Is Yosemite Bear, the burly eccentric who achieved cultural ubiquity with his famous expression of awe at the sight of a "double rainbow," really all that different from Toby Radloff, the "genuine nerd" who became something of a pre-Internet microcelebrity when he starred in a series of MTV promotional shorts in the '80s? Radloff was a coworker of comics legend Harvey Pekar, who featured Radloff in his *American Splendor* comics. Radloff was just a random weirdo who became known nationwide for a short while, not unlike Yosemite Bear and dozens of other web icons who've popped up on the mainstream's radar over the last twenty years.

While the rise of Yosemite Bear and Toby Radloff share the same "look at this random everyday weirdo" element, the means by which each achieved mainstream exposure is different. Radloff got big because some TV execs decided he was a quirky character and put him on TV. Yosemite Bear eventually made it all the way to the small screen as well, but it happened because millions of links were instant-messaged back and forth. Thousands of tweets. Hundreds of blog posts. The rise was perpetuated by an unorganized grassroots movement. If you are aware of Yosemite Bear, it's because his meme was strong enough to beat out the millions of other memes competing for your attention.

Memes had spread virally before the Internet as well. Consider the strange story of *Shut Up Little Man*, a series of recordings from the '80s made by a couple of guys living in San Francisco. Fascinating documents of bizarre humanity, the tapes captured the sounds of the guys' misanthropic neighbors hurling drunken insults at each other. The recordings were passed from friend to friend on cassette tapes. People made copies of copies. They became what we used to call "cult hits" in the burgeoning alternative West Coast zine culture. Since then, the recordings have been turned into a puppet show, a feature length drama, and a documentary that debuted in 2011.

OK, so we've established that there's nothing new under the sun. As I mentioned in the introduction, this isn't a book about explaining the way technology has changed the way we behave. The Internet didn't invent memes; it just expanded their scope and ramped up the frequency of their creation.

According to Eddie Lee Sausage, one of the guys who made the *Shut Up Little Man* recordings (whom I interviewed for urlesque.com), experimental jazz composer John Zorn sampled them in his music. And they didn't peter out with the rise of the Internet. Within two days of Mel Gibson's racist rant against his now ex-girlfriend, some anonymous YouTube user had mashed up the rant with the audio from *Shut Up Little Man*. A similar mashup was created when Christian Bale famously flipped out on some poor lighting guy on the set of *Terminator Salvation*.

Speaking of music, consider hip hop culture, which is based on sampling, the practice of taking someone else's work, mixing it with the output of others, adding some of your own bits, and fusing it all together into something fresh. Many of today's hip hop producers sample classic hip hop loops, which are themselves made up of bits of soul and jazz from the '60s and '70s. And the beats are only part of this cultural milieu. B-boy dancing, MCing (rapping), and graffiti are layered over the music in a rich sensory experience that vividly demonstrates the way all art evolves memetically.

The graffiti that evolved from hip hop culture is a prominent pre-Internet visual meme. Like many memes, graffiti is a means of showing off creativity or spreading a message. Sometimes graffiti artists just want to mark their territory. We've all probably seen "X was here" scrawled on a bathroom stall at some point. Where did that come from? Why is it observed all over the world? A suspected root of the meme is the "Kilroy was here" iteration, which features a bald-headed cartoon man with a long nose peeking over a wall.

Kilroy can be found in countless locations, scribbled on beachheads, landmarks—even the Berlin Wall. No one is quite sure who Kilroy is, and even the name is up for dispute, with variants that include Foo, Chad, Smoe, Clem, and others. Some suspect that the phrase originated among US servicemen marking places they'd been during tours of duty. Some historians place Kilroy's origins as far back as the 1930s. Regardless of where he came from, Kilroy is a wonderful example of a visual icon that motivated people to spread the meme virally, for no monetary or reputation benefit. They just wanted to be part of the meme.

Hide Ya Kids

I'll never forget the moment I first heard a woman singing The Gregory Brothers' "Bed Intruder," in a bar in the summer of 2010. For me it was a singularity that represented a shift in popular culture, the moment when Internet ephemera became solidified in the mainstream.

When people ask me what memes are I usually respond, "Have you ever heard of lolcats? You know, those funny cat photos with the misspelled captions?"

If that doesn't work, I'll say, "How about Antoine Dodson? That guy from the projects? There was that song? Hide ya kids? Hide ya wife? Nothing?"

Usually, by the time I get to "Hide ya wife," a wave of recognition washes over this uninitiated person's face, and I'm grateful I don't have to explain why an attempted rape is supposed to be funny. But that's what I'll do here.

In July 2010, Antoine Dodson was filmed by a local NBC affiliate in his Hunstville, Alabama housing project, where an unknown attacker had attempted to rape his sister the previous night. The video features an impassioned plea by Dodson:

> Well, obviously we have a rapist in Lincoln Park. He's climbin' in your windows. He's snatchin' your people up, tryna rape em. So y'all need to hide your kids, hide your wife, and hide your husbands 'cause they rapin' everybody out here.

Antoine became an overnight meme celebrity, but he rocketed to fame when his monologue was Auto-Tuned by musical comedy group The Gregory Brothers a few days later. The song was posted on iTunes and reached the Billboard charts, and The Gregory Brothers split the profits halfway with Antoine, enabling him to get out of the projects. At this point, Antoine is nearly as recognizable a pop-culture icon as Justin Bieber or Lady Gaga. He's appeared on BET, the *Today Show*, and *Lopez Tonight*.

Many people felt that the humor of the clip was derived from a near-tragedy resulting from the plight of poor urban communities. The original coverage struck many as exploitative, as though Huntsville's NBC affiliate WAFF aired Antoine's ebonics-filled tirade for no other reason than to laugh at the uneducated black guy. Feminist bloggers wondered how a guy's goofy rant so easily overshadowed his sister's painful ordeal.

Nonetheless, the video racked up millions of views, becoming one of the fastest-expanding memes in history. Antoine saw an opportunity and rode the meme celebrity train for all it was worth. Merchandise, TV spots, promotional campaigns, you name it: Antoine was all over the place. He became almost a modern-day folk hero. Thousands of YouTube videos remixed, mashed up, and otherwise parodied the original. Even if the original video had been out of his control, at least Antoine was able to own his viral fame. On his personal site he proclaimed:

> You all made me who I am today and for that I will for ever be in your debt. Once again I say thank you from me and on behalf of my entire family. I love you guys so much. You have given me this opportunity to shine so dammit I'm going to shine.

As of this writing, Dodson is working on an upcoming reality TV show.

Keeping Up With the New Language

People use the word *meme* to describe visual content like videos or photos or offbeat microcelebrities, but it's important to recognize that the meme is the concept. A photo or video might be just one execution of that concept among many. As memes evolve, they branch out in countless ways, shifting and merging with other mashed-up, mutated memes. Sometimes, in order to understand a given iteration of a meme, one must also be familiar with dozens of others.

Here's an analogy. The world of ABC's show *Lost*, which captivated TV viewers in the 2000s, demanded an unprecedented amount of attention from its fans. Each episode contained dozens of storylines, playing out bit by bit. There were so many characters and relationships to keep track of. One could not just jump into the show mid-episode, let alone mid-season. An offhand joke, or even a wordless facial expression, could be a reference calling back to an occurrence from an episode originally aired years prior. People who tried to pick up the show but hadn't watched earlier seasons were, uh, lost.

So it is in the world of memes. Keeping up with the Internet's daily output of fresh memes will likely define the watercooler conversation of tomorrow. A host of wikis, blogs, and even books have appeared over the last few years to try to make sense of it all. The structure of hypertext makes it easy to explore branching clusters of increasingly granular information. But given the availability of information on the web, the network of memetic information increasingly demands more from casual browsers. If I see something on 4chan and don't know what it means, I follow an informal process for figuring it out. This likely will start with a Google search, followed by a few quick scans of Wikipedia entries. If the meme is too obscure for Wikipedia, I might have to browse Encyclopedia Dramatica or Urban Dictionary. If it deals with entertainment I might instead opt for the Internet Movie Database or Allmusic. I may consult Google News or Technorati to see if there's been any recent related web chatter. By the time I've fully explored the information, my browser is full of tabs.

As the Internet facilitates a growing network of increasingly complex memes, the gulf expands between those in the know and those who aren't privy to meme culture. There is a new language of memes forming, and I'm not referring to lolspeak or leetspeak. What I call the language of memes is not Internet slang, but a new visual way that people succinctly communicate emotions and opinions. Cheezburger CEO Ben Huh calls it the "visual vernacular."

Those who aren't able to keep up with all the latest cultural iconography won't be able to engage in the conversation. Knowing how to source the roots of memetic language will become an increasingly valuable skill as the network of memetic imagery becomes progressively more complex and people are expected to be more familiar with obscure web phenomena. Ignoring Internet memes will be equivalent to showing up to the office watercooler having watched none of last night's primetime content.

Dude, You've Got to See This

What compels people to share this stuff? The same impulse that incites us to gossip and share jokes. We want other people to enjoy the information we've acquired, and we get a mental kick out of being the ones to share it. This is as universal and historic a human characteristic as the need to eat. Sharing information, no matter how trivial, solidifies societal bonds and deepens relationships. These shared points of reference make up life as much as our inside jokes at work or gossip at church.

Clay Shirky has made waves in the last few years as being a kind of Marshall McLuhan for the Web 2.0 era. Throughout his two books, *Cognitive Dissonance* and *Here Comes Everybody*, Shirky provides the kind of commentary that fills one with excitement for being a part of the web right now. We're making things happen! It's a new stage in human social evolution! Look at all the cool stuff the Internet lets us do!

In *Cognitive Dissonance*, Shirky uses the lolcats found at http://www.icanhascheezburger.com as a convenient representative for what he calls "the stupidest possible creative act," as opposed to, say, improving a Wikipedia entry or creating a platform for financing human rights projects in the third world. I asked him about this, and he laughed.

"Actually, I love Cheezburger."

I breathed a sigh of relief, feeling a bit less guilty for spending more time laughing at "fail" videos than I've contributed to building out Linux.

He quickly added, "I'm not going to hold them up as a paragon of human intellectual achievement, but . . ."

Fair enough. He continued.

> ... I do think there's lasting social value in it. There's a spectrum of creativity from mediocrity to excellence, but there's a gulf between doing nothing and doing something. And anyone who's slapped a few words on a picture of their cat has already crossed that gulf. The invitation to make something and share it with other people on that scale is so radically different from what we were capable of doing in the twentieth century, that even a lolcat, one of the stupidest creative acts, is still a creative act.

Clay explains that we regard lolcats as an inexplicable novelty because the network on which they happen is so new. But the drive to share funny or interesting things with each other is a deeply entrenched human (not to mention animal) trait. So people who shake their heads and say, "Why would anyone waste their time with this stuff?" don't recognize that this impulse is nothing new. What's new is the scale of the sharing.

Think of the aforementioned watercooler conversation. Or the bulletin board–covered walls of the college dorm room, festooned with satirical flyers, newspaper cutouts, editorial cartoons, and other ephemera. I remember as a kid visiting the shop floor where my dad worked, and noticing that he'd covered a filing cabinet with hundreds of magazine ads and other imagery. He'd used a Sharpie to draw mustaches and black eyes on the models, or given them speech bubbles, granting the images the ability to mock his coworkers.

I asked Buzzfeed's senior editor Scott Lamb how he responds to people who think the world of memes is a waste of time.

> Bad romantic comedies are a waste of time. But very little Internet culture counts as that—as a waste—for me. First of all, it

31

asks so little of you. Ten to fifteen seconds to scan a post, at most two minutes for a video? And most memes can be read and understood much faster than that.

It's important to remember that the cost that memes bear is almost nil compared to most other media. Who has the time for this stuff? Actually, quite a lot of people. Internet memes are bite-sized, and as more of us become handcuffed to computers throughout the day, these tiny diversions become almost necessary.

A recurring theme in Shirky's work is the idea that some human social behaviors have always existed but are latent until triggered by some new technology that allows humans to express those behaviors like never before. In many cases, cultural critics shake their heads, claiming that human society is somehow getting dumber or lazier or more debauched. Clay argues that human behavior is mostly constant, and what changes is the technology.

This explains why we didn't see a group like capital-A Anonymous, the pseudopolitical activist group spawned from 4chan, ten years ago. Clay Shirky mentions the area code hookup threads that pop up on /b/ from time to time.

> The scale at which Anonymous operates would not have been available ten years ago. When you look at area code hookup threads, the unspoken there is that obviously there's enough people here in any given area code that might be on the board. That density wasn't around ten years ago. People getting comfortable with this medium takes a lot longer than just rolling the tools out.

Clay draws my attention to Six Degrees, an early social network that had basically the same functionality as the more popular

Friendster, but years earlier. In 1996, there simply weren't enough people online to support Six Degrees, and those who were online were not sufficiently acclimated to the Internet to be comfortable with the sort of commitment to a virtual identity that profile-based social networks such as Facebook and MySpace demand. Today, a generation has grown up with the Internet, considering it as much of a given as telephone networks. This generation has pioneered social networking because a lot of younger people already feel like they are living their lives online.

The Meme Factory

So what does all this have to do with 4chan?

For eight years now, 4chan has been a powerful (if not *the* powerful) wellspring from which memes emanate, a no-rules, boundary-less forum where the funniest and most interesting content not only rises to the top, but is copied, remixed, and mashed up ad infinitum until it becomes an indelible piece of this ever-shifting new culture. On 4chan, entertainment is no longer passive. It is an interactive, living organism. 4chan behaves like the Internet, but harder, better, faster, stronger—a whirling microcosm of creativity. A fetid, bubbling meme pool.

To understand what makes 4chan tick, one must understand the language of Internet memes. 4chan didn't invent this, and is hardly the only place on the web where memes are born. Many of the memes featured in this book became viral completely independent from 4chan. But for a period of time that continues at least up to this writing, 4chan reigns as the web's primary meme factory.

Chapter 2

Discovering 4chan

GROWING UP IN rural Pennsylvania I had little exposure to the outside world, culturally speaking, except for the piddly local library. My grandparents bought my sister and I our first family computer, a Compaq Presario with a blindingly fast Pentium II processor, when I was fourteen. My ninety-year-old grandfather insisted that familiarity with a computer would define a person's ability to compete in the marketplace of tomorrow, but I had one thing on my mind: How do I get this thing to play video games?

Up until then, I had owned a few Nintendo consoles. Pop in a game cartridge and you're off. There was no installation of software, no downloading patches. Everything just *worked*. Not so with this unfamiliar contraption that miraculously landed in my room (a decision my parents apparently made without considering the implications of putting what was essentially a free porn machine in an adolescent boy's bedroom). Of course, I was terrified at the prospect of divine retribution and celestial shame, and I limited my racy searches on that computer to victorias secret.com, which still brought unimaginable guilt.

Successfully running an average game on a PC in those days often required hours of detective work. I trawled tech support pages and dug deeply into hobbyist forums, slowly loading page after page until I had gathered enough information to get back into the game.

I familiarized myself with dozens of software packages, but I was most fortunate to grow up along with simple hypertext, the nonlinear, nonhierarchical structure of ideas all connected across millions of blue sentence fragments. My search for knowledge and entertainment on the web felt like untangling a giant knot; at times screen-smashingly frustrating and at other times deeply satisfying. I would follow certain paths across twenty pages, come to a dead end, and then start over from the beginning, following a different path. Over time I became more adept at finding the fastest routes to the information I wanted, whether that meant googling various search strings, posting a question on a forum, or browsing massive downloadable user manuals.

Along the way, I learned basic computer skills. More importantly, I learned how to navigate the Internet, a skill that would come to define my career. Due to the way information is structured on the web, one can follow endless rabbit holes of information. This was the dawn of the search engine and Wikipedia, which together opened my mind to an infinite world of new questions and answers. At some point gaming became a secondary concern, and I started using the Internet for the Internet's sake.

Though my mother put strict limits on the amount of time I could spend on the Internet, I had an hour each day to chat with friends on AOL Instant Messenger, read video game news, and look at funny photos at places like Fark and Something Awful. I'd boot up the computer, dial up a connection, and open twenty windows. Then I'd putz around the house, waiting for everything to load (usually about ten minutes). Then, and only then, would I start the egg timer that my mom used to mark our Computer Time. The twenty windows would generally keep me occupied for the hour.

Over the next few years I discovered Napster, which opened my ears to indie rock. I became obsessed with punk music and its associated aesthetic. During those years I read probably thousands of music reviews and participated in countless forum arguments over the authenticity of certain bands. I got turned onto indie game development and the software piracy scene. I engaged in conversations about the nature of art, pop culture, and the web itself. I felt as though I was a part of something to which literally no one I knew in real life was privy. At home, amid miles of cornfields, I had one neighbor (a middle-aged couple), but online I was a part of a cadre of critics and tastemakers on the bleeding edge of culture. (Looking back, I was probably pretty insufferable in those days.)

And then college happened. I went to a tiny liberal arts school a few miles from my hometown. Culturally speaking, it didn't have much more to offer, but I fell in with a small group of indie rock geeks. We were *aesthetes*, silently projecting an aura of cultural superiority over the normals, who likely never noticed.

One of my friends shared my enthusiasm for the web, though his knowledge of its emerging trends dwarfed mine. He was the sort of guy who wore a fedora, started a satirical newspaper, and had dreams of developing a gossip site that would act as sort of a hyperlocal Gawker for our rinky-dink campus. Perhaps more than our shared love of the web, we had in common a basic desire to be a part of a world bigger than the one in which our bodies were trapped. We'd talk about New York business moguls and Silicon Valley upstarts, referring to industry personalities by first names though we were miles away (geographically and experientially) from either of those scenes.

This friend and I developed a habit for sending each other, via instant messenger, links to funny or interesting web content. It became a challenge to beat each other to the latest story, and since we were pretty much the only people we knew who spent most of their waking hours in front of a computer, this practice continued after college. To this day, we still IM each other stuff.

Sometime in 2006, this guy sent me a link to 4chan—to a gross-out photo of an anime (Japanese animation) character doing something unspeakable involving at least three bodily fluids. For us, the Internet was a magical ladder reaching to new heights of the human imagination, but it was also a hilarious cesspool of depravity.

"Dude, WTF," was probably my response, incredulity giving way to laughter at the existence of the kind of mind who would create such an atrocity. "Where did you find this?"

"4chan.org. It's a gold mine."

And so began my relationship with 4chan. My friend went on to write, in a blog post for Gawker, one of the first mainstream reports of 4chan as a growing phenomenon.

4chan users would likely call me a newfag (read on, offended readers) and a lurker. I've rarely ever posted anything on the site, and I came to the scene relatively late. But what I found on 4chan was a distillation of what made the web so special. It's wild and weird—a level playing field where physicists and fathers rub shoulders with horny teenagers and senior citizens who compulsively collect their belly button lint in mason jars, with photographic proof. To be honest, I often find the place generally repulsive, but sometimes repulsive things have massive influence.

On 4chan, you never quite know whom or what you're going to run into. 4chan is like that burnout teenager who asked you and your childhood friends if y'all wanted to see a dead body down by the train tracks. 4chan is that kid in your class with Asperger's who sketched out a hundred-page graphic novel based on the entire recorded output of the prog-metal band Rush. It's the lightheartedly sadistic next-door bully named Sid from Pixar's *Toy Story*. It's Brad Pitt's Tyler Durden from *Fight Club*. It's Willy Wonka and Boo Radley and Johnny Knoxville all rolled into one throbbing, sweating, oozing gob of id.

4chan is the most fascinating place on the Internet.

But What Is It?

4chan is an imageboard: a simple message board that allows users to post images in addition to text. Users can post anonymously, without setting up an account. It's hosted at http://www.4chan.org, and was launched in 2003 by a 15-year-old kid who wanted to provide his online buddies with a place to share anime.

That's it.

But somehow, 4chan has evolved into the web's foremost wellspring of pop-culture output over the last decade, spawning globally recognized iconography and serving as a base for people who conduct clandestine operations ranging from stalking cute girls to organizing global efforts of pseudopolitical "hacktivism."

As of this writing, 4chan receives 12 million hits monthly, making it one of the largest communities on the web. No small feat for a site with no marketing budget, no stated mission, no searchable index, no archives, a userbase that's famously antagonistic to outsiders, a decade-old user interface, and almost zero static content. There's something special about 4chan that keeps people coming back, in dramatically greater numbers year after year.

"Like it or hate it, 4chan is an important cultural force . . . It is a huge site, and so many Internet memes are formed there, it's hard to ignore it," said June Cohen, executive producer of TED Media, the organization that invited 4chan's founder to speak alongside impressively credentialed academics, inventors, and entrepreneurs in 2010.

I could go on telling you about it, but I'd rather show you.

Chapter 3

4chan in a Day

MOST OF THE media coverage that 4chan has received over the last year has focused on Anonymous (again, capital A Anonymous). This is the loosely organized hacker collective responsible for a variety of unrelated pranks, hacks, and protests beginning in 2007. 4chan's the sort of place where unseemly characters congregate to plan pseudopolitically motivated mischief. We'll get to them later. But what's it actually like to be there?

I spent twelve straight hours on the site, documenting my experiences in real time. Everything you're about to read actually happened as I've presented below. I haven't added a thing to make it interesting. I don't need to.

Take my hand. Call me Virgil.

The Enthusiast Boards

As of this writing, there are 49 boards that make up 4chan.org. When you read about 4chan in the news, you are most likely reading about /b/, 4chan's Random board. And for good reason. /b/'s traffic makes up more of the activity on 4chan than the other boards combined. /b/ is a no-rules board that fosters all kinds of nasty behavior. I discuss it later in this chapter. But first, some descriptions of the enthusiast boards found on 4chan that focus on specific areas of interest.

Note: All posts quoted from 4chan and elsewhere are reproduced exactly as posted.

/a/ Anime & Manga

4chan was originally conceived as a place for anime and manga (comic book) fans to talk about their hobby and share images from their favorite anime franchises. There are strict rules in place to ban those who spoil storylines. Not much to see here if you're not an anime buff.

As someone who has little personal interest in anime, I haven't spent much time on this board. But anime has had an important influence on the rest of 4chan, and on Internet culture at large. Anime fandom in the West exploded with the advent of the Internet. Before the web, fans acquired VHS tapes from pen pals in Japan and drove for days to get to annual anime conventions. Today's anime geek has millions of hours of content at his fingertips, all dubbed, subtitled, and readily available. What's more, he has a deeply informed network of superfans he can consult 24/7.

And if he can't find some obscure piece of content, he can inquire at /a/ and likely receive an answer within seconds. Still, the hobby demands a deep devotion, and this is a favorite place for fans to geek out.

Japanese culture is deeply embedded in underground Internet communities like 4chan, partially because the initial scarcity of anime in the West drove anime nerds to the web to find information about their hobby—but also because certain strains of anime lean towards the transgressive, and transgression loves company.

/adv/ Advice

One of the more recent social experiments on 4chan, the /adv/ board is a crowd-sourced advice column. Sometimes responses are genuine, even heartfelt. Sometimes they're snarky and mean, but in a lighthearted, creative way. A lot of the questions deal with nerds asking help for dealing with girls.

Here's the top question right now, verbatim:

> Ok, so here's my problem. Next fall, I got into my last year of college. I've havent declared a major, but I can finish either English or Psychology in two semesters. If I go into english, I will go to law school. If I go into psych, I'm in the long haul for a PHD. I enjoy psych alot, but I want the best for my future family and I'm concerned about money.

Advice is requested with the understanding that many of the responses will be trollish in nature. But half the fun is seeing what kind of creatively terrible advice anon (i.e., lowercase-a anonymous, the anonymous crowd on 4chan, not to be confused with Anonymous, described above) is able to come up with.

/an/ Animals & Nature

This board is for photos of plants and animals only, with frequent discussion on how to care for pets and plants.

The top post:

> So I found a baby cat on the streets yesterday, me and a friend brought him home, tried to feed him some tuna, she didn't want any of it, but she had some milk. Now I'm keeping her at my house, and, well, I'd like some advice on what to do now, for getting to shit and pee in one place and food she could eat that doesn't go to waste after two hours, and if I should bathe her. She's got no wounds or anything, but she was pretty scared yesterday night, crying and getting into my bed and in my sheet, and now she's sleeping in a box on my dad's lap.

D'aww.

/c/ Anime/Cute

Here is a place for lonely anime nerds to post cute, as opposed to erotic, anime pictures. Bookish girls with sexy librarian glasses and big eyes dominate the board.

One poster describes his crush with an enthusiasm that perfectly encapsulates the vibe:

> For me, attraction is mainly her physical appearance. She looks like a doll or a lollipop with a curl of ice cream or something

on her head. It's very appealing visually. Also she is good at doing/saying really cute things, especially things boys like.

But it's not just about looks. I stumble on one poster who insists that his infatuation with a particular anime character from a series called *Magical DoReMi* is based on the strength of her character as depicted in the show:

> A lot of it has to do with her selflessness and personal sacrifice for others. This is best showcased in the beginning of Sharp when she's taking care of Hana at night, while still juggling school and her idol work. I can barely keep up with just school on its own. Her straightforwardness can come in handy sometimes too.

I'm no psychologist, but it seems the attraction to cute, child-like anime girls is driven by a fear of real women. These cartoons don't talk back, they don't judge, and they're innocent and trusting. Best of all, they're often depicted as being into nerdy guys. The producers of these series' know their audience.

People throw the word *love* around quite a bit on this board, and they mean it. To the extent that a human being can love a cartoon character, these guys (and a few girls too!) do. It's not just a sexual thrill. One guy says that such and such a character is so beautiful he could cry, and I believe him.

/cgl/ Cosplay & EGL

This discussion board is for people who dress up like anime, video game, or other fictional characters for fun. It's called *cosplay* (costume-play). If you've ever been to a comic book or video game convention, you've probably seen these folks—

though there are also many conferences dedicated solely to cosplay culture. Hard-core cosplayers spend thousands of dollars on everything from exotic fabrics to wigs to comically massive foam swords. There are lots of women hanging around /cgl/. EGL stands for Elegant Gothic Lolita, a Japanese fashion that looks like modest, frilly Victorian garb, but is very dark and influenced by punk/goth subcultures.

It might seem at first glance as though there's something wrong with adults who dress up like comic book characters. I'm tempted to think from time to time that there's something unhealthy about cosplay fans, who obsessively ponder the history of their favorite fantasy characters, who devote most of their free time absorbing ephemera relating to their hobby, who spend a decent chunk of their disposable incomes building their identities around their hobby . . . and then I go to a football game.

/ck/ Food & Cooking

A sample:

> Alright, /ck/. I'm on a mission and I'm not quitting until I succeed. I don't like eggplant or zucchini. I'll eat them if I absolutely must, since I'm not a 5-year old, but I do not like them and have never cooked anything with either of them.
>
> But, there MUST be a way to prepare eggplant or zucchini that I will enjoy. Not tolerate, but actually enjoy. I want to be able to say, "Fuck yes, I want to eat more of this shit!" So I come to /ck/ for suggestions on delicious ways to prepare eggplant or zucchini. I will NOT give up and you WILL hear from me again,

either asking for more suggestions or to confirm that I've succeeded in my quest to enjoy these two vegetables.

4chan's cooking board allows users to share recipes, kitchenware deals, and cooking tips. It's all very macho, as though the boys are attempting to compensate for their interest in a traditionally domestic hobby.

/cm/ Cute/Male

Another anime board. This one's full of photos of male anime characters—a gay-male and hetero-female counterpart to /c/.

/co/ Comics & Cartoons

A home for images and discussion regarding Western comics. This includes everything from superhero fare to graphic novels to Spongebob Squarepants. The current top thread began with someone writing "Meanwhile at Taco Bell." Hundreds of responses follow, each taking on the persona of a comic book character, writing what, say, Spider-Man would say if he was chilling at Taco Bell.

/d/ Hentai/Alternative

This is where things start to get *really* weird. Hentai is hardcore pornographic animation. The "alternative" part means tentacle rape (a slippery fetish that goes back centuries in Japanese art) and a host of other deviant sexual fantasies played out in ink.

Here you will find sexualized depictions of women who are half-arachnid; cannibalism; and massive, intricately drawn monsters covered in genitalia from head to toe like some kind of Lovecraftian nightmare creature. The psychology behind these fetishes runs far deeper than the scope of this book.

/e/ Ecchi

Ecchi is the soft-core alternative to /d/. So if you'd rather see a Sailor Moon nip-slip than tentacle rape, welcome. The current top thread is a "pillow" gallery. These are anime girls who are embracing, and sometimes humping, pillows.

/fa/ Fashion

4chan's fashion board blows my mind. It's populated by super-stylish people asking each other questions about $300 dress shoes. I guess not all 4chan users are dragon shirt-wearing neckbeards. A popular meme on this board is to post a photo of oneself trying on outfits. It's like having a room full of stylists telling you what to wear each morning. Right now someone is giving a hilarious tutorial on how to fold clothes ("Don't use Japanese folding techniques? You don't know shit about clothes").

/fit/ Fitness

Physical fitness tips and photos of weight loss progress are just a few of the discussion topics you'll find on 4chan's fitness board. Some are more serious than others.

The current top thread:

> Okay so every other weekend i get shitfaced. I'm trying to re-
> duce bodyfat at the moment, however i understand getting shit-
> faced is VERY bad ... But .... is it still possible reduce
> bodyfat while drinking every other weekend?

/g/ Technology

Of course 4chan has a gadget and tech board. The conversation here isn't much different than what you'd find in the comments section of an average tech blog. Users often post photos of
their "battle stations" (i.e., home computer setups featuring
massive screens and gaming peripherals).

/gif/ Animated GIF

A place to share animated GIFs; the board is generally flooded
with porn. GIFs are small animated image files that are used on
4chan either to isolate a tiny portion of a video clip or to string
together several images to form a slideshow.

GIFs are found all over 4chan, and increasingly on the web at
large, as many blog-commenting platforms and message boards
allow users to submit animated GIFs as comments. Sites like
GIF Soup allow people to easily convert YouTube footage into
GIFs so they can share them with friends on blogs and social
networking pages.

Over the last few years I've noticed people using GIFs in lieu
of text to convey an emotional reaction to someone else's content.
A GIF of *Sesame Street*'s Bert looking nonplussed is a more con-

cise, clever way to express one's reaction than saying, "Wow, I don't know what to say." On 4chan, people will post a GIF image with the caption, "MFW [My Face When] ____." It becomes a game to find, or make, new GIF images to represent emotions.

/h/ Hentai

Yet another board for sharing hard-core cartoon porn, though this one's more about Princess Mononoke having sex with a fellow human being as opposed to a sea monster.

Positioning myself as a reporter, I asked the board what they get out of cartoon sex and these are some of the responses I got.

> we don't have to explain shit to you. GTFO. [Get The Fuck Out]
> It's kind of like how you look at :) and you see a smiling face. Just because it's less detailed doesn't mean it's not attractive to us. Why don't you go talk to people who read erotic fiction.
> With hentai, you're getting an artists representation. the models are cute and flawless. so much better than real porn.
> because hentai characters aren't faking it.

I hit refresh. Uh oh.

> You are banned! ;_;
> You have been banned from all boards for the following reason: posting irrelevant garbage - report on your ban, seymore hersh

I'm used to /b/, where you're allowed to say whatever you want. Not so with the other boards. I should have known better than to mess with hentai fans. I won't be able to access 4chan for another two days.

2 days later . . .

/hr/ High Resolution

High-resolution 2D/3D artwork, scans, photography, and images. Mostly safe-for-work eye candy, like close-up pictures of eyeballs, nature scenes, and cityscapes. People typically use this imagery as desktop backgrounds.

/int/ International

One can expect to find at least one thread dedicated to comparing the average penis size in different countries, and a lot of "USA rules, UK drools!," but sometimes /int/ surprises with an informed discussion about geopolitics or world trade.

/jp/ Otaku Culture

Otaku is a catchall term used to describe people who are obsessed with Japanese pop culture. One would expect this board to veer into less commonly discussed elements of Japanese culture, but it is dominated by anime.

The word *otaku* is derived from the Japanese word for home, and loosely implies that otaku people spend all their time at home watching anime, playing video games, and otherwise obsessing over nerd culture. Calling someone "otaku" in Japan is an insult, but in the West the term has been embraced as a badge of honor among people who possess a passion for all things Japanese. They are stereotyped as basement-dwelling, unhygienic virgins who sleep with body pillows fashioned to resemble Japanese pop stars, surrounded by massive collections of action fig-ures and DVDs. On 4chan you can find masses of people who are into Japanese pop culture, but you can also find a strong anti-otaku vibe. People who post anime on /b/ are often told to "Go back to /jp/."

On 4chan, otaku are often called *wapanese*, or *white Japa-nese*, in the same way that white people who emulate African-American culture are derisively called *wiggers*. Otaku are also called *weeaboos*, which is a term created by a wordfilter—a bit of code that automatically changes one word to another, in this case instituted by 4chan founder Christopher "moot" Poole—that automatically changed *wapanese* to *weeaboo*. Weeaboo is a reference to a nonsense word from a Perry Bible Fellowship web comic strip that has nothing to do with Japan or Japanese culture. I suspect moot just thought the word sounded funny.

/k/ Weapons

If you own nine samurai swords, this is the board for you. A popular thread on the front page reads:

> guys you have a grizzly charging you at 100 yards what gun do you want and you only have one round left what cal and what make is it?

There are always a few threads on /k/ that are dedicated to arguing about specific aspects of gun control.

/lit/ Literature

Despite being populated by Randroids (Ayn Rand devotees) and sci-fi geeks, 4chan's literature board is another that continually surprises with clever content. A common game is "Honest Covers," wherein players post Photoshopped images of novels with blunter titles. Nabokov's *Lolita* becomes *Likeable Rapist*. Hemingway's *The Sun Also Rises* becomes *Jews Ruin Parties*. This board probably has the highest ratio of quality content to garbage content, since it's frequented by people who have read at least one book.

/m/ Mecha

Mecha culture is made up of dozens of different sci-fi universes all based on bipedal fighting robots, like the zords from *Mighty Morphin' Power Rangers*. Mecha vehicles are often piloted by humans, and anthropomorphized so that fans will be able to bond emotionally with hunks of metal. The genre is extremely popular in Japan, encompassing feature films, comics, toys, novels, and more.

/mu/ Music

4chan's music board gives music geeks a platform to engage in the age-old practice of cultural snobbery. It's dominated heavily by metalheads, the one true music of computer nerds. People post what's currently on their turntables, take glamour shots of their hi-fi setups, and create lists upon lists that quantify specific eras and genres.

/n/ Transportation

Photos and information about planes, trains, and automobiles. Looks like most people use it as a forum to talk about bicycles. There appear to be some commercial pilots in here talking with some air traffic controllers. It's of course impossible to verify, but the language they are using implies that the discussion is legit.

/o/ Auto

Car talk and slick photos of cars. A lot of arguing about the relative merits of NASCAR vs. Formula 1 racing. I once saw a lengthy thread where people debated which parts they'd use were they given the ability to perform maintenance and repairs on the Batmobile.

/p/ Photography

Personal photography only. Users are encouraged to include a description of when and where photos were taken along with a description of the camera used. This board has a few fun games, like "Take a photo of the view from your window."

/po/ Papercraft & Origami

Dedicated to the ancient Japanese art of folding paper so it looks like cool stuff, usually related to video games or anime here. 4chan founder moot claims that this is one of his favorite boards.

/s/ Sexy Beautiful Women

Yet another porn board. This one's just for soft-core nudes of actual human females, which makes it something of an anomaly on 4chan.

/sci/ Science & Math

People arguing about science. Trolls trying to rile up math nerds. Kids looking to get quick answers for their homework. Armchair physicists pondering the nature of time and space.

/soc/

moot posted the following message to 4chan in January 2011:

1. Created to get "rate me," meetup, report in, cam, etc. threads out of /b/.
2. No whining (aka "BAWWW") threads.
3. Post only pictures of yourself-not others. This isn't a cam-whore dump board.
4. Per the above rule, nudity is allowed so long as it is of your-self. AGAIN-THIS IS NOT A PORN DUMP BOARD.

So this board is meant for "Rate Me" threads ("Am I hot or not?") and "Report In" threads ("All NYCfags report in!"). More importantly, it was created to remove such social-related clutter from the rest of 4chan. This board is active, but it hasn't stopped /b/tards from posting stuff on /b/ that moot would prefer be relegated to /soc/.

Hookup threads are rampant in /soc/. These threads are

kicked off when someone writes, "412 report in!" Everyone who lives within or near that area code will chime in, and more granular, regional discussion ensues. In some cases, threads are more specific. People looking for drugs or prostitutes or just buddies to catch a movie with can find folks within their area codes here.

/sp/ Sports

A place for sports fans to talk sports. Like this:

> Hey /sp/, I'd like to have a discussion on stadiums. Specifically, what do you think is the best stadium in each sport. Seriously give it some thought. The things to take in account can be things like History, Atmosphere, Design, Location, Amenities, etc.
> This is NOT a comparison of teams. This NOT about how one fanbase is worse than another. Its figuring out whats the best stadium in each sport.

/t/ Torrents

Here people share links to torrents of usually pirated content.

/tg/ Traditional Games

Board games, paper games, war games, card games, etc., go here—another of moot's favorites. Right now, there appears to be an interactive narrative/role-playing game happening within the board itself.

You are Osyki, newly promoted Totemist and first line of defense for your village against the rabid Behemoths wandering the land. Your master, the previous Totemist, fell in a battle against a terrible Basilisk Wyrm, leaving the duty of defending your settlement to you.

The post goes on to explain the different weapons and skills at your character's disposal. The thread has over a hundred responses, and the original poster, or OP, acts as a dungeon master, accepting responses as turns and responding accordingly. It's unclear if the OP picks a response at random or if there's a system in place to decide which of the chiming voices gets to choose the hero's next course of action.

You glance around at the assembled items, deciding on one more experiment before you return to the forest to speak with Boand, the Spring Spirit. You pick the Skull Focus from the pile, holding the long scrap of Drake Wing in the other hand. Speaking the Ritual of Binding, you close your eyes.

The game boils down to a choose-your-own-adventure with some puzzle-oriented combat mechanics, but the narrative is as strong as any proprietary role-playing system I've encountered. Epic geekery.

/toy/ Toys

A place to talk about, buy, sell, and trade toys. Mostly action figures and the sort of collectibles so expensive no actual kid would own them. Remember the Comic Book Guy from *The*

Simpsons? He'd hang out here. One guy is using it at the moment to find an obscure, beloved toy truck from his childhood.

Having yearned for what was (and still is) one of the most poseable Star Wars figures in the entire line, I was elated to have acquired a Vintage Collection Commander Gree a few days ago. Much to my disappointment, his legs were floppy and his movement was severely restricted, so I decided to take him to the work desk for some modification.

/trv/ Travel

The travel board is mostly made of people asking for travel recommendations. There are a few creeps a-creepin'. Here's the current top post:

Looking for a country with you-know-what kind of tourism in place. Is Cambodia any good? Or maybe Thailand? Any advices? No specifics, of course. We don't want a ban, do we?

This post is accompanied by a photo of a little girl tiptoeing on her father's shoes. We are to assume the poster, possibly a troll, is looking for a country where he can find child prostitutes.

Thankfully, only smartasses reply, although it's possible that this guy is playing along, using *ruins* as code:

I will assume that you are talking about old ruins and yes, Thailand and Cambodia has plenty. Ankor Wat is in Cambodia and is a beautiful sight, but it is best to visit there from a tour in Bangkok because it is just across the border and cambodia as a country sucks ass. While in Bangkok, you could also check out Ayutthaya, it is a beautiful place with lots of old wat ruins.

Another simply replies, "Reported." 4chan is usually pretty self-policing when it comes to this sort of thing.

/tv/ Television & Film

A place to talk about TV and film. As of this writing, actress Elisabeth Sladen, who once played a character on British TV's *Dr. Who*, has just died. A thread commemorating the death beat reports from most media outlets. A lot of the discussion is dedicated to TV shows that are airing currently. People also use the board more like a real-time chat room, sharing spoilers, projections, and interpretations about shows as they unfold.

/u/ Yuri

Somehow, even more cartoon porn. This one's specifically for soft-core animated images depicting two or more women.

/v/ Video Games

Well duh. There ain't much more central to the nerd aesthetic than video games. /v/ is known for being populated by rabid fanboys who angrily flame and troll each other all day. Because a lot of kids are into video games, /v/ is often plagued by the most banal discourse. This board is also incidentally famous for launching the Rickrolling meme. After lolcats, the most recognizable 4chan meme is undoubtedly Rickrolling.

It was a happy accident. moot instituted a wordfilter which changed the word *egg* to *duck*, so when someone typed the word *eggroll* in a post, the word *duckroll* would show up instead.

Duckroll became a silly prank meme when 4chan users started linking their friends to an ostensibly cool site, only to be met with a picture of a duck on wheels with the word *duckroll* written on it.

So you'd send a friend a link with, "Hey, check out these new screenshots of the Playstation 4," but when they clicked on the link, BAM, duckroll'd. In the spring of 2007, duckroll morphed into Rickroll when someone posted a link that was claimed to be the hotly anticipated *Grand Theft Auto IV* trailer, but instead led the victim to a YouTube page hosting Rick Astley's 1987 smash hit "Never Gonna Give You Up." It was the Internet equivalent of sending someone on a snipe hunt, with a much more immediate payoff. Beyond the troll, the music video itself was parodied and mashed up thousands of times over.

When moot was voted into the TIME 100 in 2009, Rick Astley wrote a blurb about 4chan.

Before I heard about moot—the mysterious 21-year-old creator of the influential Web message board 4chan.org, who just happened to win Time.com's online poll to determine the world's most influential people—I used to think some young kid had stumbled across my video and thought it would be funny to send it to his mates, and it just kind of caught on. I suppose at first I was a little embarrassed by it. I always liken it to when people look through their photo albums or home videos from 20 years ago and think, Gosh, did I really wear that? The difference is, thankfully on the one hand and perhaps a bit scarily on the other, mine are out there for the public to see whenever they want. I find some Rickrolls really funny. Have you seen the one with President Barack Obama? Someone has cut up his speeches and put them together so that he sings "Never Gonna Give You Up." It's totally amazing. I find it bonkers, by the way!

I visited New York last fall to do a surprise live Rickroll as part of the Macy's Thanksgiving Day Parade. I thought it would be a really good and funny thing to be a part of. I called up a few of my friends in the States, and they said, "You've got to do it!" So I did! Thanks, moot.

/vp/ Pokémon

This is your spot if you're into Pokémon. This forum reveals the surprising complexity of the game, as the discussions get pretty lengthy and heated. Pokémon is very social. Here people exchange information so they can battle against each other and trade cards. On /vp/ and a few other boards, using a constant identity is actually encouraged in order to facilitate trades and meet-ups IRL (In Real Life).

/w/ Anime/Wallpapers

Weeaboo wallpapers galore. Lots of sparkles and blue hair.

/wg/ Wallpapers/General

High-resolution images used for desktops. One powerful trend is the "alternative art" movement, in which artists recontextualize pop-culture icons. For example, what would Mickey Mouse look like in the Star Wars universe? What would the Mario Bros. do if they found themselves in a world of gothic horror? The Simpsons recast as anime characters? The Reservoir Dogs, but with boobs?

/y/ Yaoi

A one-stop shop for naked male anime characters. Currently there is a "nipple" thread going strong. This is a thread that features images of cartoon men with extra-good-looking nipples, I guess.

/x/ Paranormal

Creepypasta, which is a variant of copypasta (content that's been "copy-pasted" from other sources) focused on scary or disturbing stories, can be found here, along with information about UFOs and other paranormal sightings. Right now, there is a heated thread about a spooky "lost" Beatles album:

> At a fan event, I managed to follow Ringo after he spoke to the crowd, and eventually had a chance to talk to him alone as he was leaving the building. He didn't seem upset that I had followed him, probably expected a typical encounter with an obsessive fan. When I mentioned the lost album though, all color drained from his face and he started trembling.
>
> When I asked him if he could tell me any details, he sounded like he was on the verge of tears. He grabbed a piece of paper, wrote something on it, and handed it to me. He begged me never to mention the album again. The piece of paper had a website address on it, I would rather not say what it was, for reasons you'll see in a second. I entered the address into my browser, and I came to a site that was completely black, except for a line of yellow text, a download link. I clicked on it, and a file started downloading. Once the file was downloaded, my computer went crazy, it was the worst virus I had ever seen. System

restore didn't work, the entire computer had to be rebooted. Before doing this though, I copied the file onto a CD. I tried to open it on my now empty computer, and as I suspected, there was an MP3 file . . .

But it's more than just campfire ghost stories. Some people spread guides that explain how to summon demons.

Messeth will not perform any requests unless you offer some kind of payment and will not perform major requests (making someone fall in love with you). Feel free to ask for relatively simple things like good luck, a good night's sleep, confidence to talk to a girl. After making a request, dismith Messeth by saying "Thank you for your services, Messeth. You are free to leave." Do you really want a lesser demon following you around and causing havoc? Don't forget to dismiss him!

/x/ reminds me of going to camp and hearing stories about people who'd dare say "Bloody Mary" three times in front of a mirror or something. I think there was a candle involved?

/i/ Oekaki

Oekaki (Japanese for *to draw*) is a place for 4channers to share their own artwork. Right now a post reads, "ITT [In this thread]: Draw your favorite actor eating your favorite fruit." I see images of Robin Williams munching on an orange. Jack Black eyeing up a pineapple. Simon Pegg requesting an apple, mate.

Oekaki is a fun board because it's all so immediate. People

request drawings and others comply for the sheer communal fun of it. The distinct topic of each thread limits one's ability to post old drawings, so you know you're getting fresh artwork.

Further down the page, a post reads, "Draw batman with your eyes closed!" There are 85 hilariously crude responses. In another thread, a man draws fantastically detailed anthropomorphic figures of countries. The thread opens with Albania, a gaunt, winged figure wearing a ceremonial headdress and what appears to be period clothing.

A more interesting game is afoot. It's a participatory drawing thread. Someone uploads a simple shape or sketch, encouraging the board to add to his drawing. The image explodes in a dozen different directions, some cute, some macabre. Before I know it, the image has been augmented and mashed together with other iterations. It's an impressive spectacle, as 4channers with wildly varying levels of talent and imagination work together.

/ic/ Artwork/Critique

Another board for sharing art, only this one allows all kinds of art, including tattoos, crafts, photography, and more. One man leads an art class. He posts a portrait of a woman and encourages his "students" to recreate the image using a pencil. Over a hundred people give it a shot. The work on display leans heavily toward sci-fi/fantasy drawings, but there is some impressive abstract art as well.

/f/ Flash

4channers upload Flash files here, including short videos, games, animations, and interactive stuff like soundboards and e-cards. You click on a file and you never know what it's going to be.

I click a random file. It's an animation featuring a *Ren & Stimpy*-like character doing appalling things to his genitals to an upbeat J-pop soundtrack. Another is a clip of a cat freaking out at a strobe light. Most of the content on /f/ seems to be aiming for a WTF reaction.

I click on one more for good measure. It's called "This is a Short Flash About the Man Who Thought He Was Bill Murray." It's a stick-figure animation about a man who goes around asking people, "Why hello, how does it feel to be talking to Bill Murray?" They play along, but snicker behind his back. Then one day he overhears their laughter. "So," he says, "you don't think I'm Bill Murray?" Then he begins to shake as operatic music swells. Hundreds of disembodied Bill Murray heads explode from within him, then dance around the screen to the epic sounds of a choir. The man turns into a shining ball of light. The heads encircle him and spin, forming two giant columns. They eventually come together to form one giant Bill Murray head, peering off into the horizon as the music reaches its resolution. This is the sort of bizarre humor for which the Internet was made.

/rs/ RapidShares

This board is for posting links to downloads available on RapidShare, a hosting service. There are three reasons why someone would want to download something directly from RapidShare as opposed to using torrent software. First, it's much faster. The company claims download speeds at 240GB per second. Second, RapidShare is less traceable, so people use it to download illegal content—and I'm not talking about run-of-the-mill pirated content, though 4chan has rules in place to prevent people from uploading anything that could get them in trouble. Last, you don't have to wait for people to "seed" content, as you do with torrents. This means that even the most rare niche content will download as quickly as the latest summer blockbuster.

/b/

/b/, also called *random*, is 4chan's most popular board, both in terms of traffic and notoriety. /b/ is significant because it's the only board on 4chan that has no rules (the only thing prohibited is committing or plotting actual crimes, the same rules that apply to any public forum on or offline). There's no topical focus, and every day brings new memes, microcelebrities, and drama.

When the mainstream media talks about 4chan, they are almost always talking about /b/ specifically. /b/ is where the trolls tend to gather in search of *lulz*, or laughs. (Lulz is a derivative of LOL, or "laughing out loud.")

"I did it for the lulz" is a phrase popularized on 4chan, used as a blanket excuse for anything from lighthearted trolling to heinous real-world bullying.

Lulz is certainly the main reason that most people keep coming back to /b/. Its popularity was built by bored, Internet-savvy teenage boys. These kids are generally smart, living in suburban wastelands, and writhing with hormonal energy. What else are they supposed to do? /b/ is the new "railroad tracks down by the river." The new "out behind the 7-11." It's where bored kids craving cheap thrills go to experience something, *anything* that might surprise them or subvert their expectations. Of course, teen boys aren't the only ones hanging out on /b/. I've personally observed soldiers, pilots, cops, zookeepers (at least, people *claiming* to be these things) on /b/. Yes, most people who use /b/ fall into a very narrow demographic, but the site attracts folks from all walks of life.

Rule #34

People also flock to /b/ to find porn. But wait, aren't there other boards specifically designated for porn? Yes, but they don't take into account Rule #34.

Rule #34 of the Internet
"If it exists, there is porn of it."

I just saw a drawing of Bart and Homer Simpson engaged in sexual intercourse. You think that's bizarre? How about the kid from Shel Silverstein's *The Giving Tree* somehow penetrating his deciduous patron? /b/ is a clearinghouse for messed-up porn. The sort of thing that would make any sane person wonder, "Just who exactly is getting off to this stuff?"

Answer: Probably someone. But not necessarily. Rule #34 has become a game on /b/, whereby someone will throw out a few pop-culture icons (The Brave Little Toaster and . . . Simon from *American Idol*!) and a specific sex act. Depending on the complexity of the challenge, everyone else participating in the thread will rush to find an image matching the description. If it doesn't exist, generally some hero will whip something up in Photoshop, or at least MS Paint.

Of course it's not all cartoon porn. /b/ has midget porn, bestiality, S&M, all things scatological, people popping intentionally nurtured zits, people picking noses, men injecting saline into their scrotums until they're the size of softballs, girls crushing fruit while wearing stilettos . . . The more bizarre it is, the more sought after.

Are there really that many deviants out there?

Probably yes, but at some point activity on /b/ becomes less about titillation and more about the thrill of discovering yet another terrifying demonstration of human deviance. Just when you thought you'd seen it all, BAM, here is grainy security camera footage of a man having actual penetrative intercourse with a dolphin in what appears to be a zoo aquarium. You can either retreat in terror or laugh at our shared human depravity.

There's a common joke on /b/, where someone will find a photo of a crowd of people with faces contorted in horror, except for one guy who bears a condescending smirk. "Spot the 4chan user," says the caption. The idea is that the average /b/tard has borne witness to so many unspeakable horrors that his general reaction to things most people find repulsive is a smug grin.

This Is Happening!

Along with that thrill of the unknown comes the feeling that only you and a handful of others are experiencing something as it's happening. It's a visceral sensation that solidifies the social bond (i.e., I was there, man). On /b/, you're thinking, "We are seeing something no one else has ever seen in human history! This is actually happening!" Of course it's not always exciting, but it happens often enough to keep people interested.

This sensation isn't limited to content of a sexual nature. By sheer luck, I once stumbled onto a thread in which a guy claimed to have just robbed a jewelry store. He provided images of the automatic rifle he used to hold the place up along with his loot— hundreds of rings.

> SUP /b/!
> I just robbed a jewelry store with an M4 assault rifle. Feeling excited but kind of scared.
> wat [should I] do now?

The thread was ablaze in minutes. People called him out as a fraud, but no one could firmly dispute his claims. The gun was real. He even took it apart, performing a fieldstrip to show the bolt carrier, firing pin, and extractor to confirm the gun's authenticity. He posted close-up shots of the rings to prove they were real. Someone found a link to a news story about a jewelry store that had in fact been robbed. We'll never know for sure, but it seemed legit. Imagine the thrill this moment brought to thousands of bored teens across the globe. It's like reality television, but unscripted, uncensored, and interactive.

/b/ has become a place for interesting, offbeat things like this that lack an institutionalized venue that's willing and able to display them.

When there isn't anything exciting happening, people make their own fun. Right now there is a thread titled "Give yourself from 10 years ago advice." Responses range from hilarious to heartbreaking.

> "Video games will all be the same repetitive shit in ten years so just stop now."
> "FUCKING INVEST IN APPLE."
> "Don't marry that asshole. Oh, and tell Dad that Mom is going to shoot him and make it look like a suicide."

We move on. Here's an invitation to participate in "Operation Holy Shit." It's an image of a Quran accompanied by the following message:

> "Do you see this piece of shit right here? Yep, that's a motherfucking quran. It's the guide radical muslims use when they want to learn how to be even more hateful. It incites violence against peoples of all religions. If we ever want peace in this world we must let the extremist muslims know that we will not put up with their bullshit.
> Your mission is to burn a copy of the quran, videotape the burning and post it on youtube. The results will be intense. Qurans are easy to acquire. Go to your local muslim student association and ask for a free copy and ask for one at your local mosque.
> APRIL 16TH. THE DAY /b/ FOUGHT AGAINST RADICAL ISLAM."

This sort of call to action appears now and then on /b/, and is generally what leads the press to believe that 4chan fosters hatred. Los Angeles Fox affiliate KTTV did an investigative report in 2007 about the burgeoning Anonymous hacker movement, referring to 4chan as an "Internet hate machine." 4chan of course found this hysterical and now many use the moniker as a badge of honor—as well as "hackers on steroids," another term used in the report. Most posts like this fizzle out before they pick up any momentum, but this thread has over two hundred replies in two hours. Sure enough, a few are linking to videos of Quran burnings. But not everyone is on board. Here, there be *moralfags*.

> "If you carry through with this, inoccent people will die! last time someone did this, 2 sweedish UN workers got decapitaded."

One poster suggests that /b/tards sully the holy books of all religions in various ways. Why stop at burning the Quran when you can defecate on the Torah? The suggestion ends in frustration, with the poster unable to come up with a way to offend Buddhists. It becomes a game to see who can be the most offensive. I'd bet that 95 percent of these people have no specific beef with Islam, they're just doing it for the lulz. These calls to action can be as far-reaching as "Let's bring down Islam" and as personal as "Let's all post nasty messages on the Facebook page of this girl who rejected me." Anyone can put together one of these posters.

This effort, as almost all calls to action on 4chan do, went nowhere. There was no media coverage. The operation was dead in the water. When a particular cause fails to garner support on /b/, people will respond, "/b/ is not your personal army." This usually results when people try to harness the trolling power of /b/ so they can terrorize someone who called them fat. /b/tards need motivation to attack, and some random guy's personal agenda usually doesn't cut it.

N*gg*rf*gg*ts, One and All

4chan users often call each other names with the suffix -*fag*. Christians are called *Christfags*. New 4chan users are called *newfags*. Let's examine the term *moralfag*, used to disparage people who express reservations about the antisocial behavior outside of 4chan. They are often called enemies of the lulz for claiming that /b/ has gone "too far."

The idea is that these people love morality so much that they are "gay for it." The reference is sophomoric, but in most cases it's not meant as a direct slur against homosexuals—/b/tards will often refer to themselves as being *oldfags* (veteran users) but the implicit meaning is there nonetheless. Another term bandied about quite frequently is *nigger*, which is used to describe just about anything. Some enterprising linguists have combined the two most offensive words in the English language together to form the repugnant moniker *niggerfaggot*, a term so succinctly offensive that I can almost appreciate its elegance. Almost.

I talked to Lisa Nakamura, the director of the Asian American Studies Program and professor in the Institute of Communication Research and Media and Cinema Studies Department at the University of Illinois, Urbana-Champaign. She's written at length about racial identity on the web in several books. We talked about the rampant use of racial and homophobic slurs on 4chan.

They want the benefit of the shock value or the ability to anger people but they don't want to be responsible for what they actually said, which is not fair. The line between someone who is a racist and someone who behaves like a racist is pretty thin, especially in online discourse, where pretty much what you write is what you are.

"Have you ever seen the movie *Office Space?*" she went on. She reminded me of a scene in the film where a white office drone blasts gangsta rap music from his sensible car's stereo while stuck in traffic on his way to work. He raps along to the violent lyrics, caught up in the dynamic beat, when he spots a black guy selling flowers, walking towards his vehicle along the median. He panics, locking the door and turning down the music until the harmless guy passes out of earshot.

"That's 4chan," laughs Nakamura.

A lot of people are happy to consume the media products and enjoy the spectacle of "blackness" or kung fu movies. But the reality of people of color is not often something people want to confront at all. A lot of disenfranchised, disaffected white people feel like they're also fighting the man, they're also on the edges, but in some really important way they're not.

I've personally observed that homosexuality seems to be much more accepted on 4chan than non-whiteness. You can't last ten minutes on /b/ without coming across a thread devoted to gay porn or cute boys or even friendly, accommodating discussion about the homosexual lifestyle. Whereas, the US seems to have gotten over its fear of racial minorities to a much larger degree than its fear of gays.

I believe, along with writer and NYU professor Clay Shirky,

that this is because gays are members of every community. There is no explicit gay-straight segregation, at least not in the Western world, yet there are still miles and miles of geography that contain people of only one race. When the people from these areas come face to face with people of other races on places like 4chan, it can get ugly. Secondly, minorities are so infrequently open about their race on 4chan that any time they prove their identity with a time-stamped photo, the thread inevitably veers to responses like, "Whoa, a black guy on 4chan?!" There's no guarantee of tolerance on /b/.

And yet, I keep coming across minorities there, and at many Anonymous-organized protests. I spoke about 4chan hate speech with author and journalist Julian Dibbell, whose pioneering coverage of troll culture has appeared in *Wired*, *The New York Times*, and elsewhere. He agrees with Nakamura that the reception of racist content is more important than the intent of the "fake racist." But he feels that once people enter the world of 4chan, the perspective of the receiver adjusts along with the trollish intent of those who would post racist content.

> The racist stuff would not keep coming up if it didn't have a charge to it. But once you enter into the world of 4chan and you're able to recognize what the intent is, you're able to recognize that it's different. I used to wonder why the minorities that I've spoken with hang out on /b/ and are a part of Anonymous. And you look on the board and you start to realize the kind of game that's going on.

That's a key word, *game*.

Blink And You Miss It

Moving on, we see a weed hookup thread, in which people post their location and contact info in order to score or sell pot. Another thread reads, "Ask a German Anything," wherein people inquire, "Why must your country be so awesome but your language sound so angry and phlegmy?"

"Ask Me Anything" posts are popular on 4chan. I've seen police officers, soldiers in Iraq, transvestites, prostitutes, midgets, scientists, ex-cons, porn actors, people who have attempted suicide, and roadies for popular bands post AMAs. It's a fun way to peek inside someone's life, though you can never be completely sure of the authenticity. People ask very specific questions in order to prove the veracity of AMA claims. In a few hours, I'm going to post my first AMA: "Ask a Guy Who Is Writing a Book About 4chan Anything." Should be fun!

Upon refreshing the page, I see an adult diaper fetish thread, an "America > Europe" thread, and an argument about gay marriage. There has been a running joke on the web since the advent of social networking that by the time you've caught up on your Facebook news feed, RSS reader, Twitter, Tumblr, Reddit, and whatever else, your Facebook news feed is already full of fresh content again. You could spend your entire day (your entire life!) reading updates on content aggregators and social networks.

One of the most striking things about 4chan, especially on its /b/ board, is that you can refresh the page a few *seconds* after it loads and be presented with an entirely new page of content. Unpopular posts are deleted in just a few minutes.

When a person adds to a discussion thread, it "bumps" the thread to the top of the board. The 4chan FAQ reads:

> All threads have a set bump limit (varies board to board). When this limit is reached, a thread will no longer "bump" to the top of the board, causing the thread to descend through the pages until it is marked for deletion and pruned. This method of post-limiting, while sometimes inconvenient, assures that content is kept fresh on the boards.

If no one is bumping the thread up to the top, it will descend to the bottom of the board, soon to be deleted. 4chan keeps no archives, so if you miss something, you miss it forever, unless someone's saved it on their hard drive or posted it somewhere else online.

Picture 4chan like a moving stream with kids placing boats made out of newspaper (these are the discussion threads) in the water. When someone posts something uninteresting, the thread behaves like a boat that's left to float down the stream until it eventually drops off a waterfall, never to be seen again. When someone bumps a thread by posting, it's as if a kid picks up the boat and places it back at the mouth of the stream. If enough people post in a thread, the boat can live on that stream for as long as a few hours—but will eventually, inevitably, be left to reach the edge of the waterfall.

Even the most popular posts are deleted, creating a perpetual churn of new information. Trying to capture it all would be missing the point. You just jump in somewhere and climb out when you get bored. There is no hierarchy of content to help you find the best bits. You can't search or filter the content in any way. The site flies in the face of every user experience trend and rule that's ever been codified. It's just a massive, unorganized jumble of unrelated information. Your experience with 4chan at any given moment will be completely different from someone else's, even if you're on the same board.

4chan users deal with the ephemerality of content by maintaining "/b/ folders," which are collections of previously posted favorite images, GIFs, and copypasta that they keep on their hard drives. In the years before the rest of the web started documenting meme culture (in Know Your Meme, Memegenerator, etc.), having a stockpile of /b/-worthy images on hand was essential. Sometimes /b/tards play a game where someone will write, "Post the fourth image in your /b/ folder," or "Post the scariest image you have in your /b/ folder."

I spoke with a 4chan user who goes by Jkid, who recently created a wiki site called Yotsuba Society (Yotsuba is Japanese for *4channel*), which he envisions as a database of information about chan culture, managed by a team of die-hard "chanthropologists." Yotsuba Society, according to Jkid, is made for people who are deeply into imageboard culture, not just lulz. I asked Jkid about his /b/ folder.

> There are many rare pictures that you can't find on Google search. What you see on 4chan, even on the slow boards, you may not see for a long time, if ever. That's why I archive every thread I click on.

Jkid calls this impulse the "prime imageboard directive." He sees himself as a historical archivist, having collected over 87 gigabytes of material from 4chan alone. He also collects information from other chan boards. Eventually he hopes to document the history of chan culture, from the perspective of the moderators behind the scenes. He manages a volunteer staff of nine, all who hope to create value for the community by documenting their corner of the web.

Another way /b/tards preserve 4chan culture is by submitting particularly epic threads to http://www.4chanarchive.org, a site that accepts user submissions and allows the community to vote on a given thread's worthiness for inclusion in the archive. It basically serves as a "best-of-4chan" collection, and browsing the site can in some ways be a much more fulfilling experience than slogging through 4chan. I often feel that one must trudge through miles of garbage on /b/ to find the occasional gem—though perusing old threads at 4chanarchive lacks the suspense of seeing stuff go down in real time. 4chanarchive not only saves the page, but all of the images hosted on the page as well. According to the FAQ, the site receives between six thousand and eight thousand daily unique visitors. The top viewed thread on /b/ right now at 4chanarchive is "Men laughing alone with fruitsalad." /b/tards have collected dozens of stock photo images featuring men laughing while eating fruit salad. I can't not laugh as I scroll down the page, seeing these cornball shots with the same bizarre theme.

The MIT Computer Science and Artificial Intelligence Lab and University of Southampton researchers recently performed a comprehensive analysis of 4chan's anonymity and ephemerality called *"4chan and /b/: An Analysis of Anonymity and Ephemerality in a Large Online Community."* They collected data for two weeks, compiling 576,096 posts in 482,559 threads. Their findings confirm how different the 4chan experience can be for everyone involved. Researchers discovered that the median life of a thread is just under four minutes. The most ephemeral threads last less than thirty seconds, often due to being posted at a high-volume time of day and inciting no replies. Furthermore, the median thread spends just five seconds on the first page over its lifetime. Only posts that are able to grab the attention of the group have any chance of staying on the front page for any length of time. They also found that /b/ hosts thirty-five thousand threads and four hundred thousand posts *every day*. Most shocking, 43 percent of posts get no replies at all—nearly half of everything posted to /b/ is summarily ignored.

The study also examined the subject matter of the threads, broken down this way.

- 27% Themed—"ITT, we post pictures of ex-girlfriends."
- 19% Sharing—"Check out this lizard that was on my front porch this morning."
- 10% Questions—"I just got a $300 Christmas bonus and I want to spend it all on Amazon. What should I buy?"
- 9% Personal Info Sharing—"This is my new motorcycle. Does /b/ like?"
- 8% Discussion—"What does /b/ think about the new *World of Warcraft* expansion?"
- 8% Request for Item—"Does anyone have any high-res *Green Lantern* screenshots?"
- 7% Request for Action—"This is the phone number of the jerk who stole my girl. Make me proud, /b/."
- 5% Meta—"/b/ sucks these days. Full of newfags."
- 6% Other.

Back to /b/. I refresh the page again, and I'm presented with a dozen new threads. The one on top features a beautiful feline in repose and reads:

My cat tiga died today /b/. She was 15. A mean mother fucker but I still loved her. Can it be cat teim?

The thread already has over 150 responses. People post condolences along with photos of cute cats.

Cats, Camgirls, and Comics

Speaking of cute cats, I should probably mention here that they are one of 4chan's defining obsessions. If I come across someone who's never heard of Internet memes, the first thing I usually say is, "Have you ever seen lolcats?" That's because it's not only the biggest thing to come out of 4chan, it's the undisputed biggest Internet meme.

Here's the idea: A humorous photo of a cat accompanied by a caption written in a pidgin English derived from rushed IM speak. The stupidly funny broken English coupled with the inherent cuteness of the cat images made for a viral phenomenon. lolcats were dumb, catchy, and approachable enough that anyone could pick up on the humor after seeing a few.

lolcats first showed up on 4chan in 2005 as a cute joke contrasting with the site's usual stream of gross-out content, but they did not achieve cultural ubiquity until 2007, when Ben Huh bought http://www.icanhazcheezburger.com and formed the site around lolcats. Now there are millions of lolcat images all over the web, generating millions of dollars. And it all came from /b/'s "Caturday" tradition of posting cute captioned cats each Saturday.

Ah, here's a big 4chan obsession: a camgirl thread. The words *camgirl* or *camwhore* describe a girl on the Internet who attracts the attention of men by using her beauty for fun or profit.

Girls on 4chan will post photos of themselves on /b/, usually holding up a piece of paper (or sometimes drawing directly on their bodies with a Sharpie) that reads something along the lines of "APRIL 5TH, 4:47PM Sup /b/" in order to prove the authenticity of the photo. Without this accompanying message, people will immediately claim that it's just some guy posing as a girl with a random photo he found on the web. But with a time stamp indicating that it's happening right now, they start bleating "TITS or GTFO [get the fuck out]." This practice is considered proof of authenticity, and girls need it more than anyone, since the 4chan adage "There are no girls on the Internet" suggests that anyone claiming to be a woman is actually a man either trolling or getting a sexual thrill out of posting as a woman.

After proving her identity as a female, the girl will generally tease the boys for a while, removing one article of clothing at a time, or responding to various requests. The thread eventually expires when there's nothing left to show, and the boys move on to the next camgirl to come along. Of course, these girls don't always disrobe. Sometimes they just show up for the attention and leave after posting a few innocent pics.

Some camgirls become famous. Some of them are known for being drop-dead gorgeous while others gain attention by being quirky and weird. Whatever the reason, these camgirls often become 4chan microcelebrities. They are given nicknames and love to show up once in a while, presumably for a self-esteem boost.

4chan's relationship with women is weird and sad. Some use the word *cumdumpster* as a synonym for *female*. Girls even refer to themselves this way. When women appear on 4chan, the men bombard them with commands to disrobe or perform sex acts, but the moment they deliver the goods, they are booed off stage. (Then again, so are men who have nothing interesting to offer.)

I asked Lisa Nakamura what she thinks about the term.

> Part of trying to blend into a transgressive social group is trying to prove that you're more transgressive than them. This is a technique of countering sexism by applying it to yourself first. I don't think it's a harmless practice. I think it's a form of self-abasement that's pretty similar to what women often have to do in the military, which is a heavily masculine environment. The only way to show that you deserve to belong in a masculine environment is to insult yourself so other people can't do it. It's kind of a preemptive sexism. You protect yourself, but it's the same thing; you've just been co-opted into doing it first.

In early 2009 a teen girl calling herself BoxxyBabee (real name: Catherine Wayne) uploaded a series of videos on YouTube that featured her face against a black background, yapping for five minutes about virtually nothing. Her spastic delivery and cutesy demeanor resembled a hyperactive anime girl, and she was quickly declared by many to be The Queen of /b/. This distinction brought not loyalty, but hostility, stalking, and threatening phone calls. The response on 4chan was so strong that Boxxy did something few in her position are able to do: she left the Internet. For a few years, anyway.

Boxxy resurfaced in November 2010 on an anonymous imageboard called Unichan in order to promote an eBay auction. She was selling a bag and wanted to drum up some buzz. She posted a photo of her holding a placard reading "lwayne202@comcast.

net" (presumably so 4chan users could send her cash directly through Paypal) and the message "i'm sorry i've been so scared. I LOVE YOU! <3" along with the date and time stamp to prove her authenticity. Touched by her return, some anons launched "Operation Give to Boxxy Till it Hurts," urging 4chan users to send Boxxy cash. /b/tards bid the bag up to tens of thousands of dollars, eBay naturally canceled the auction, and Boxxy disappeared once again.

Boxxy's place in 4chan mythology is solidified among a long line of young women who have caught the attention of /b/ for being both supercute and superannoying. More recently, the teen pop sensation Rebecca Black was targeted by 4chan trolls. Black achieved instant global celebrity, partially on the strength of hatred coming from 4chan, since the mainstream media was able to position the story as a young girl's triumph over cyberbullying.

Black's mother paid a few thousand bucks to a vanity record label called Ark Music Factory, which specializes in recording saccharine pop songs sung by precocious tweens. In exchange, Ark wrote, produced, and recorded a pop song for Rebecca along with an accompanying video. The result was "Friday," a teen ode to good clean weekend fun. Within a few days, Rebecca went from suburban anonymity to YouTube oddity to global pop sensation. And it annoyed anons to no end. They launched Operation Black Friday, encouraging /b/tards to fax bestiality porn to Rebecca's school under her name, attack Ark Music Factory's website, flood her YouTube channel with antisocial comments, and find out where she lived. Nothing noteworthy came of these efforts.

The minimal press coverage of 4chan that I've seen over the

last few years focuses primarily on the idea of 4chan as a racist and homophobic hate group. The words *faggot* and *nigger* are used so frequently, and in situations so far removed from a hateful context, that at times it's almost difficult to see them as slurs. People open conversations with "Greetings, faggots . . ." or "Have any of you niggers heard the new Metallica album?" The use is so indiscriminate that regular users might see them as terms of endearment. It's as if they're saying, "We're all faggots and niggers here."

I'm reminded of punk poet Patti Smith's "Rock and Roll Nigger," which defiantly declared, "Outside of society, that's where I want to be," going on to declare that Jesus Christ, Jackson Pollock, and even Grandma were niggers too. Remember, most 4chan users are computer nerds. The language operates as a way for 4chan users to bond over their shared status as social misfits, friendly monikers for those who see themselves as marginalized.

Lisa Nakamura is skeptical.

Comedians like Richard Pryor and Paul Mooney have done pretty high-profile interviews about why they've chosen to stop using the word *nigger*, even though they have pretty rich comedic histories of using them. People who make the argument that the words are harmless are often white people. I tend to take this argument a little more seriously when it's coming from minorities.

I refresh /b/ again and find:

Lets make a thread where you go wikipedia and select random article, whatever comes upp, that will be the new name of your dick. ill start: Château Grand-Puy-Ducasse . . .

Further down the page I spot a RageToon thread. These are four-panel comics that highlight subtle things that enrage everyone. They showed up on 4chan in late 2008 and have become one of the most recognizable Internet memes, expanding to places like Tumblr and Reddit.

The comics start with three blank panels and a fourth featuring a crudely drawn, screaming face with the caption, "FFFFFFFFFUUUUUUUUU-" The artist fills in the first three panels with something that is typically enraging, like when you accidentally rip into a page of notebook paper while removing the perforated edge. They're simple, catchy, and infinitely shareable because they touch on commonly held but seldom-discussed frustrations. Because they're so easy to create, their stick-figure template has spawned dozens of variations, including:

- Stoner Comics—Hilarious stories about pie-eyed misadventures.
- Troll Physics—Pseudoscientific explanations for impossible physical phenomena.
- Everything Went Better Than Expected—The opposite of RageToons.
- Forever Alone—A guy in humorous denial of his loneliness.

These are just a handful of examples. Today the form stars a cast of characters numbering several dozen. The important thing about these comics is their status as *exploitables,* or images that serve as semiblank canvases for the imagination of the hivemind. An exploitable could be a man's face with a blank thought bubble overhead; everyone can fill in the bubble with their own text. It's kind of like the *New Yorker* caption contest. It becomes a game to creatively fill in the blanks.

And it doesn't stop at text. Photoshop wizards augment the imagery itself, for hilarious results. Exploitables allow anyone to engage in the communal meme pool that is 4chan, with a very low barrier to entry. All you need is some basic image-editing prowess and a sense of humor, and you too can achieve maximum lulz. Some of the comics that come out of these threads surpass anything I've seen in the Sunday funnies.

A Meme Pool For Participatory Culture

There are many words used to describe this kind of interactive entertainment. Some call it riffing; others call it remixing. Media scholar Henry Jenkins calls it participatory culture. Before the web, most content was produced by professional content producers and broadcast by professional broadcasters until it reached you and millions of other consumers. The web has obliterated that process.

Consider a recent meme called Nyan Cat, aka Pop Tart Cat. Nyan Cat is an animation depicting a cat with a Pop Tart body flying in space with a rainbow contrail. It was originally posted to a comics site, then made its way to Tumblr in GIF form. Someone else set it to a hyperactive electronic pop song created with a vocal synthesizer that sounds like a person saying "nyan nyan nyan" over and over, and uploaded it to YouTube. Then 4chan and Internet culture blogs like Buzzfeed picked it up. Since it was uploaded, someone mashed it up with heavy metal band Slipknot's music video for "Psychosocial." Dozens of alternate animations and parodies were created. A bunch of musicians independently covered the song with piano, guitar, and Japanese lute. There's a dubstep remix. There's a video of a guy on an exercise bike dressed up as Nyan Cat, pedaling to the music. There is a Nyan Cat flash video game. Between the image parodies, video mashups, audio remixes, games, and other references, the flying cat with the Pop Tart body is a memetic sensation with tens of thousands of iterations—and it's only been viral for a month, as of this writing.

Another example of participatory culture is Advice Animals, which also began in 4chan but has seeped out into the broader web. The Advice Animals are some of the most visually arresting and immediately satisfying image macros on 4chan, and, like Ragetoons, have expanded to places like Reddit and Tumblr. It all started with Advice Dog, a cheerful puppy against a bursting rainbow backdrop. Nothing could be cuter. And then, you read the caption, which consists of two lines; a command above and below the dog's adorable face:

STEAL THE CANDY
FROM THE MEDICINE CABINET

The cutesy image of a dog juxtaposed with horrific "advice," made for a powerful meme. Then came Courage Wolf, a snarling beast that offers extreme platitudes:

THE DOCTOR SAID IT WAS CANCER
I CALL IT A CHALLENGE

And Insanity Wolf:

> YOU SAY KIDNAPPING
> I SAY "SURPRISE ADOPTION"

And Courage Pup, a miniature version of Courage Wolf:

> DAD SAYS NO LUNCHABLES
> PUT IN CART ANYWAY

The meme soon expanded to include dozens of other animals and people. There's Bachelor Frog, a stereotype of the slacker lifestyle:

> CAN'T HEAR TV
> CHEW CHIPS SLOWER

Business Cat, who spouts business cliches:

> I NEED YOU TO STAY LATE TONIGHT
> WE REALLY HAVE TO CATCH THAT RED DOT

And Socially Awkward Penguin, who's always saying the wrong thing at the wrong time:

> WAITRESS TELLS YOU TO ENJOY YOUR FOOD
> SAY "YOU TOO"

And so on. Now there are millions of variations of the Advice Animal meme encompassing Hipster Disney Princesses, OCD Otter, and more. They usually derive their humor in one of two ways: Either they speak universally recognized but seldom spoken little truths, or they rely on pure shock value. The closest pop-culture equivalent to these diptychs would probably be editorial cartoons.

I've described just a few of the simpler visual memes. They're not examples I'd point to if I wanted to demonstrate the intellectual vibrancy of the medium; they're just case studies in virality. Nyan Cat is not only a video, but an experience in which thousands of people are actively participating.

Today, most consumers have the ability to be producers, and communication channels no longer move information in just one direction, from few to many, but can move information back and forth and back again. Pieces of content rub up against one another in melting pots like YouTube, DeviantArt, Tumblr, and Reddit. Users recut their favorite films, make custom music videos for new pop songs, and develop sprawling fan fiction based on beloved literature. The experience of consuming entertainment is now only part of the fun. Today, we can make the entertainment our own, and it happens nowhere more dynamically than at 4chan.

Mini-Games

"You Barf You Lose" reads the description of a newly christened thread. Accompanying this caption is a photo of a corpse; the top half, anyway. Threads like this are called "gore threads." The object of this game is to find revolting images featuring mutilated bodies, autopsy photos, animated GIFs of suicides caught by security cameras, and so on. Gore threads are a parade of death and dismemberment, drawing on the adolescent male impulse to gross out one's friends. Perhaps it's a way to laugh in the face of death. Maybe it's just the visceral thrill of seeing something you're not meant to see. Call it /b/-horror.

"You Barf You Lose" is only one of the many iterations of the "You Lose" games. The most popular is "You Laugh You Lose," in which players compete to post the most hilarious, freshest images. In "You Bawww You Lose," players post the saddest pictures they can find in order to make people bawww, or cry. One that immediately comes to mind is a devastating image of a loyal dog lying next to a body bag, presumably his recently deceased owner. "You Rage You Lose" has people posting links to pages containing troll-baiting content, like some 14-year-old kid's ADD YouTube rant about libertarianism or a woman complaining about misogyny in the workplace.

One of the more fascinating games is "You Fall In Love You Lose," which pits players against each other to find not so much the hottest girls, but photographs of women that they'd like to hold hands with while strolling along a promenade. It's interesting how these /b/tards, who have long been desensitized to the most extreme forms of pornography, tend to gravitate toward photographs that depict women as innocent, carefree, and generally wholesome. The girls featured prominently in these threads are almost always fully clothed. There are several more "You Lose" games, all designed to elicit strong, specific emotions such as nostalgia, lust, or bewilderment. 4chan is defined by its users' desire to outdo each other, and these threads capture that mentality.

Another example of a game 4chan likes to play is called "Delicious Cake." Someone will post a crude MS Paint drawing of a man and a cake separated by whirling blades, deadly spikes, monsters, pits of lava, and the like. Then everyone else in the thread will augment the image, explaining how they will overcome the obstacles in order to acquire the delicious cake.

There's also "3 Items That Make the Cashier Wat." *Wat* is a catchall response to anything mind-blowingly bizarre. It's like saying "What?" but comes across as more deadpan. The challenge here is to come up with three items that would freak out a cashier. Some examples:

- A pregnancy test, a metal clothes hanger, a goldfish.
- A wooden crate, a rope, and an ice-cream cake.
- A hunting knife, duct tape, six boxes of Lunchables.

The best ones don't imply gross sex or murder, like "A box of Cheerios, milk, and a single spoon."

Other games include "Make This Face," "Read The 3rd Sentence on the Last Page of the Book Nearest to You," and "Finish This Drawing." New games are being created every day. The /b/ community is constantly coming up with new ways to defeat boredom.

You're just as likely to come across a thread with guys comparing pictures of their dicks as you are an example of wildly creative storytelling or deep philosophical debate. It's true that the lion's share of content on /b/ tends to be sophomoric, but it is random after all, so there are pleasant surprises.

Delicious Copypasta

Here we go. I've just found some *copypasta*, which is content that's been "copy-pasted" from other sources. I know it's old content because I googled it and found a match.

Okay so I am starting to have a panic attack because I am afraid the fucking FBI is going to kick my door down any second so if this is my last post on /b/ I hope it's epic. To start it all off I live in a pretty quiet, secure, suburban town. I have a cat that I love more than life itself and a neighbor that is dumb as fuck. next door to me lives a New Family that just moved in a year ago or so, they have a child thats probably 18 months or so old. This kid is the fucking devil. He has cause more problems than any other kid I have ever heard of. Anyway, I have observed on several occasions the child torturing my cat. The parents let the child play outside alone quite a bit, I imagine they supervise from the kitchen or patio, I can never really tell from my vantage point, I just assume so since the child is so young. I have seen my cat (who is so friendly he literally goes up to everyone he see's and rubs against them) wander over to the child and get friendly only to witness Satan smaching the cat, punching him, ripping out clumps of fur, and grabbing his tail and not letting go. The cat is so nice that he doesn't even try to attack the child, just squirm away in pain as best he can. I always have to run outside and save my cat, but there have been times this happened when I was not around. Now I know this makes my cat look stupid but the fucking kid actually goes out there trying to catch him, my cat learned from the first encounter but since then his parents have given the child some cat nip and other such treats to try and lure that cat over. So finally I snapped today after I saw the kid throw a rock at my cat. It hit him on his hind leg and I imagine it's broken, I saw the cat limp away whining with his leg literally being dragged behind him. I went on my computer and pulled up Earth Caller.

I called up the neighbor (I knew the mother was the only one home). And as soon as it started to ring I played some music on my computer near the mic and bolted out the door. I ran to the back yard, looked in the window and saw the mother with her back turned walking to the phone. I snatched the kid and bolted out of there. I know she did not see me. I cupped his mouth so the bastard would not make any noise. I ran inside and grabbed a black trash bag from my house. I literally stuffed the fucker in there and went for my car in the front. I threw the bag in my car and drove off non-chalantly. I drove for a while and got out in a wooded area and literally just through the bag in the woods. The kid screamed so loud. I herd the thud and then took off. I went to a friends house from there so I had some kind of alibi and then I came home and started typing this. Am I fucked /b/? I am pretty sure the kid is dead . . .

People make up freak-out tales like this, and responses range from ironic support to outrage to bored yawns. Some of them turn out to be elaborate shaggy-dog stories.

Copypasta is also used as a template for riffing. Consider the Bel-Air meme, based on the lyrics of the opening theme of Will Smith's sitcom *The Fresh Prince of Bel-Air*, which are recontextualized in different situations.

They've been remixed for Darth Vader:

> Now this a story all about how
> My life got flipped turned upside down
> And you should take a minute just listen to this
> About how I became apprentice to the Dark Lord of Sith.
>
> In West Tatooine I was born and raised . . .

You get the idea. Here's another version, spoken like a carica-ture of a real British gentleman.

> To begin, this is a tale of how my very existence was twisted and transformed in a most peculiar way. Please have a seat, for I wish to take a moment to relate to you the fascinating odyssey which ultimately led to my reign as the Prince of Bel-Air. I was sired and reared in West Philadelphia. As a lad, most of my time was spent at the neighborhood recreation center where I would laze about and relax in a most charming manner—that is, when I was not engaging my chums in a friendly game of basketball at the schoolhouse. Around this time, two young hooligans had begun to stage a campaign of vandalism and intimidation in my neighborhood. When my mother discovered I had had a bit of an altercation with the ruffians, she insisted I leave town at once and take up lodgings with my aunt and uncle in Bel-Air.

There are hundreds, maybe even thousands, of these things. Any time a major news event occurs centering on a specific per-son, some /b/tard will inevitably create a Bel-Air meme to com-memorate the event.

Know Your Trolls

Now is probably a good time to explore the world of trolls. Trolling is the act of agitating or fooling people for fun under false pretenses. It's derived from fishing lexicon, in which troll-ing refers to slowly dragging a baited hook or lure from a moving boat in order to simulate the natural movement of, say, a min-now, in order to trick a fish. The modern definition may also come from the mischievous trolls of European folklore. 4chan didn't invent Internet trolling, but 4chan attracts trolls like no other community before it.

There are a few types of trolls:

- The Deceiver—Tries to get you to believe something that's not true.
- The Know-nothing—Pretends to be dumb so you waste time explaining something. Uses bad grammar so you take the time to correct him.
- The Pottymouth—Uses offensive words to annoy.
- The Contrarian—Plays devil's advocate to an obviously unreasonable perspective.
- The Hissy Fit—Throws a fake tantrum so you expend energy convincing him to calm down.
- The Accuser—Accuses you of being a troll, knowing you aren't.

The troll is an interesting creature with a long heritage dating back to the trickster characters of ancient mythology. The Greek prankster Pan, the Norse god Loki, and the conniving Native American Coyote are a few older examples. One could argue that even the Biblical Satan primarily exists to troll humanity. The trickster's mark is all over modern Western popular culture, from Brer Rabbit to Bugs Bunny to Bart Simpson. Trolls pester, poke, and prod until they get what they want: control of your emotions.

I spoke with Ted Frank, legendary Usenet troll, though he's more famous today as a leading tort reform advocate and founder of the Center for Class Action Fairness.

Frank's name came up multiple times when I researched the

history of trolling. He replied quickly to my request for an interview, but immediately insisted that we define our terms.

> *Trolling* meant one thing in the small close-knit Usenet community of the 1990s, where it was used to describe innocent pranking of know-it-all Cliff Claven types with subtle disingenuous displays of ironic ignorance—by making the sort of mistakes that could only be made by someone who was actually knowledgeable about the subject, and a close reading of the post would demonstrate that the writer couldn't possibly be serious about his mistake.
>
> The know-it-all newbie would arrogantly correct the troller (often making a mistake of his own), and everyone would laugh. That was an art form of sorts, but the term also started getting used to describe more malicious provocations. When spam overran Usenet (and Usenet itself became superseded by more sophisticated web forums), there wasn't really a forum for the innocent version, because the dynamic of new people entering an Internet community changed. Usenet always had a large ratio of experienced posters to newbies.

Frank insists that the relationship between the trolling on 4chan and the trolling on Usenet can be explained as nothing more than an etymological coincidence. The trolling of his day was bitingly clever, with relatively mild pranking. He draws comparisons to comedian Don Novello's Laszlo Toth letters, in which the entertainer wrote prankish letters to famous businessmen and politicians.

> Don Novello would write absurd consumer complaints to starchy corporate customer-relations departments and get ramrod-straight by-the-book letters back that were entirely inappropriate to the original missive.

This sort of trolling isn't completely without social value in the right context.

It served as an educational tool to newcomers not to be condescending to the regulars. In a larger community where most people are strangers, I doubt it has any social value; when it is done purely to provoke, it has no value at all.

Ted Frank palled around with Dave and Barbara Mikkelsons, who went on to found Snopes, the rumor-debunking site that's served as a trusted source of obscura for 16 years. The Mikkelsons met on Usenet, developed a relationship based on their shared fascination with urban legends, and eventually married. According to Frank, Dave Mikkelson ("Snopes" on Usenet) was a pro troll, who was known to have called candy companies to complain that their products did nothing to relieve his headaches.

Now, the type of personality that engages in snopes-like trolling is the kind of personality that doesn't mind going into a room and being told by everyone there that he's wrong, questions authority, and starts up a snopes.com or a Center for Class Action Fairness, but that's a different issue.

Today, heinous forms of harassment are lumped in with this clever pranksterism. Usually, trolls on 4chan use a little bit of both. In 2008, Oprah ran a segment on Internet predators. Leading up the show, a /b/tard posted the following message to Oprah's message board:

We do not forgive. We do not forget. We have OVER 9000 penises and they are all raping children.

Cue disbelieving gasps from the audience. Who knew such evils were lurking in the family computer room? As it turns out, OVER 9000 is an old 4chan meme from the anime *Dragon Ball Z*, in which a character humorously screams the phrase. The quote was an obvious troll to anyone who spent any time on 4chan, but to Oprah's producers the quote contained the perfect amount of cold-blooded evil for their fear-mongering segment.

Oprah repeated the quote on her show, attributing the quote to a "known pedophile network" that was both organized and systematic. Meanwhile, Anonymous had itself a hearty lol. There are currently hundreds of videos on YouTube making fun of Oprah for the incident. Tricking a celebrity into acknowledging the existence of Anonymous was funny, but doing it under the pretense of a fake army of over nine thousand organized pedophiles was considered an epic win for the trolls. I often wonder if anyone told poor Oprah afterwards that she'd been had.

Troll Heritage

Perhaps the finest example of a pre-Internet troll is the late comedian and entertainer Andy Kaufman, who made a career out of subversive multilayered publicity stunts so convincing that some fans still doubt the authenticity of his 1984 death from kidney failure. Kaufman would concoct elaborate hoaxes and practical jokes. He once appeared on *The Dating Game* as a sweating, stuttering foreign man whose awkward delivery confounded the other participants.

In one highly publicized troll, Kaufman sparred with professional wrestler Jerry Lawler. He claimed to have suffered a neck injury and wore a neck brace wherever he went, including a legendary on-air fight with Lawler on the set of *Late Night with David Letterman*. Not even his close comedian buddies knew for sure if the neck brace was worn genuinely. Kaufman's feud with Lawler was later revealed to be 100 percent staged.

Kaufman's jokes were often on his audience. He delighted in messing with people's heads. He once read *The Great Gatsby* aloud to an audience expecting standup. At first they laughed, but he refused to stop, even as they booed and left the auditorium.

Check the monologue from *I'm From Hollywood*, a documentary which included a promotional video Kaufman made to rile up Southern wrestling fans.

I want to talk to you. And I want to help you. Every week I'm going to be coming here, on this station. And I'm going to be giving you little tips about how you can better your lives. And how I can bring you up from the level you're in right now. And how I can bring you up from the squalor that you're living in, in the gutter, and the garbage that your lives are.

This is a bar of soap. Now, does it look familiar to any of you? I know that you probably don't know what this is and probably you don't have ever seen one of these before. But it is called soap. Matter of fact, if you're sitting at home now, you can maybe repeat after me and say: "Soap." Say "soap." S-O-A-P, soap. Not "sowp." Not "say-owp." It's "soap." okay?

You people, your hands are so greasy and slimy. I mean, I don't wanna shake 'em. You ask me for an autograph, I'll sign you an autograph. But please, don't put out your hand and shake it until you can wash your hands. That is what you do: Wet your hands, okay, then wet the soap. Wash the soap, rub it on your hands, rub it around and your hands will get clean.

The video continues with Kaufman condescendingly instructing his audience in basic hygiene, intercut with reaction footage of enraged Southern good ol' boys claiming, "If I saw 'im right now I'd kick 'is ass!" During his wrestling matches, thousands would shriek for Andy's head on a platter. And the footage shows he's loving every minute of it.

In the same documentary, comedian Robin Williams declares, "Andy made himself the premise and the entire world was the punchline."

If Andy Kaufman is a spiritual ancestor of /b/'s penchant for outlandish stunts, then alternative rock stalwart Steve Albini plays godfather to the site's more subdued smartass. I mean, the guy had a band called Rapeman, which provoked picket lines and news crews crowding the band's small indie rock gigs.

In an interview with Adam Dolgins, author of *Rock Names*, Albini clarifies that he discovered an obscure Japanese comic book featuring a hero called Rapeman, who rapes women who've wronged his clients. Albini writes songs about serial killers, wife beaters, and gruesome executions. His first band, Big Black, had an EP named after Budd Dwyer, a Pennsylvania politician who shot himself in the mouth on live TV. Very /b/.

What interests me the most about Steve Albini's dark brand of trolling is that he's operating within the realm of rock and roll, which is supposed to shock and offend . . . parents. Albini takes it a step further. He wants to mess with feminist studies students and went straight for the throats of liberal progressives and the alt-rock elite, calling universally revered bands tedious, for example. *Very* /b/.

Now, imagine a world full of millions of would-be Andy Kaufmans and Steve Albinis loosely working together. Only these trolls are all faceless, with no reputations to protect and nothing on the line. That's the environment in which I'm about to expose my identity.

Here goes nothing.

Are You There /b/? It's Me, Cole

My publisher recently posted a page about my book with a cover mockup on the site, so I'm able to give 4chan a teaser. I type out a simple message.

> Oh hai /b/,
> What do we think of this?

I type out the CAPTCHA (an authentication process instituted by moot to limit SPAM that made /b/ practically unreadable for a while in 2010) and exhale. Click.

Nothing.

I hit refresh. One response:

> That it's a book

Refresh again.

> Awww shit!
> seems legit
> who the fuck cares? Somebody wrote a book about 4chan. This isn't a secret underground organization.

Of course, it'll be distributed threw BitTorrent right?
Oh fuck me. I hate this little cunt.

I make a follow-up post, unlikely to be believed. "I'm writing a book about you. What do you think about that?"

That's pretty cool, OP.
We think you're asking for more trouble than it's worth. Seriously.
Rule 1 and 2. you will die soon
OP, kindly an hero [that is, kill yourself] immediately. As if anyone gives a fuck other than cancerous summerfags [also called noobs] like you
I'd love to help you out with the book in any way, writing it or just online distibution/marketing, or design. Willing to get some help?
OP, are you ready for the potential shitstorm aimed at you?
Cool story, bro.

The thread continues with various empty threats, insults, and a few surprisingly sincere optimists who tell me they can't wait to read the book. One person Photoshops a pirate mustache onto my face and posts it. Another writes:

Don't publish your book, you faggot. You probably suck at writing and are trying to scrounge money together because you know you'll never have an actual job because you majored in journalism. Your days are numbered, Cole.

The thread continues, devolving into a loose argument about whether 4chan is worth writing a book about. Soon, someone posts an inappropriately graffitied photo of me, yanked from my personal blog. Time will tell if the /b/tards actually try to find out where I live or target me in any way. Probably not, but I'm not going to go any further out of my way to invite harassment.

Calvinball

I have used the word *game* to describe the experience of /b/, and more broadly, 4chan and the Anonymous movement. I believe people are drawn to /b/ because it's a ludic playground, where the rules are perpetually being redefined.

Play can be defined as any activity that is done for personal enjoyment. In its barest definition, a game is structured play. (Unstructured play being something like daydreaming, blowing bubbles, or frolicking in a field.) A game must have an achievable goal, with walls erected between the player and the goal that make it a challenge to reach. These walls are rules that define the game. One could say that 4chan is a game in which the rules are in a constant state of flux.

It reminds me of Calvinball, from the comic strip *Calvin and Hobbes*. In the first Calvinball-related strip, creator Bill Watterson defined the only permanent rule of Calvinball: You can't play it the same way twice. So Calvin and his imaginary tiger pal Hobbes are constantly reinventing the game, bickering over the rules every step of the way. The strip lampooned the childhood tendency for groups of kids to make up their rules as they went along, when tempers, politicking, cheating, and boredom make strict rules difficult to uphold.

There are very specific games happening within each individual thread of 4chan, and one can observe 4chan as an ongoing global metagame like Calvinball. Sometimes the goal is to piss people off. Sometimes it's to make some specific person's life miserable . . . or wonderful. Other times the object of the game is to confuse outsiders or wreck others' idea of what the game is about.

Mine is a generation raised by video games, which teach children to test the boundaries of their rule sets, mess with their environments, and memorize entire tiny universes until they're able to spot and exploit holes and glitches. Computer hackers identify with this impulse to a large degree. For them, systems are made to be mastered, broken, and messed with. When playing a game the way it's supposed to be played gets boring, they seek out cheat codes and other ways of essentially "breaking" the game. It's one thing to beat or win a game, but can you say you've truly mastered a game until you've broken it?

This kind of metagaming is not limited to video games. Think of all the various ways people find to enjoy professional football, for instance. They place bets on teams, they play fantasy football, they engage in playful taunting with the fans of opposing teams. The football happening on the field is just a small part of the game experience.

You Just Lost The Game

In April 2009, *Time* magazine held its annual TIME 100 poll, part of which was dedicated to the most influential people on the planet. Candidates included the likes of Tina Fey, Hu Jintao, Gamal Mubarak, and other luminaries of art, science, business, government, and philanthropy. *Time* opened up the list to online voting, and the 4chan hivemind set to work putting moot at the top of the list. When they accomplished that, they decided it wasn't fun enough. They eventually gamed the whole list, ensuring that the top twenty names would spell out a coded message to fellow /b/tards that they had indeed accomplished an epic win.

It all started when 4chan discovered that moot had been included as one of the many candidates in the TIME 100 poll. 4chan hackers (and this is low-level hacking to be sure) found that they could game the poll with a series of custom autovoter URLs associated with each candidate. The /b/tards spammed the URLs far and wide, including a limit for each, so the candidates would appear in the proper order. *Time* spotted the shenanigans, reset the poll, and changed the URL protocol in order to authenticate votes.

Now the challenge was really on. The hackers set up an IRC channel to discuss the hack, eventually figuring out how to bypass the authentication process (Internet Relay Chat, or IRC, is an early form of real-time chat favored by Anonymous because it's easy to hide one's IP address). Some autovoters were created that could vote one hundred times per minute. Others created apps that would cycle through IP addresses so the *Time* site wouldn't be able to detect that the spam votes were coming from a single computer. Eventually the hackers were able to craft scripts that would easily manipulate the poll's order. Their final list began:

1. moot
2. Anwar Ibrahim
3. Rick Warren
4. Baitulla Mehsud
5. Larry Brilliant

And so on, with the first letter of each name spelling out MARBLECAKEALSOTHEGAME.

Marblecake is a probably fictional scatological sex act defined (if you are prepared to brave it) at urbandictionary.com. But what about The Game? This is a popular 4chan meme that presages the site. The point is to make the victim think of something or notice something very specific, with the moment of realization delivering a sense of having been had. The object of the game is to avoid thinking about The Game.

According to http://www.losethegame.net, The Game was invented in 1977 by members of the Cambridge University Science Fiction Society (CUSFS) as a variant of the White Bear Game, in which participants try to think of anything other than a white bear, which the human mind makes difficult in a mental phenomenon called ironic processing.

So it becomes a competition to make people recognize The Game in clever ways. On /b/, people will craft sprawling posts culminating in the anticlimax, "Oh, btw, you just lost the game." They write "You Lost The Game" on currency and spray paint it on walls.

I first lost The Game when someone on /b/ urged me, "Check the TV Guide for 6:00pm on Thursday you won't believe it!" I played along, and sure enough the broadcast description for that slot was a mere two words: The Game, a 1997 thriller starring Michael Douglas.

4chan's gaming of the TIME 100 poll has gone down in history as one of the most epic Game-related wins, since they were able to make millions of people cognizant of The Game. Furthermore, they arguably established Anonymous as the true winner of the TIME 100 most influential poll.

Chapter 4

Tracing 4chan Ancestry

LIKE EVERY OTHER web community, 4chan didn't simply materialize fully formed out of the ether. In order to understand the motivations and interests of 4chan users, it's helpful to know where 4chan came from. The history of the web isn't so much a story about technology as it is a story about people, and how the ways they interact with one another change when new technology allows them to try new things.

Phone Phreaks: Pre-Internet Hackers

One might argue that the roots of 4chan go all the way back to the '50s, when a bunch of kids figured out how to get free long-distance phone calls by whistling a specific pitch into the receiver. These kids called themselves phone phreaks. Many of the phreaks were blind, with increased sensitivity to sound that enabled them to quickly learn the right pitch to mimic the phone companies' control tones. Many were also social misfits, drawn together from across the US by their shared interest in technology, and more importantly, in breaking the technology.

In the late 1960s, one phreaker, John Draper—known by the nickname "Captain Crunch" after he discovered that a plastic toy whistle distributed in boxes of Captain Crunch cereal perfectly produced the right tone to hack into the phone network—helped to spread the hobby, which eventually permeated the MIT tech community, where the practice of hacking into communication systems continued, along with the rise of . . .

The Wild West: Usenet & BBSes

A lot of 4chan users laud their platform for hearkening back to the early days of the Internet. "Back then it was like the Wild West. There weren't these structures in place to make sure that people stayed in line," one anon told me. Another said, "And forget about the thirty-page terms of service documents." If you stepped out of line, either you got banned or your transgression became the new law of the land.

Dating the birth of the Internet depends on your criteria. It's difficult to pinpoint where a bunch of nerds playing around with modems stopped and "the Internet" began. Bulletin Board Systems (BBSes) started appearing in the late '70s. These were mostly local communities, since dialing into a BBS outside of your local calling area would have brought hefty long distance charges. I've talked to a few dozen people about those early days, from community managers to hackers to system operators, and they all agree on two things: the Internet in that era was expensive and slow.

BBSes were simple text-based precursors to message boards, where people could post messages to everyone else who happened to dial in. The boards often dealt with local interests and specific hobbies like fishing or philosophy. There were also boards dedicated to computing and hacking. It was in these that the first instances of what would come to be known as *leetspeak* bubbled to the surface. This pidgin English was used by hackers to get around wordfilters and, eventually, to avoid the prying eyes of search engines. *Hackers* became *h4x0rz,* for example. This argot is very common on 4chan, though it has been co-opted by people with no hacking ability and is now either used ironically or by noobs attempting to emulate the hackers of yore. Anyone who says things like, "ph34r my 1337 h4x0rz ski11z" isn't going to bring down Bank of America any time soon.

In 1979, three grad students developed Usenet, a file-transferring network that ran on the Unix operating system. Users gathered in "newsgroups" with threaded discussions much like the message boards of today. Usenet differed from previous BBSes because it lacked a central server and system administrator. Apart from leetspeak, Usenet is known for being an early breeding ground for memes, though at the time they were limited to in-jokes and slang such as sockpuppet, cleanfeed, flaming, trolling, and sporgery. Despite the rise of more technologically advanced forms of online community, Usenet has experienced significant growth year to year.

Brad Templeton is a software architect and the creator of Usenet's "Emily Postnews" (Postnews is a double pun referring to etiquette expert Emily Post and to postnews, a piece of Usenet software), a character he created in order to establish basic Usenet etiquette, or netiquette. Some of the principles he laid down came from as far back as the '70s and pre-Internet mailing lists. He explained to me that with so many people struggling to figure out how to best use the Internet, it took time to recognize how easy it was to offend with text.

Today, we take antisocial behavior on the Internet as a given. We routinely read and say things that we'd never say in real life. When someone lets loose with a string of expletives in a comments section I roll my eyes and keep scrolling. But if someone said those things to me on the street my heart would stop. During the early days on the Internet, there were no agreed-upon standards of etiquette. Templeton helped to define the way people would behave for decades to come.

The Virtual Community: The Well

In 1985 Stewart Brand and Larry Brilliant founded the Whole Earth 'Lectronic Link, or WELL. The WELL was made up of a new breed of techno-utopian ex-hippies who'd been experimenting with communal living and other alternative lifestyles. These baby boomers had grown up a bit, and where their '60s brethren had failed, they believed they'd succeed, with the power of network technology. It was all very back-to-the-earth, but with a focus on the power of computing. Words like *cybernetic* and *transhumanism* were thrown around. Many of the community's first users were subscribers to Brand's *Whole Earth Catalog*, a magazine devoted to topics like alternative shelter, nomadics, and telecommunications. These subscribers were already on the forefront of technology, and very smart. This early user base would come to have a tremendous influence on the quality of discourse.

In 1995, a decade into the WELL's history, *Wired* magazine called the WELL the world's most influential online community. It was a hyperintellectual environment that bore significant structural barriers to entry. It was slow. It was complicated. And perhaps most importantly, it was expensive. Between the monthly fee ($8), the hourly fee ($2), and any additional fees exacted by telephone companies (to say nothing of the cost of a computer and modem in those days), it wasn't uncommon for power users to burn through $300+ per month.

The WELL provided free access to reporters, which not only rewarded the WELL with plenty of press, but also infused the community with a sense of journalistic integrity.

I talked with former WELL Director Cliff Figallo, who can be considered one of the first community managers. Today the field is one of the tech industry's hottest careers and a necessary component of nearly all consumer-facing companies' online strategies. Back then it wasn't so glamorous, and Cliff doesn't have a whole lot of nostalgia for those days. He's quick to point out how much a pain in the neck running the WELL could be. And he quickly dispels any image of the pre-AOL Internet as an anarchic proto-4chan.

> I only had to ban one person in ten years at the Well. It was too expensive and difficult to dial in; the people who were there had a good reason to be there. We were very friendly, but very hands off.

I asked Stewart Brand, cofounder of the WELL and editor of the *Whole Earth Catalog*, about the nature of anonymity in an effort to draw parallels between 4chan and the infancy of the Internet. Unlike other Internet communities of the day, the WELL forced identity on its users. Stewart attributes the success of the community to "continuity of community and absence of anonymity"—what he calls "the main preventatives of destructive flaming." The people on the WELL were mostly friends who knew each other well. He says, "There was a fair amount of raucous name-calling still, but there was also enough community shaming of name-callers to keep it tolerable."

> I made the no-anonymity rule specifically to avoid online vileness. After a while we did experiment with one anonymous conference, and it was so immediately destructive it was shut down within the week by popular demand.

Where Usenet had newsgroups, the WELL had "conferences," subject areas devoted to computing, religion, politics, whatever. The community *was* like the Wild West in the sense that it was writing the rules as it went along. This new territory didn't have any mores. One defining maxim that Stewart Brand coined for the WELL was, "You own your own words," which reinforced personal responsibility.

Cliff told me a story about cantaloupes and how this early community dealt with unsubstantiated claims.

> Just after I was named Director of the WELL in August 1986, one of the WELL's earliest members openly discussed her idea of starting an online news service using USENET (not the WELL) as her platform. This was more than five years before the Internet connected existing networks into a privately run commercial system. There had just been a big story in the news

about watermelons grown in California containing pesticides. The aspiring reporter posted on the WELL that she'd received "unsubstantiated" reports of the same pesticides being found in cantaloupe.

The reactions of pretty much everyone on the WELL could be summed up as, "That's interesting. Maybe I'll stop eating cantaloupe, at least until the story is proven false." But one founding member of the WELL felt that we had opened the door to the spread of evil net rumors, and that we at the WELL were obligated to nip this unethical behavioral trend in the bud. A week-long argument ensued among interested WELLers, most of whom questioned what amount of damage could possibly be done by sharing secondhand knowledge with a virtual audience in a private online community. The court of popular opinion decided in favor of the aspiring reporter and eventually the plaintiff quit the WELL.

To me, "the tainted cantaloupe incident" was one of the most important formative social discoveries we made in the WELL's early experimental phase. As Director of the WELL I spent considerable time trying to understand how ad hoc groups worked things out in cyberspace, and how people attempted to achieve their purposes through monitors and keyboards.

There is still no bright line separating casual from professional conversation on the Web. The answer to the question, "Who IS a journalist?" only gets hazier every day. Every day millions of false rumors are intentionally planted on the web. Tools are being invented to help support the social web's ability to self-correct.

Given that the WELL was founded by optimistic hippies, I assumed these geeks on the forefront of technology would have high hopes for their hobby, but I was surprised to find the opposite.

"I had no idea the Internet would expand to the scale it is today. Absolutely no idea," says Figallo.

The Eternal September

Throughout the late '80s and early '90s, universities granted their students access to Usenet and other BBSes. Every September these online communities would be flooded with new users who hadn't learned the lingo or the etiquette. The veterans would naturally look down on these noobs with disdain, and dreaded the coming of September. In many cases, trolling was an effective remedy.

In 1993, America Online began offering its customers Usenet access, which brought the community thousands, and eventually millions, of new users. These users were often the children of net-savvy parents who were relatively less equipped than university students to provide value to the Usenet communities. And the influx didn't stop. The AOL users just kept coming. Waves upon waves of noobs. Trolling isn't as effective a form of social engineering when the noobs outnumber the old war horses.

On January 26, 1994, Dave Fischer posted a message to the alt.folklore.computers newsgroup: "September 1993 will go down in net.history as the September that never ended."

And thus the phrase *eternal September* was born. It's something that every successful Internet community experiences, but this represented a massive shift in demographics for the web.

The Internet was no longer an exclusive haven for geeks; and a bit of magic was lost forever along with the countercultural exclusivity of the web. Rather than accept the mainstreamification, some geeks burrowed deeper into weirder territory.

Rotten, Stile Project and . . . Gaping Holes

Enter Rotten.com. I was first introduced to this portal to hell when my meth head coworker at a fast food restaurant told me about this site that "has, like, dead bodies and shit." The site's current header includes a pretty clear disclaimer:

> The soft white underbelly of the net, eviscerated for all to see: Rotten dot com collects images and information from many sources to present the viewer with a truly unpleasant experience. Pure evil since 1996.

In 1999, the site added a regular column called "The Daily Rotten," a news feed dedicated to macabre stories of terrorism, abuse, disfigurement, and perversion. A photo of a Chinese man supposedly eating a fried human fetus was one particularly scandalous photo. An image that still haunts my memory depicted a man who'd been nearly consumed from the inside out by parasitic worms. The site is full of tumors, birth defects, rashes, cysts, and other bodily terrors. Rotten was disgusting, but the Internet was captivated. In the early '00s, the site received two hundred thousand rubbernecking visitors every day.

Tim Hwang, who went on to found the meme-centric ROFL-Con convention, admits Rotten's peculiar appeal:

> In middle school, we were spending a lot of time online. And a big part of the attraction of the Internet is finding really nasty things to send to your friends. So, at the time we were passing around a lot of Rotten links.

For a wide swath of my generation, Rotten was a gateway drug that would eventually introduce users to places like 4chan. More importantly, Rotten served as an early whipping boy for censorship crusaders. In 1997, the Rotten staff unleashed a manifesto that would shape the way people approached censorship on the web:

> The definition of obscenity, according to the Supreme Court and known informally as the Miller test, is:
>
> - must appeal to the prurient interest of the average person,
> - must describe sexual conduct in a way that is "patently offensive" to community standards, and
> - when taken as a whole, it "must lack serious literary, artistic, political, or scientific value."
>
> Certain people (including parents and schoolteachers) have complained to us and stated that rotten.com should not be "allowed" on the net, since children can view images on our site.
>
> One US schoolteacher wrote us a very angry email that complained some of her students had bookmarked images on this site, that our site shouldn't be on the net, and other claptrap.
>
> This is our response. The net is not a babysitter! Children should not be roaming the Internet unsupervised any more than they should be roaming the streets of New York City unsupervised.
>
> We cannot dumb the Internet down to the level of playground. Rotten dot com serves as a beacon to demonstrate that censorship of the Internet is impractical, unethical, and wrong. To censor this site, it is necessary to censor medical texts, history texts, evidence rooms, courtrooms, art museums, libraries, and other sources of information vital to functioning of free society.
>
> Nearly all of the images which we have online are not even prurient, and would thus not fall under any definition of obscen-

ity. Any images which we have of a sexual nature are in a context which render them far from obscene, in any United States jurisdiction. Some of the images may be offensive, but that has never been a crime. Life is sometimes offensive. You have to expect that.

The images we find most obscene are those of book burnings.

In 2001 the Rotten staff launched The Gaping Maw, which offered biting cultural commentary and satire, like a bizarre, adults-only *Mad* magazine. Because The Gaping Maw was hosted on Rotten, a site that was routinely threatened with lawsuits, its writers could get away with just about anything, providing some of the freshest commentary on the web.

A similarly rude site called Stile Project was founded in 1998 by a teenager named Jonathan Biderman. In 2001, it gained notoriety for hosting a video of a kitten being killed and prepared for a meal. PETA naturally flipped out and attempted to shut down the site. Strangely enough, Stile Project had been nominated for a Webby award the year before. Stile warned, "This is quite possible [sic] the single most offensive thing I have ever seen" in the video's description; however, he felt the video exposed people's hypocrisy toward their food.

> To us it seems like the ultimate taboo. How could those Godless Asians do such a thing to such a beautiful creature? Well, I'm sure Indians wonder the same thing about us, but you don't see North Americans shedding a tear every time a cow is slaughtered. . . . When's the last time you cried over a Big Mac?
>
> I do not condone animal abuse, and I view the video more as an educational tool than one of shock value. For us to say it is wrong, it would just make us all hypocrites since most of us eat meat. I never get hate mail when posting images of dead people . . .

Rotten and Stile represent two sites that were built upon a larger web trend of gross-out content. When I was a freshman in college, I remember someone telling me to visit lemonparty.org (Don't do it). The URL of course leads to another shock site, this time a photo of three elderly gentlemen tangled in bed. (And in the last US presidential election, 4chan trolls posted signs on telephone poles reading, "Politics left you bitter? lemonparty .org." Another sign read, "Sick of gas prices? www.lemonparty .org.")

For many, the experience of Internet shock sites began with goatse, a notoriously repulsive image that is considered the king of shock sites. It features a hirsute gentleman bending over and stretching his anus wider than you'd think was humanly possible. The image was originally hosted at goatse.cx (as in goat sex). The link to goatse.cx was passed around by giggling teen boys, mostly, and used to troll unsuspecting browsers.

In 2010, a group of trollish hackers associated with Encyclopedia Dramatica, a wiki site focusing on 4chan culture, exposed a flaw in AT&T's security, revealing the email addresses of iPad users. They called themselves Goatse Security (themselves an offshoot of the Gay Nigger Association of America troll collective). Their logo was a cartoonish parody of the goatse shock image, and their motto was "Gaping Holes Exposed."

Nerd News: Slashdot & Metafilter

Slashdot founder Rob Malda, aka "Commander Taco," says that he created Slashdot because he missed the high-minded technical community he enjoyed in the BBS era that discussed the sort of "news for nerds, stuff that matters" that interested him.

In 1997, Slashdot offered something new: user-submitted stories. Each story became its own discussion thread. The site became so popular that when a story was linked by Slashdot, the site's host would often buckle under the weight of all the traffic. This phenomenon became known as the Slashdot Effect. This phenomenon is not unique to Slashdot, but Slashdot was one of the first to be routinely recognized as a server killer. Other sites can be *farked*, for example, or undergo the Digg Effect, demonstrating the power that content aggregators wield.

Malda says that Slashdot developed its own unique memetic culture almost instantly. He remembers lots of gross-out memes popping up in addition to stuff from the *Star Wars* prequels, which were hugely popular during Slashdot's early years. I asked him if there was a specific moment when he realized that memes were a thing. He replied, "Long before I heard the word, that's for sure." Many of Slashdot's memes deal with ultra geeky science and computing puns.

Malda claims that since he started Slashdot, the corporations have taken over, our rights are on the decline, and our privacy is gone. Back in the early days it was chaotic, but free. He recognizes the value in anonymity, and feels that there's something special about 4chan's community.

I love that they interact anonymously. Slashdot was similarly completely anonymous for the first year of our existence, and still today we allow anyone to post without any identifying information whatsoever.

I think a registered pseudonym is useful because it gives you continuity if not accountability. You might not know that

"CmdrTaco" is actually a dude named Rob, but on Slashdot at least, you know that each time you see a post with that name attached, you know it's the same guy. I felt for Slashdot that it was important to provide that for people that wanted it. I don't think that creates a sense of "personal responsibility" in any sort of globalized sense, but it allows you to build a reputation and history which might be important if you want to be taken seriously.

Interestingly, anonymous posters on Slashdot are jokingly labeled "Anonymous Coward."

Matt Haughey was a big fan of Slashdot, but he wasn't crazy about the interface. Slashdot had editors that picked from submitted stories. Matt was looking for something more democratic, so he created MetaFilter, a community where anyone's story could land on the front page.

The community blog became most notable for its Ask Metafilter section, which was an early example of information crowdsourcing. You could ask an obscure question and, due to the size and quality of the community, sometimes get surprisingly informed answers. This kind of querying would influence sites like Yahoo Answers, Quora, Reddit, and, to an extent, even 4chan.

According to Haughey, MetaFilter also developed its own memespeak pretty early on.

Probably in the first year, 2000 or so, I noticed people shouting "double post!" to something they'd seen before became a sort of game for people, where they wanted to be first to notice something was old and demonstrate their expertise at MetaFilter. There was also this early meme where a post that was really awful or boring would elicit a response of someone saying "I really like pancakes" and then everyone would talk about pancakes and we sort of had a pancakes-as-mascot thing for a while.

My favorite meme is the current one where someone overanalyzes something at MetaFilter, people tell them they are "beanplating" which started with one user poking fun at another by saying "HI I'M ON METAFILTER AND I COULD OVERTHINK A PLATE OF BEANS."

MetaFilter users were known for being creative smartypantses, which was reinforced by a simple decision by Haughey to charge users $5 to participate for life. It's a modest fee, but according to Haughey it worked wonders in keeping out trolls and casual passersby who would contribute nothing of value to the conversation.

Haughey is fascinated by 4chan, especially how it produces interesting memes "from a place of total fuck-off anonymity." Like most online communities, MetaFilter asks its users to post under usernames, but Matt recognizes the value in namelessness.

I do appreciate moot's point about how anonymity lets you be ok with failing, while a username feels more like "everything is on your permanent record" and people might be afraid to ever try something. I'm a big fan of failure and I think everyone should be terrible at everything they love for the first year or so they do it. I guess I'd rather see a world where everyone has a username and a permanent record and we all have these embarrassing beginnings where we openly failed again and again before we started to figure things out.

Slashdot and Metafilter were the first big content aggregators, and their elegant feature sets have had a massive impact on the way all media now behaves on the web. Long before

Digg and Reddit came along, Slashdot and MetaFilter provided users with a way to define what their news would look like. This democratization of the media has influenced not only the way news is consumed, but how it is formed, framed, and distributed.

But what about all the news for nerds that *doesn't* matter? What if it's not news, but . . . something else?

"It's Not News. It's Fark"

In 1999, Drew Curtis unleashed Fark (a purposefully misspelled euphemism for a word you can probably guess), an offbeat news aggregator that would become a meme creation powerhouse. The formula was simple: Fark's community submitted articles to the site's admins, who then green-lighted the best ones for inclusion in the site's news feed. Each news story had an accompanying discussion thread that allowed the users to engage in witty banter on very specific, immediate topics.

Before Fark, Curtis often read news stories on the web and emailed the best ones to his friends, which he found to be a cumbersome way to share and discuss information. So he created Fark, allowing millions to share what essentially amounted to a giant global "News of the Weird" section.

Curtis was attending college in Iowa but living in Kentucky during the early '90s. A friend advised him to check out email, a cheap way to circumvent expensive phone calls to campus. So he got an account and started using email to correspond with his contacts in the Midwest. He remembers a conversation with some friends:

I asked, "What is the Internet good for other than chat and text games?" They couldn't think of anything. Even porn wasn't doing all that great. Conventional wisdom was free porn sites had no chance of working because the minute people found out about them they crashed under the traffic.

Because every news story provided a comment thread full of geeks trying to outwit each other, Fark was an early breeding ground for Internet memes. The comment fields allowed for images, so clever Photoshops and wordplay abounded. One early meme was "Still no cure for cancer," which would append stories dealing with scientific advances in obscure, seemingly useless fields of interest.

Curtis remembers when he first became acquainted with the term *meme*, recalling the development of Memepool in 1999 and rattling off some older memes that dried up long ago, such as Troops and I Kiss You. "It's how I know I'm old," he says. One meme that sticks out most in Drew's mind is the legendary All Your Base Are Belong to Us, a garbled bit of Engrish (i.e., badly translated Japanese often found in video games) spoken by a villain from an old coin-operated arcade game called *Zero Wing*. The phrase took off on Something Awful and was further popularized by Fark. It eventually became a popular taunt in online gaming, a way to tell your opponent that they'd just been *pwned*. (This was another goof from video game land: in the frenetic pace of online play, people wishing to taunt their opponents with "hahaha owned," as in "You've been owned," easily made the mistake of typing *pwned* instead, as the *p* and *o* keys are adjacent on most keyboards.) Today there are thousands of photoshopped All Your Base images, and even T-shirts. It was one of the first image memes to be endlessly remixed.

Curtis claims that this insular Internet culture went mainstream around the advent of the big social networking sites MySpace and Facebook, which brought so many people online and made it easy for average joes to share content.

> One thing I find interesting is that there isn't another Fark. There's stuff that kind of looks like Fark but nothing really exactly like it . . . Right now I'm pushing the fact that the entire social Internet is set up to give you what it thinks you want—Fark gives you what you don't know you want. It's about the only place out there which intentionally isn't putting you into an echo chamber of like-minded sheep.

Curtis says that the social aspect of the site wasn't really his goal from the beginning. He just wanted a place to share funny, interesting links with friends, not much different than lots of link aggregation sites of the day. He had a "Submit a Link" option on Fark from day one, but after a year it became obvious that the site's future was in user submissions, so he made it a more prominent and integral feature.

> It became apparent that people were submitting material faster than I could find it manually. So I switched to selecting from the submission queue as opposed to searching the broader Internet. Wasn't really a plan so much as I'm just lazy.

Curtis eventually discovered that the crowd's ability to provide the best bits of information vastly outpaced his own ability to curate content. This rest of the media caught up to his discovery in the Web 2.0 revolution that occurred several years later.

It wasn't just the unique features of his site that made it a success; it was the changing infrastructure of the web as a whole. Blog software was becoming popular and increasingly approachable, even for tech noobs. It enabled unpaid, amateur writers and commentators to compete with mainstream news sites, and aggregators like Fark, Slashdot, and Metafilter gave them equal standing in terms of traffic. It wasn't who you were, it was what you were saying.

Curtis doesn't have a lot of nostalgia for the good old days ("Things were clunky and didn't work all that great"). But things are always changing:

> Another interesting thing I've noticed is that the VC [venture capital] dollars seem to scramble around based on the rules of web statistics. Look at all the money that poured into content farms [Demand Media, Associated Content], and now Google changed the rules and made them more or less moot (for now).

Curtis defines two major changes in the web since he started out: Tons more people, and the presence of a generation of folks who grew up online. Today, people are much more well-equipped to share the things they like, and companies are being forced to come to terms with the reality that their content has to be good, and that there is no secret formula for creating a viral sensation.

Fark was the first of the big content aggregators with a focus on the sort of offbeat stuff that people eventually recognized as being "from the Internet"—in other words, Internet memes. One popular Fark meme was a Photoshopped image of a kitten frolicking in a field, being chased by two Domos (a creepy Japanese TV mascot that looks like a brown rectangle with sharp teeth and beady eyes). The caption reads, "Every time you masturbate, god kills a kitten. Please, think of the kittens." Farkers didn't invent the phrase, which dates back to a 1996 student newspaper, but the goofy image coupled with the amusingly sacrilegious phrase went viral.

Another was the infamous UFIA, or Unsolicited Finger in Anus, which derives from a news story posted to Fark about a high school football player who poked a teammate's butthole in a bit of jocular fun. The other kid didn't think it was so funny and pressed charges, prompting a judge to eventually declare that an "unsolicited finger in anus is crude, not criminal."

Farkers gleefully beat this catchphrase to death, culminating in Drew Curtis's purchase of the naming rights to Boston's Fleet Center for a day, hoping to rename it the Fark.com UFIA Center. The Fleet Center caught wind of the prank and opted to not use the name. However, a Farker was able to convince the Tennessee Department of Transportation to put up an "Adopt a Highway" sign that read "Drew Curtis TotalFark UFIA," which he explained stood for Uniting Friends in America. The sign lasted a few days.

"The Internet Makes You Stupid": Something Awful

I discovered Something Awful, a wonderland of bizarre online culture, almost immediately after getting online in the late '90s. Its community of "goons" thrived, providing perhaps the most direct Western antecedent to 4chan, which was eventually spawned from its anime forum. Launched in 1999, the site charged a one-time $9.95 fee for forum access, which thousands willingly paid to be a part of the strangest community on the web.

Something Awful was a repository for lowbrow humor, with condescending editorial commentary tacked on. Founded in 1999 by Richard "Lowtax" Kyanka, the site featured daily essays about everything on the web perceived as awful, with a focus on nerd stuff like video games, anime, and script kiddie culture (script kiddies, or skriddies, are teenagers who've learned a few basic hacking techniques and think they're capable of bringing down the Pentagon. Rather than hacking manually and writing their own code, they use prefab scripts with little understanding of what they're doing). A trademark feature was the site's "Awful Link of the Day," which shined a spotlight on some hilariously dumb corner of the web. It might be a website fetishizing girls sucking on ice cubes or some guy's exhaustively researched argument about how the biblical hell is geographically located within the earth's molten core.

Other features on Something Awful include "Photoshop Phriday," a weekly image gallery that lampoons any old thing using image editing tools. 4chan users have turned this practice into something approaching an Olympic sport. "Your Band Sucks," a recurring column, offers hilariously provocative essays taking down highly regarded bands. The "Weekend Web" gathers quotes from weird message boards devoted to topics like urine consumption as a spiritual exercise, white supremacy, or support groups for those with self-diagnosed Asperger's.

If there was something awful on the web, the guys at Something Awful eventually found it and skewered it with unparalleled wit. But beyond the collation and parody, Something Awful's vibrant community eventually began to form a unique creative culture of its own, which included a collection of powerful memes. Perhaps more than any web community before it, Something Awful harnessed the power of its community's creative abilities. With a bit of editorial direction, Something Awful managed to skim the cream from the top of its goon community, creating grade-A comedic content for web geeks.

Longtime contributor David Thorpe describes the site's unique appeal.

> I think a fair number of people who wound up fascinated by weird Internet fringe stuff came from Stile Project. Something Awful was on the rise right around the time Stile Project was on the decline, and the two sites had a few crossovers once in a while. Something Awful was much more appealing because it was funnier and way less sleazy. Rich Kyanka, the guy who started it, was making fun of the Internet from the perspective of a legitimately funny and fairly normal dude, whereas Stile presented himself as the kind of C.H.U.D. [Cannibalistic Humanoid Underground Dweller, named after a cult classic b-horror flick] who was only one step above the people he was making fun of.

Thorpe joined the Something Awful forums in 2001 and hung around for a while, simply because it was a community of fun people that he could joke with. Zack Parsons, the closest thing Something Awful has to an editor-in-chief, eventually offered him a gig writing for the site.

I asked Thorpe if he thought it was weird how mainstream meme culture has gotten. When he started at Something Awful, a lot of the jokes and slang that are now featured on MTV were solely the realm of these hellaciously witty geeks on obscure Internet forums.

I always sort of figured it would happen. The fact that people are making tons of money on it now is kind of depressing, partially because the stuff that's making money is a lot of the dumbest stuff, the worst of "Internet humor," like the lolcat shit. Another reason it's depressing is because I'm not one of the people making money off it.

Thorpe points to the creation of image macros, which used to be popular on Something Awful but have since died out due to their mainstream popularity. These are basically images with text plastered on top; lolcats are the most popular example. They were called macros because it used to be possible to post popular ones by typing a code in the post that would automatically generate the image. This is loosely based on the computer science concept of macros by which input sequences are linked to output sequences. In this case, code in, funny photo out.

Eventually, they developed into what a lot of people would call memes, like all the lolcat stuff. A good example of SA's influence on that development was that my friend Jon, another writer for Something Awful, made this picture of Spider Man looking confused, with the caption "How do I shot web?" That was one of the first examples of the kind of broken language thing that slowly evolved into the lolcat phenomenon. Jon is pretty ashamed to have indirectly influenced the development of something so idiotic.

How Do I Shot Web is a massively popular meme, with thousands of iterations. It might be idiotic, but it's a tangible part of web culture that makes up the memescape. The non sequiturs and obsession with human eccentricity were two powerful themes that defined Something Awful, and later 4chan and Internet pop culture as a whole.

The Birth of the Chans: Ayashii World, Amezou, and 2channel

Meanwhile, an enterprising Japanese slacker named Hiroyuki Nishimura developed a message board in 1999 called 2channel, a text-only anonymous forum that would eventually become a popular place for emotionally repressed Japanese to vent. But what made 2channel special was its almost complete lack of rules and anonymity.

2channel was based on a previous text board called Ayashii World, the first big anonymous text board in Japan. It was an outgrowth of Japanese Usenet culture, created by Shiba Masayuki in 1996. Because it was an extension of Usenet, its subject matter was deeply nerdy, focusing on hacking, pirating, porn, and other black market information. Ayashii World, like 4chan, was unique for two reasons: anonymous posting and meme creation. Ayashii World even had an equivalent to /b/, called the "scum board," which was used exclusively to plan raids (attacks on other sites through hacking, spamming, or other destructive means).

The first image board meme, Giko-neko, was created here. It was represented in ASCII art, a form of illustration using text characters, as a cat, usually saying *itte yoshi* (Japanese for *fuck off*). Because the cat could be easily copy-pasted elsewhere, with new captions, it was easy for other users to make Giko-neko their own.

Ayashii World, like many anonymous chan boards, experienced so much downtime that its owner began to receive death threats, prompting him to shut down the board in 1998. When Ayashii World was shut down, many of its users created their own textboards in an effort to create a new home for *nanashi*, Japanese for *anonymous*.

The anonymous creator of one of the splinter boards, Amezou World, added a new style of discussion threading called floating threads, which displayed discussions in one chronological stream rather than in branching conversations. Secondly, he integrated bumping.

As Amezou became more popular, it was increasingly targeted by trolls. When violent threats eventually forced the creator of Amezou to shut down his board, another round of splinter groups popped up to meet the demand for anonymous community. Among these was 2channel, which brought chan culture to the mainstream.

"I created a free space, and what people did with it was up to them," Nishimura told *Wired* in 2008, his laissez-faire approach mirroring that of 4chan's founder. In order to understand why 2channel was such a raging success, it's important to know a bit about Japanese culture. We're talking about a society wherein face-to-face confrontation and emotional expression are actively discouraged. In the United States, straight talk and audacity are prized as character traits. In Japan, they are often interpreted as rudeness or disrespect.

It's the culture of the salaryman, the lonely wage slave who lives to work, with the few social pleasures he allows himself often related to corporate team-building. The image of a salaryman is certainly a stereotype (sleeping in a suit on a subway, late-night corporate-sponsored karaoke), but there's no question that this socially repressed caricature represented a community that was waiting for a platform like 2channel to come along. Today, the Japanese-only site draws several million daily page views—more than four times the traffic of 4chan, which is global. 2channel gives the people of Japan a place to say what they're really thinking, with no real-life consequences.

The 2channel welcome screen message reads, "Welcome to the large group of bulletin boards that extensively covers topics from 'hacking' to 'supper.'" More than six hundred individual boards are listed in a scrolling column on the left, including "Large Special Vehicles," "I Love Dogs and Cats," "Romantically Challenged," and one of the most popular, a board dedicated to the recent Japanese earthquakes.

One board, "Solitary Man," seems to be a place for lonely males to commiserate. I've found a thread in this board titled "What do you prefer in the opposite sex?" The first post, penned by an alleged 16-year-old boy, details different characteristics, like height, age, education, and attractiveness. The thread continues with people contributing characteristics like "kind person," "looks like Cameron Diaz," "likes housework," "loves animals," and "beautiful Japanese." Within ten replies, a troll offers his idea of an ideal woman, with wings growing from her head, raptor claw hands and feet, and, of course, beautiful breasts.

Because the site doesn't allow images of any kind, the users have developed a form of visual communication based on ASCII art.

These can be simple emoticons, like this angry fella, a 2channel emoticon, or *kaomoji*:

(>Д<)

Some of them contain thousands of characters in order to create almost photo-realistic visual representations.

Each discussion thread can potentially contain up to a thousand posts, which either "age" or "sage." Saged posts (from the Japanese *sageru*) move down to the bottom of the thread, while aged, or bumped, posts float to the top. This dynamic method of arranging content was eventually borrowed by 4chan's founder.

2channel is a place to argue, vent, cajole, insult, and goof around. The users are sarcastic and sophomoric, and have developed a dense internal lexicon. Those who aren't in the know are said to be *kuku yomenai*, or someone who "can't read the air." In other words, a noob or newfag.

2channel can get pretty dark. In 2000, a 17-year-old kid posted a message claiming that he was about to hijack a bus, an act that he carried out an hour later, stabbing one passenger to death. Racism, especially toward Koreans, is rampant. Mass suicides have been organized on the site, and criminals have boasted about their plans before committing crimes hours later. Interestingly, many notable documented events resulting from or announced on 2channel has a Western analogue on 4chan. The cultures are so different, but the technology influences human behavior on a deeply similar level.

2channel also has a heartwarming side. Consider Trainman, an anonymous 2channel user who regaled the community with a story fit for a romance novel. While sitting on a train he noticed an attractive woman. A drunk man boarded the train and began to harass the other passengers, who ignored him. Then he began to sexually harass the woman. Despite being an introverted geek,

Trainman took action, fighting off the man until the other passengers were able to alert the conductor.

The woman thanked him profusely and asked for his address so she could send him a token of appreciation. A few days later Trainman received a beautiful French tea set. Overwhelmed by her thoughtfulness, he returned to 2channel to update an expanding group of interested fans and ask for advice. As a self-conscious nerd, he had no idea how to respond appropriately. The folks on 2channel convinced him to contact the woman. He eventually worked up the courage to ask her out on a date, his first.

Then, per 2channel's advice, he got a new haircut, bought a snazzy outfit, and picked up some contact lenses. His first date was a success, and he continued to keep 2channel abreast of his progress. After a few more dates he and the woman began texting regularly, and eventually Trainman confessed his love, which she returned. Trainman triumphantly announced their shared affection to 2channel, whose users banded together for an ecstatic online celebration.

Trainman's story is now folklore in Japan, having been adapted for television, film, and manga. Though many are convinced of the story's authenticity, it's never been proven, and neither Trainman nor his lover have ever come forward in real life.

In a 2003 interview with *Japan Media Review*, Nishimura laid out the site's appeal.

Q: Why did you decide to use perfect anonymity, not even requiring a user name?

A: Because delivering news without taking any risk is very important to us. There is a lot of information disclosure or secret news gathered on Channel 2. Few people would post that kind of information by taking a risk. Moreover, people can only truly discuss something when they don't know each other.

If there is a user ID attached to a user, a discussion tends to become a criticizing game. On the other hand, under the anonymous system, even though your opinion/information is criticized, you don't know with whom to be upset. Also with a user ID, those who participate in the site for a long time tend to have authority, and it becomes difficult for a user to disagree with them. Under a perfectly anonymous system, you can say, "it's boring," if it is actually boring. All information is treated equally; only an accurate argument will work.

2channel is now considered a media powerhouse on par with the country's biggest magazines and TV channels. And it's completely open and free for everyone, not just for viewing but for contributing and collaborating. 2channel behaves not only as an alternative media source, but as an ombudsman that is continuously keeping the Japanese mainstream media in check.

4chan Godfather: Futaba Channel

Futaba Channel, or 2ch, is an image board that was launched in 2001. The community is more focused on otaku culture than 2channel is. Futaba Channel contains around one hundred boards, some of which are devoted to images, some of which are text only.

I wander onto Futaba Channel and sure enough, it looks almost exactly like 4chan. I pick a board at random: "Two-dimensional Gro." I'm met with a warning page:

You are about to enter the grotesque image board.

Images on the grotesque image board may cause serious consequences.

I enter the board, consequences be damned. It's full of images of anime girls being suspended by hooks, or stretched out on examination tables while being disemboweled, or smiling sweetly while bleeding, apparently from having been recently quadruply amputated. Yuck.

I try the newest board, called "Nuclear." It's a forum for people to discuss the potential for nuclear fallout, primarily related to the Fukushima power plant. There seems to be a lot of anger being expressed toward the Tokyo Electric Power Company, the fourth-largest in the world, regarding its handling of the Fukushima nuclear accident in the March 2011 earthquake and tsunami.

"No nuclear power plants should be up and running properly in a country that cannot handle a nuclear accident," writes one understandably resentful poster. Everyone seems to be arguing about who is to blame for the perceived lack of preparedness in the aftermath of the disaster.

This kind of venting is something that Japanese people probably wouldn't feel comfortable with in real life. Futaba Channel and 2channel, with all their oddities, seem to offer a release valve for the Japanese.

The forums also provide an opportunity to achieve social good. In October of 2004, thousands of 2channel users rallied to help in the aftermath of the Niigata Prefecture Chuetsu earthquake. Right now, I'm seeing hundreds of threads buzzing with people sharing information and offering to help one another in the wake of the recent tsunami and earthquakes.

Collecting Bite-Sized Memes:
You're The Man Now Dog

In 2001, back in the United States, Max Goldberg launched the online community You're the Man Now Dog.

The site began as nothing but the words "You're the man now dog" written in ASCII text on a black background, at http://www.yourethemannowdog.com. The line is prominently spoken by Sean Connery in the trailer for the 2000 film *Finding Forrester*. By the end of the year, Goldberg had changed the site to include a tiled image of Connery, an audio clip of him saying the quote, and accompanying text reading the same. It was absurd and useless, and people appreciated it for exactly those reasons.

I remember someone sent me a link to it back in 2002. By the time the audio clip had repeated a third time I'd thrown my head back in laughter. Who made this? What does this mean? Why that specific line? The ludicrousness of it all. YTMND is an early example of the single-serving site, a URL reserved for an exceedingly singular, and usually trivial, purpose.

Over the next few years, creative goofs would apply the YTMND model (a pic, a sound clip, and text) to different weird pop-culture icons. So many people created derivatives that Max eventually decided to set up a site to host all of them, and //www.ytmnd.com was born.

The top-viewed YTMND is a clip of a prank call that was originally recorded by comedian Tom Mabe. The second is a massive animated GIF image created collectively by some clever Something Awful goons. The YTMND wiki explains:

The Blue Ball Machine is one of the most frequently-viewed pages on all of YTMND. The site is a patchwork of animated GIFs linked together accompanied by a looping hook of the song Breakfast Machine from the film Pee-wee's Big Adventure. The concept was conceived by Andorion, who created a template and some sample tiles and a thread for others to contribute, and the individual images were created by hundreds of Something Awful forums goons. Each image has three balls enter and leave at particular spots at any frame which is a multiple of 30, but otherwise the content is up to the creator. It has earned this title by accruing a staggering four million pageviews since its inception in October of 2005.

The third is called "Breakup Letter: Dramatic Reading," which features a narrator reading an inarticulate breakup letter as though it were a dramatic Shakespearean monologue, while trying not to giggle:

> Dear Loser,[Chris]~~~~!!!!!
> I thought you liked me you said it yourself I hate you. People only say you asked me out because you needed a date for the dance and that after the dance you would dump me well guess what bastert i dumped you cause you were thinking that i cheated on you i didnt so like idiots that you guys are and so smart that you are you called me a slut. I hung up on you cause you tol me it on the phone

That's a small taste, but you get the idea. Moving down the list I see an animated GIF of Paris Hilton that shows her using the same facial expression in every photo. Another has the opening sequence of "Cowboy Bebop," only with audio of a Bill Cosby soundalike scatting over the original music (Cosby Bebop).

The appeal of YTMND is that it allowed users to crystallize a single, self-contained bit of absurdity into a unique URL that they could easily share with their friends. There was also a feature that allowed people to rate the clips, so the best ones rose to the top. For a time in the mid-2000s, YTMND was one of the most powerful Internet meme aggregators.

The Memesphere Expands

From the mid-1990s to the mid-2000s, the Internet birthed hundreds of smaller sites that have come to be known as early Internet memes themselves, or that hosted viral content before viral content was recognized as something new. I've already told you about "Gonads and Strife," a cartoon from Threebrain, a flash animator who also released such viral sensations as "Sorry Your Mom Died" and "Monkey Salad."

realultimatepower.com is a good example, and it somehow remains intact after all these years. The homepage begins:

Hi, this site is all about ninjas, REAL NINJAS. This site is awesome. My name is Robert and I can't stop thinking about ninjas. These guys are cool; and by cool, I mean totally sweet.
Facts:
1. Ninjas are mammals.
2. Ninjas fight ALL the time.
3. The purpose of the ninja is to flip out and kill people.

It goes on like this. I distinctly remember the pure delight the childlike wording of this home page brought to my college dorm. This stuff was our generation's *Monty Python*. It was fresh and funny and it felt like nobody seemed to quite get it but us.

In 2004, Quiznos ran a campaign featuring the Spongmonkeys, who had achieved viral fame with an animation called "We Like the Moon." Joel Vietch had originally created the video for his goofy animation site http://www.rathergood.com in 2003. The ads featured the bizarre creatures singing "We Love the Subs." The monkeys were among the first, if not *the* first, Internet memes to be used in advertising. The bizarre nature of the Spongmonkeys ads confused many TV viewers, and the requisite explanation was, "Oh, it's just this weird thing from the Internet."

This phenomenon would reoccur a few years later, when one of the first YouTube sensations capitalized on the strength of 4chan's meme-spreading capabilities. In the spring of 2007, a guy called Tay Zonday recorded himself singing an original song called "Chocolate Rain." The video features an almost childlike Zonday crooning a surprising baritone into a microphone over a cheesy drum loop. Zonday's face contorts with effort as he sings the utterly ungroovy tune. That November, Zonday licensed the song to Comedy Central and released a spoof called "Cherry Chocolate Rain" as part of an ad campaign for Cherry Chocolate Diet Dr. Pepper.

Newgrounds, eBaums World, and Albino Blacksheep, three successful web communities, hosted videos, flash games, and animations from thousands of independent content creators. Sites like these enabled people to create one-off pieces of content that had the potential to go superviral. At the time, there was a lot of arguing about content attribution. eBaums World especially came under fire for hosting video content it didn't own. Today, these arguments seem almost quaint. There are so many places to host content these days that it's virtually impossible to prevent people from sharing copyrighted content.

During this time the memesphere expanded rapidly through-out the web, and people began to see pieces of entertaining content from the Internet as a fresh new medium—but most people didn't have a word for it yet. If asked "What the hell is this?" we'd say, "Oh it's just something I found online." Today we use the word *meme*.

Each of the communities I've just described is part of the gradual progression in the evolution of the online community that created the mother of all Internet in-groups, 4chan. Of course, online community branched forward in different directions, mutating into mainstream social networks like Facebook and Twitter too—but if you look closely, you can spot the countercultural strains of the freaky, outsider's web community coming to a head when, in 2003, a 15-year-old kid decided he was going to create the best site on the Internet.

Chapter 5

The Rise of 4chan

BY 2003 THERE were plenty of English-speaking communities in place where one could share cool stuff from the Internet, but for some they just didn't move fast enough.

Christopher Poole was a teenage anime geek who would frequent Something Awful's anime forum under the name "moot," and occasionally lurk Japanese forums like 2channel and Futaba. He appreciated the quick pace of these sites. As soon as you get to the bottom of a page, you can hit refresh and be hit with a page of completely new content. But because Poole didn't speak Japanese, he could only check out the images.

So he lifted Futaba Channel's code wholesale and created 4chan.net, an English-speaking forum that would bring the dynamic culture of 2channel and Futaba Channel to the West. The site launched on October 1, 2003.

Poole posted a message to the Something Awful forums announcing the creation of the image board. It was met with immediate positive reception. No logins, no profiles, no hierarchy of users. Just a frenzy of streamlined fun. With 4chan it wasn't about who you were, it was about what you knew, a pure meritocracy. People loved it. 4chan.org received millions of hits in the first few weeks of its existence. Eventually Futaba and 2channel users became aware of 4chan, which brought in a flood of traffic, taking down the site's servers.

I tracked down a guy who calls himself "Shii," who is credited with writing the software for 4chan's text boards. On his personal site, he claims, "I wrote the suck-ass anonymous message board software that they still use today, despite never having taken a programming class ever." In 2003 Shii learned of the existence of the Japanese chan boards and was excited to bring that style of forum to the West. That October, Shii met moot online, who had announced the development of 4chan on the Something Awful anime forum they both frequented called Anime Death Tentacle Rape Whorehouse (ADTRW), a jokingly offensive name poking fun at the medium's extreme fringes.

Shii vividly remembers moot calling him up to deliver an hour-long monologue about how 4chan was going to be the best site on the Internet. moot made Shii a volunteer moderator, but according to Shii, they began to butt heads when moot tried to turn the site into a business—though he admits, "I've always had trouble consulting others before I do stuff and I was not very professional, so he banned me from the site in 2005."

Shii tells me 4chan was a very different place back in its infancy.

4chan in 2003 was utterly different from the familiar culture that's developed today. It was a fairly friendly place where everyone used nicknames, re-posted memes from 2chan, and dug up interesting pictures. The signal-to-noise ratio was very high; users would start drama about each other; but the tone of discussion was casual but polite. In other words, it was similar to any other Internet forum.

But it wasn't always anonymous.

Originally, the 4chan mod team wanted people to fill in their names with tripcodes [an optional feature on 4chan that allows users to create an ID code that remains constant throughout the board. This is looked down on by most 4chan users, who prefer that everyone be anonymous] . . . The overwhelming majority of 4channers used their names; people who criticized others anonymously were called cowards who didn't want responsibility for their actions. The shift towards condoning anonymity was a combination of bottom-up organic change (some people were anonymous from the beginning) and a change in attitude from the mod team.

Shii claims he was enamored with 2chan's culture of anonymity and promoted it passionately on ADTRW and the Raspberry Heaven forums. ADTRW contained a thread dedicated to Futaba Channel, where users posted the weirdest stuff they could find, introducing thousands of Westerners to the most bizarre stuff coming out of Japan. Shii says that most of 4chan's earliest memes were mostly copied directly from Futaba Channel.

Raspberry Heaven was a DC++ file-sharing hub for ADTRW users that eventually became a gathering place for those purged from ADTRW when Something Awful attempted to clean up some of the nastier content from its boards.

Today you might better dub the site Something Sensitive— and Raspberry Heaven became the gathering place for people, like me, who were purged. There is a huge gulf between RH, which continues on today with most of its original userbase, and the ADTRW of today which is full of the most pretentious, self-hating Serious Anime Fans you could find anywhere.

Anyway, Shii thought 4chan was the future.

> [I was] claiming that it was a panacea for everything that was wrong with American message boards, etc. I was actually a bull-headed 16-year-old and was making stuff up, not because I believed 4chan could be the greatest accomplishment in human history (it was obvious from the start that would not happen), but because I wanted to create something new and make the Internet change.

Over the next few months moot would add and remove different boards according to demand. He created a Guro board, catering to audiences who were after animated depictions of sexualized violence and gore, and Lolicon, for sexualized depictions of underage children. He would eventually shut down both, possibly to appeal to advertisers and to Paypal, who processed donations. The Lolicon board was also shut down due to occasional floods of actual child pornography.

Shii admits that the availability of extreme pornography played a massive role in 4chan's growth.

> This was the first time a forum for such things had been created on the English-speaking Internet, since they were beyond the pale on any other kind of website. It is hard to imagine now but this was in fact an entirely new realm of obscenity on the Western Internet, a category of pictures which would get you banned forever from any respectable website, and which had

previously only ever been pulled out by the worst kind of trolls to shock people.

After about a month moot began to ask for donations so that he could maintain the onslaught of new traffic to the site. 4chan was plagued by downtime throughout its early history, which would inspire others to set up dozens of competing chan-style image boards like iChan, Infinitychan, and Desuchan; these experienced temporary flares of traffic whenever 4chan was down, subsiding when 4chan went back online.

I got in touch with David Ashby, who runs an anime-centric chan site called iiichan. Like Shii, he's got a lot of nostalgia for 4chan's early days.

It felt like you were part of a really clever mob, in those days. There was high volume, but not to the insane levels you see on /b/ these days—you could refresh the page and still find the thread you'd just been looking at. The most liberating, incredible thing about it was how easy it was. To see a site like that, with no registration, no names, no history, basically . . . just cleverness and images.

The lack of history and the general impermanence was, and I guess still is, the most fun thing about 4chan. Everywhere else was concerned with building up a reputation, working your way into the important cliques on the site, getting noticed for who you were rather than what you knew. There were explicit hierarchies all around you, all the time. With imageboards, one can actually assume everyone else on the board is as smart and clever as you are—you find yourself talking up to the room, as opposed to down to it.

Before getting involved in the imageboard subculture, Ashby spent time on Megatokyo, a massive otaku forum, but was frustrated with how inefficient the average forum structure was, with the majority of space on pages devoted to "extraneous nonsense" like gaudy signatures, user profile images, and unnecessary bio information. He loved the community found in message board culture, but not the bloat.

Clash of the Chans

Ashby started iiichan along with several other 4chan refugees who were tired of dealing with the site's frequent downtime.

> Soon after I started paying attention to the idea of imageboards in detail, 4chan went down for something like two weeks, and a number of smaller refugee sites popped up, the longest-lived of those being iichan . . . The idea was floated for the users of the board to each take over their own board and run the site as a federation . . . That's how I started running my own imageboard. I think the splintering occurred at first because of downtime but quickly morphed into an ideological separation just based on who found out about them. After all, there wasn't any way for 4chan [being down] to advertise them; knowledge of their existence traveled via IRC and other sites, each drawing on a unique subset of 4chan users.

4chan was the first and most well-known, and no other English-speaking chan-style image board would ever come close to usurping it in terms of traffic or influence.

> "Lain," one of the early admins of iichan, posted on 4chan a message for moot, saying he could help out with servers and the like. moot posted back: "Who the hell are you?"—honestly curi-

ous, I think, and not trying to be dismissive. But iichan just wasn't on moot's radar; he had enough stuff to deal with just with 4chan.

During this period there was antagonism between 4chan users and those of other chan-style boards, wherein they would flood other boards with porn and other spam. Ashby recounts conflicts that have been dubbed the Chan Wars:

> Those sorts of floods were often the work of one or two individuals with either some imagined grudge or a hankering to troll the users of another site. It was never between the admins of the boards themselves. They could be triggered by any number of things: perceived mocking of another site, "theft" of memes or jokes, or simply a dislike of the content being posted.

According to Shii, the Chan Wars began as a result of a porn site called HentaiKey whose owner was personally annoyed with moot for distributing porn for free on 4chan. He sent complaints to PayPal and moot's domain registrar, which led to 4chan losing its hosting and original 4chan.net domain—which gave rise to iichan as a replacement site for anime geeks.

According to one anon, some of the more overtly trollish /b/tards left for 7chan en masse because this new site gave them more freedom to engage in illegal activity. In other cases, 4chan users were drawn to alternative chan boards because they had other boards discussing topics like law, philosophy, politics, and history. Encyclopedia Dramatica casts the birth of 7chan, one of the biggest alternatives to 4chan, in biblical proportions:

> Anonymous toiled under Moot's harsh rule for over 9000 years, building great pyramids unto him on many hectares of

land. Anonymous cried out "When shall we be freed of this tyrant king, who so punishes us for our beliefs?"

The Internet spoke unto Anonymous: "There shall be a baby born amongst you, a child prophet, and he shall be called Ian, and he shall lead you from this place. There will be some other guys too, but they will turn out to be faggots."

Upon his 17th year, the prophet Ian came before Moot and brought plagues of DDoSing and rebellion on his head. Ian parted the Internet, and led his people to freedom. Forty days and forty nights they traveled through the desert. Finally, on the last day, Ian dropped his GBC and proclaimed "This, my followers, is our new land. It shall be called 7chan." And lol, the Internet saw that it was good.

This is just a snippet of the staggering amount of lore dedicated to the different chan boards. Despite the tension between the different chans, /b/ reached one hundred thousand posts in April 2004, one of the first notable "gets." Each post is given a number, and nice round ones are often sought after in get threads (as in "I got it!"). The random anon who posted the hundred-thousandth post wrote "lol Internet," which became an instant meme, as many get posts do. That summer 4chan had its longest stretch of downtime, a full six weeks, which was triggered by a complaint sent to PayPal, who had been processing 4chan's donations. moot was eventually able to get the site back online with some new features and boards in August.

One Million Get!

In 2005, /b/ reached one million posts. moot experimented further with the site's principles of anonymity by removing the name fields entirely. The site continued to suffer from hacks and downtime, but by spring of 2006 the site had reached ten million posts.

At this point 4chan's tomfoolery began to extend outside of /b/. /b/tards began to target Internet personalities, for varying reasons. They attacked furries. (People who like to dress up in cartoonish animal costumes called fursuits. Furries' attraction to animals is often sexual, but many furries insist otherwise. 4chan is especially antagonistic to furries, though every Friday /b/tards post massive furry porn threads, calling it Furry Friday.) They attacked pro-anorexia message boards, washed-up celebrities, and the MySpace-profile-turned-online-memorial of a seventh grader who took his own life. Thrill-seeking /b/tards would find an easy target on the web, post related info to 4chan, and mobilize dozens, sometimes even hundreds, of anons in order to troll Internet users who'd caught their attention.

In August 2006, moot posted a message to /b/, declaring that anyone who posted illegal content (e.g., child pornography, personal information, and raid-related calls to action) would be banned permanently from 4chan, and anyone who posted within illicit discussion threads would be banned for two weeks. This led many users leave 4chan for other chan boards. It has gone down in chan lore as *lb/day*.

4chan's Eternal September Moment

If one had to pick an eternal September period for 4chan, it began in 2007. That was the year of lolcats and Tay "Chocolate Rain" Zonday. Most importantly, it was the year of the Internet Hate Machine.

A Los Angeles Fox affiliate put together a breathless exposé on Anonymous. It starts off like this:

> Anonymous. This is what "they" call themselves. They are hackers on steroids, treating the web like a real-life video game. Sacking websites, invading Myspace accounts, disrupting innocent people's lives—and if you fight back, watch out.

At this point, the ominous music begins.

> "Destroy. Die. Attack." Threats from a gang of computer hackers calling themselves Anonymous . . . They attack innocent people like an Internet hate machine.

"Hackers on Steroids" and "Internet Hate Machine" became instant memes. I can imagine the howls of laughter that met this sensationalized news report.

> Those who fight back face death threats. Anonymous has even threatened to bomb sports stadiums. Their name comes from their secret websites. It requires anyone posting on the site to remain anonymous.
>
> MySpace users are among their favorite targets. People like David. Anonymous hacked his site and plastered it with gay sex pictures. His girlfriend left him. They crashed his computer with

a virus and used his own email to infect everyone on his friend list.

The report doesn't mention 4chan by name, instead calling it "an underground hacker site linked to Anonymous."

Anonymous gets big lulz from pulling random pranks. For example, messing with online children's games like Habbo Hotel. The pranks are often anti-Semitic or racist, and always posted on the Internet. But truly epic lulz come from raids and invasion.

Their most notorious stunt? A bomb threat against seven football stadiums, which drew national media attention.

Cut to a woman drawing her curtains, presumably to keep out lurking members of Anonymous.

This mother's also fighting Anonymous. Her whole family's been under attack.

"They posted pictures of all of us."

Anonymous has posted their home address and phone number.

"Pretty much said that 'You've got all the information now. Do what you need to do. Go go go.'"

Death threats started pouring in.

"Your heart is breaking. You need to keep your family safe."

She installed electronic security, a phone tracing system, and bought a dog. Then she started tracking down Anonymous members and brought in the FBI.

"Buy a dog" has become another legendary meme. It's used as a catchall for mocking advice. If someone asks "What can I do to save money on my tax return?" on Yahoo Answers, some /b/tard will inevitably reply, "Maybe you should buy a dog."

This news story set the tone for the media's relationship with 4chan for years to come. It's marked by a weak grasp of Anonymous's structure, histrionic sound bites from supposed victims, and ham-fisted usage of 4chan lingo.

Slashdot founder Rob Malda posted the video, commenting, "Cringe as you watch this video explain terms like 'LULZ' and show inspirational poster parodies as evidence of the evils of this terrifying 'Group'." The thread received over five hundred comments, nearly all making fun of the report, which conflated comparatively harmless Anonymous trolling with actual domestic terrorism.

One anonymous Slashdot commenter nailed the sea change:

> Seriously, /b/ is so mainstream now, it beggars belief. Here is a Slashdot article that mentions it in passing without so much as stopping to explain the term . . .
>
> It's a shame really. For a short while, /b/ was a great little Internet phenomenon. Anonymity, with all its baggage, and somehow no lawsuits. Now, though, the old guard is quickly moving on. Anybody who's frequented the site can attest to this . . .
>
> Despite my pessimistic tone, I predict that "Anonymous" will continue to grow. As more and more attention is given to these "secret websites," more and more people are clamoring to become "hackers on steroids." This new Anonymous will be larger, with more brute force at his call, but at the same time stupider, and less apt to create entertaining content. And paradoxically, he'll be less anonymous than before. I see threads where a bunch of high-schoolers recognize each other based on posted photos and local memes.

A prescient analysis. Meanwhile, 4chan continued to grow as curious onlookers who caught the news coverage wandered onto

/b/ to see what all the fuss was about. *Wired* ran a piece in January 2008 called "Mutilated Furries, Flying Phalluses: Put the Blame on Griefers, the Sociopaths of the Virtual World." This article, written by Julian Dibbell, mentioned 4chan and finally provided noobs with a reasoned analysis of troll culture.

Meanwhile at Gawker, my friend Nick Douglas (the college buddy who turned me on to 4chan), wrote "What the Hell Are 4chan, ED, Something Awful, and 'b'?"—a report that remains the top source cited on 4chan's Wikipedia entry.

And so, shortly after its fourth birthday, and now with more than fifty million posts, /b/ was flooded with new users like never before. Many veteran users bemoaned that the newfags were only interested in trolling, and cared not for meme creation and ultranerdy culture. This constant grumbling about the "cancer of newfaggotry" became a recurring theme on 4chan. You can barely scroll to the bottom of a page on /b/ without seeing someone complain about how newfags are ruining the board.

"Newfags can't triforce" is a meme that began as a way for old users to assert their authority over the noobs, and more importantly it showed new users that they have a lot to learn before they can mess around on 4chan. The triforce is a bit of video game iconography, an ancient source of power from the *Legend of Zelda* franchise that looks like three triangles arranged in a triangular pattern. Oldfags will post the symbol along with "Newfags can't triforce." New users who try to copy-paste the symbol in their reply to prove their worth will learn that the pasted symbol appears misaligned. The only way to properly display the triforce is by using a complex set of Unicode characters.

From here, 4chan continued to garner news coverage for various trolls and hacks, culminating in the anti-Scientology movement Project Chanology, which made Anonymous, if not 4chan itself, a household name. (See Chapter 8.)

Meet Moot

On July 9, 2008, moot's identity was revealed in a *Wall Street Journal* article, "Modest Web Site Is Behind a Bevy of Memes." The article followed the template for 4chan exposés, starting off with a brief introduction to memes (e.g., Have you seen these lolcats things the kids are into?), easing into 4chan culture, highlighting Anonymous, and dropping a few quotes from eggheads and anons that demonstrate the surprising influence and size of the site. This was the first time moot, now unmasked as a handsome young man named Christopher Poole, showed his face in the media.

In the following three years, Project Chanology would peter out, with Anonymous moving on to other targets (everything from Paypal and Mastercard to Oprah and the Recording Industry Association of America). 4chan continued to churn out memes, and sites like Know Your Meme, Buzzfeed, Urlesque, and the Cheezburger Network rose up to serve as gateways between 4chan and the rest of the Internet. In 2010, Christopher Poole announced a new project called Canvas.

Shii has mixed feelings about 4chan today, and he hasn't followed the site closely since 2005.

Before 4chan, posting online meant developing an Internet reputation, no matter what you wanted to say. I only saw this as a negative thing, because I could only see the downside of tradi-

---

tional forums; self-aggrandizing egos became famous while interesting voices were drowned out, and pointless and exhausting Internet drama was constant. Anything that would shake up that banality was interesting to me. But I don't think I could have foreseen the shape it would take beyond mere entertainment, which 4chan certainly invented and improved tremendously.

Shii explains that 4chan has created both good and bad: Anonymous as social activist and Anonymous as stalker and harasser. Technology has served the group well in both directions, with members becoming skilled in initiating "life-ruining" attacks as well as impressive feats of social good. He says that both types of activity are now coordinated outside of 4chan in places like IRC and AnonOps. "4chan itself is not really innovative anymore," he says.

Today moot's busy with Canvas, though he occasionally gives an interview about the still-growing popularity of his first endeavor. In April 2011, moot gave an AMA on Reddit, where he engaged with the community in a Q&A session about Canvas and 4chan.

Someone asked him, "What do you think, ten years from now, the lasting cultural legacy of 4chan will be?"

He replied, "That it shaped 'net and IRL culture in a way that few other communities/websites have."

Quite an accomplishment for a 15-year-old kid.

Chapter 6

The Meme Industry

$\mathbf{B}$ECAUSE 4CHAN HAS no archives, a host of websites have sprung up around it in order to analyze and document meme culture. Some of these sites act almost like museums, adding sociological commentary and in-depth research in order to place memes in context. Others behave more like comedy sites that go straight for the lulz. As Internet culture becomes mainstream, even massive media organizations like CNN dedicate more space to viral content.

Consider the following two case studies in meme celebrity.

In the fall of 2002, a chubby Canadian student named Ghyslain Raza filmed himself wielding a golf ball retriever like a lightsaber in his high school film production studio. Providing his own sound effects, the poor kid spins and kicks his way through a clumsy martial arts routine. It was perhaps the most pitifully nerdy thing committed to film in a pre-YouTube era. Of course, one of his friends discovered the tape and passed it around.

Eventually, one of his classmates uploaded a file called Jackass_starwars_funny.wmv. This was during the height of *Star Wars* prequel mania, and the video went on to become one of the most viral clips in history.

If the Star Wars Kid video had been uploaded today, the kid probably would have been featured on *Good Morning America*, done a parody video for the comedy site Funny or Die, guested on *Late Night with Jimmy Fallon*, and been given a low-budget reality TV show in which he judged martial arts routines across America. That's because today, there's a massive infrastructure built around the memesphere that's driven by the media's insatiable desire to be first to market with the next big viral craze. Being first can make the difference between hundreds of page views and millions.

But there was none of that around back then. Instead the clip was parodied on a few dozen TV shows against his will—just a humiliating experience for Raza all around. His family filed a $250,000 lawsuit against the families of the classmates who distributed the video, eventually settling out of court.

Two years later, a video of 19-year-old Gary Brolsma hilariously gesticulating and lip synching to a Romanian pop song went viral. The "Numa Numa" phenomenon brought immediate media attention. Brolsma appeared on *Good Morning America*, but soon decided to reject his designated fifteen minutes of fame, shunning all interviews. Brolsma reappeared in 2006 with his own website, merch, and a remix of the original song: a cash-in attempt that smartly coincided with the birth of You-Tube, which allowed countless others to upload renditions of the legendary meme.

In a way, Star Wars Kid is an artifact of a bygone era. Meme fame is so easy to monetize now, it's unlikely we'll ever see meme celebrities of that magnitude shun fame the way Star Wars Kid did way back in 2002.

Encyclopedia Dramatica

For several years, Encyclopedia Dramatica was the only place to go to read about 4chan culture. It's a wiki site that contains thousands of entries dedicated to all things drama. Like 4chan, it's almost incomprehensible to outsiders, as every entry is written in an intensely mean-spirited tone, peppered with obscure Internet slang and populated by lolcows.

A lolcow is someone who offers lulz like a cow offers milk. People who just never learn, who post their hysterics on the web, who try to fight back against Anonymous and lose. Lolcows are people who play by the old rules, who smugly declare that they're going to sue 4chan, or tearfully threaten to call the police.

Lolcows just don't know when to give up, and Encyclopedia Dramatica made documenting lolcow behavior its mission. For example, here's an excerpt from the entry on Asperger's Syndrome:

> Assburgers is a made-up disease, most common in overachieving middle-class families, because little Johnny is either a social outcast, or is just acting fucking retarded. The parents diagnose their child, and the "doctors" go along with and encourage it because of the money it generates. Fuckers. The truth is, the Assburgers diagnosis has become popular with parents because they need a good excuse as to why their "fucktard children are dumb faggots who will be dying alone."

While each entry is intended to provide some informational content, it's conveyed in such a way as to troll the unsuspecting reader and delight those who are in the know.

It surprised me to find that Encyclopedia Dramatica's creator, Sherrod DeGrippo, has absolutely zero interest in 4chan.

> Just so you aren't shocked or disappointed . . . I am not a walking encyclopedia of memes. I don't really follow Anonymous or 4chan or anything like that.

What? This woman runs a site that behaves as the definitive repository for 4chan culture, and is telling me that she could not care less about 4chan? As it turns out, she launched the site in order to chronicle the hilarious drama she saw on LiveJournal, the online diary/social network that predated the blog revolution. DeGrippo discovered LJ in 2000, when it was mostly "people posting pictures of their cats and detailing what they had for breakfast."

DeGrippo quickly became fascinated by LJdrama, a community on the site that eventually got booted off, and later resurfaced with its own domain. An Urban Dictionary entry describes the site as "the high school cafeteria of the Internet." DeGrippo and her cohorts posted reports of LJ gossip. Their coverage of the community acted as a Gawker or a TMZ for the LiveJournal community, and gained notoriety quickly.

The rise of LJdrama coincided with the rise of reality television and the blogging revolution, when regular folks began to garner headlines alongside Hollywood A-listers and pop stars. It was a huge shift in the nature of celebrity and tabloid culture. LiveJournal users soon learned that if they stirred up drama on their journals, they could build bigger fanbases. Some went as far as to threaten suicide or document their mental imbalances.

People were accessible and it was bidirectional. Voyeurs and exhibitionists were able to interact in a way that was normalized. That's why I started ED. It was mostly just personalities that were just so nuts and fascinating.

Technology gave us an environment in which people are empowered to project their dysfunction to millions of viewers. DeGrippo found this environment intoxicating. The lolcow who started it all was mediacrat, aka Joshua Williams, a student at the University of Washington, Seattle.

In 2002, Williams began a relationship with another LJ user, Andrewpants. The relationship soured, and drama ensued. When LJdrama documented Williams's online histrionics, he threatened to sue. He even went so far as to drive to Portland, Oregon, to talk to LiveJournal's abuse team about the matter. He claimed that he underwent online harassment when unflattering pictures of him were posted online.

Williams contacted a local TV news station to report the harassment. He threatened to press charges and get restraining orders. The drama resounded throughout the Internet until July 19, 2002, when Williams updated his LiveJournal account for the last time, leaving the controversy behind. Encyclopedia Dramatica was born in the wake of this scandal. According to DeGrippo, there were a lot of people on LiveJournal faking pregnancies, diseases, and relationships to get attention. People had become fascinated with these lolcows in the same way they used to obsess over the antics of Elizabeth Taylor or fictional drama like *Dallas*'s "Who shot JR?" phenomenon. "It turns regular people into paparazzi," says DeGrippo.

She defines an lolcow as "someone who just doesn't know when to stop. They just won't wise up and stop posting pictures of themselves naked, or [writing] insane posts, or whatever. They just keep fanning the flames of the fire they claim to hate." She considers Courtney Love to be a prominent celebrity lolcow, given her perpetual legal trouble, drug addiction, public mental instability, and seemingly insatiable lust for the limelight. A more recent example would be Charlie Sheen, whose recent manic downward spiral has been documented in real time via streaming video, live performances, and Twitter feeds throughout 2011.

"You want to just grab them and be like, 'Look! Just STOP it! For your own good!'" says DeGrippo, but of course there is a certain voyeuristic pleasure in rubbernecking at the celebrity train wreck. And the Internet offers much more delicious schadenfreude than Hollywood does. But TV is catching up.

DeGrippo is really into reality TV gossip, especially the various iterations of the *Real Housewives* franchise, which is basically built around lolcows. But the experience of enjoying the shows doesn't stop when the credits roll. In fact, for DeGrippo, the real fun begins the following morning, when Gawker's Richard Lawson posts snarky commentary of the previous night's drama. The mayhem continues in the comments following the article.

Producers recognize this phenomenon, and they facilitate it with crazier, more dramatic content. Because now Demi Lovato isn't just competing with Miley Cyrus for your attention; she's competing with Jessi Slaughter, and Kiki Kannibal (teen webcam microcelebs who were recently targeted by trolls). This forces Hollywood celebs to make themselves more accessible, offering the public their illicit cell phone photos, for instance. Celebrities used to be unattainable demigods, and now we're watching them fart and philander on YouTube.

According to DeGrippo, LiveJournal became such fertile ground for drama because it was particularly open, making it easy for noobs to spew their dysfunction into the world. It provided an early example of the "follow" function called "friendslist," which created a chronological feed for users to browse their favorite LJ personalities. This functionality would come to define social blogging platforms like Twitter and Tumblr years later. It also included a clever threaded commenting structure, making it easy for people to keep discussion threads going for years.

Which is of course the exact opposite of how 4chan works. 4chan feels more like a fire hose of unrelated content hitting you all at once and then disappearing down a storm drain. Speaking of which, how is it that Encyclopedia Dramatica is so inextricably linked to 4chan rather than to LiveJournal? DeGrippo claims she created ED to house one article about LiveJournal, and completely lost interest after that.

> I think this is something that many 4chan users wring their hands and tear their hair about. I still use LJ every day. Ha! I have never been a 4chan user, so I just assumed these people were seeing stuff on the Internet. As long as something wasn't submitted as illegal or an abuse complaint, I didn't even see it. Wikis are something that you either closely, closely monitor and manage, or you just let it go.

And let it go she did, allowing Encyclopedia Dramatica to mutate into a museum of 4chan-related lulz and drama. It also acts as a troll hall of fame.

In 2006, Seattle-area network administrator Jason Fortuny, who described himself as "a normal person who does insane things on the Internet," became an Encyclopedia Dramatica microceleb when he posed as a woman seeking a partner for some rough sex in the "Casual Encounters" section of the Seattle Craigslist personals. Fortuny then posted each response, many of which included personal and contact information, to Encyclopedia Dramatica, calling it the Craigslist Experiment. A few respondents were fired when companies caught wind of the information dump. This scandal gave ED its first taste of mainstream media attention. Fortuny was required to pay one victim $74,252.56 in damages, attorney fees, and costs.

When the focus of Encyclopedia Dramatica shifted away from LiveJournal, that's when DeGrippo stopped having fun. She kept paying for server space because she thought maybe it might turn back around to focus on lighthearted, sarcastic LJ drama again, rather than the mean-spirited trolling of 4chan.

Encyclopedia Dramatica never turned a profit. Like 4chan, it had just too much vile content to turn the heads of any serious advertisers. DeGrippo never set out to make millions, and never used the popularity of the site to further any personal agenda. Despite her fascination with Internet celebrity, she prefers to keep her identity under wraps, so much so that I had no idea she was a woman in her 40s when I was first able to track her down. She's spoken to the press twice in the last seven years.

DeGrippo loved the Internet because of the interesting personalities she found there, ever since she discovered BBSes at age 13 in the back of *Thrasher*, a skateboarding themed counterculture rag. Her dad was a "mega hard-core smarty type," who taught her basic computing. But she wasn't a shut-in. She was also on homecoming court and president of several clubs in high school.

Her experience with BBSes and IRC was controlled chaos. She claims that people were generally friendly and wanted to collaborate, but Internet users back then were much more equipped to fight back against antisocial behavior, since the very fact that they were on the Internet at the time meant that they knew a thing or two about the technology. Plus the online experience was slow. "Being a dick took forever, so why bother?" she says.

DeGrippo always suspected the Internet would go mainstream, but not exactly the way it has.

> Technology is cheap and ubiquitous now. It's just assumed. I used to think that everyone would be programming C and writing their own operating systems. File systems would be taught in middle school, kids would all be kernel committers.
>
> But in reality it went the way of television. The populous wasn't elevated. The entry was dumbed down. No one knows how to fix their television, or cares. They just want to watch it.

DeGrippo came to hate ED, so in April 2011, she killed it. In its place she built Oh Internet (as in, "Oh, Internet, you so crazy!"), a sanitized, approachable version of ED—if not for social value, then at least for entertainment value. She believes that collecting and archiving content is valuable. And this time, she's doing it on her own terms. It's still a user-edited wiki site, but it will be more closely monitored and moderated. She believes that if a person wants to upload embarrassing information to the Internet, all that content is fair game, but she doesn't want Oh Internet to be a place where personal info and dirty laundry is easily posted and distributed. Leave that to 4chan.

The Cheezburger Network

It started with a supremely stupid image macro featuring a chubby British Shorthair cat. The happy cat photo was captioned with the line "I Can Has Cheezburger?" and eventually launched a media empire. The image was originally posted to Something Awful in the tradition of 4chan's lolcats. A blogger named Eric Nakagawa thought the lolcat was hilarious, so he created a blog to document funny cat photos.

Meanwhile, in Seattle, a start-up kid named Ben Huh was running a tiny blog about being a pet owner in Seattle. Fate struck when Nakagawa hot-linked one of Ben Huh's animal photos and brought down Huh's server with an avalanche of traffic. Also known as inline linking, this means Nakagawa linked directly to Huh's image rather than hosting the image on his own server. It's considered a supremely dickish move because the hot-linker gets to benefit from featuring the image while the other guy has to deal with the traffic it generates. Huh called Nakagawa and told him to cut it out.

Huh's initial annoyance gave way to curiosity. If this goofy site had crashed his server, it must be getting a ton of traffic. So he helped Nakagawa manage the site for a while, and then offered to buy it.

The blog was already hugely popular, but Huh spun the thing into a network of meme-oriented blogs that had the sort of numbers major newspapers would envy, with the flagship site achieving over ten million daily hits.

Huh insists that he wasn't buying a site so much as the potential for a vibrant community. He'd seen the way online communities like 4chan work together to create a vast canon of something approaching modern folk art. The trick was getting the fad out of /b/ and into mom's and dad's laps.

Huh expanded the network to include a site for loldogs called I Has a Hotdog. There's Daily Squee, a site for cute pictures of all kinds (not just animals). You can probably guess what My Food Looks Funny is about.

Then there's FAIL Blog. The use of *fail* as a noun began to pop up on the web in 2008. It derives from a bit of Engrish from a video game called *Blazing Star*. If you lose, the game tells you, "You fail it! Your skill is not enough! See you next time! Bye bye!" The term eventually evolved to include the mirror term *win*, and related terms *epic fail* and—you guessed it—*epic win*.

FAIL Blog is one of the biggest sites in the Cheezburger roster, essentially an *America's Funniest Home Videos*–style clearinghouse for videos and images illustrating extreme human stupidity. This expansion of the Cheezburger brand has itself spawned Failbook (Facebook fails), Engrish Funny (self-explanatory), There I Fixed It (dangerously lazy or inept repairs), and After 12 (party fails).

There's also The Daily What, a tremendously popular Tumblr blog, which in just a few years cornered the market on meme-oriented news with its staggering publishing speed, though much of its coverage is scraped directly from Reddit. TDW has recently diversified into TDW Geek and TDW Tease, which cover geek news and racy content, respectively.

A handful of other random meme-oriented sites rounds out the Cheezburger Network. Advice animal memes, demotivational posters, GIFs, trolls, RageToons, and more. Basically, if Huh sees a meme trending on 4chan or Reddit and he thinks it's strong enough, he builds a blog around it. These blogs print money, and this is where Huh starts to draw criticism.

"You're stealing our memes!" screams 4chan. "You're profiting off our hard work!" cries Reddit. That's a big question guys like Ben Huh are facing right now. Who owns these memes? The person who created the source material? The person who Photoshopped or otherwise augmented it? The community where it was originally posted? The community that helped it go viral? These are questions that content producers and intellectual property lawyers are currently wrestling with.

The Hitler biopic *Downfall* features a scene in which Adolf goes on a tirade, realizing that he's lost the war. Hundreds of YouTube parodists used the video and audio footage from the scene, but changed the subtitles to suggest Hitler was freaking out over something else, like the price of the iPad. As the meme spread, the producers of the film tried to have the clips removed. But the more they fought to suppress the meme, the faster it spread. The conflict between the memesters and the creators of the source material ended with the creators throwing up their hands in defeat. It was simply impossible for YouTube to keep the stuff down. One particularly meta iteration of the meme showcased Hitler bemoaning the takedown notices. Today, the meme is recreated in the wake of every major controversy or hot topic. If something's big in the news, there almost certainly will be a *Downfall* parody.

Imagine a guy spends two hours creating a *Downfall* parody

video that gets posted all over Reddit and eventually Gawker, which doesn't give the remixer credit. The guy sends a furious complaint to Gawker, claiming that he put his heart and soul into that remix and he should receive credit for his work. But what about the community that made the clip go viral? And while we're at it, what about the original film studio? The actors, director, producer, makeup artist, and on and on down the line? Who deserves credit when there are so many people involved in meme creation, even some who never wanted to create a viral hit?

Huh admits that he'll catch flak no matter who gets credit.

> People say, "I am part of this community, which had a hand in making the meme, it's to our credit, even though I personally had nothing to do with it" [or] "Hey, that image came from Reddit!" It didn't come from Reddit. We do the best we can; even though, in this example, Reddit is the popularizer, credit belongs elsewhere.

Ben Huh can't remember life before the web. His father was computer savvy, teaching his young son how to take apart a computer and put it back together. But it wasn't until Huh saw ICHC that he recognized something special was happening online. It was while he worked for Eric Nakagawa that Huh discovered 4chan.

> I initially assumed it was just another forum, but it was like, "Oh my God." Very eye opening. It gave me some insight as to how memes formed there and why it's such a breeding ground. You would post something and have to rely on the digital and psychological memory of someone else.

I asked Huh why he thinks his sites have been such successes, and he draws from an offline analogy, the celebrity sighting.

> Think of you telling a friend, "I just saw Brett Favre." There's no benefit to you sharing that information, but there is, biologically speaking, when you associate yourself with something greater than you. Not because you're giving them a piece of advice. I can tell you something funny or show you what's popular; therefore my status in the community increases somewhat. There's that powerful association.

This powerful association is what drives the memesphere.

Buzzfeed

In the mid-2000s, pretty much every media portal came up with some kind of web 2.0 strategy that would help it harness and monetize user-generated content. No site pulled this off better than Buzzfeed, though it had the advantage of starting from scratch. Co-founder Jonah Peretti was also responsible for the Contagious Media Festival and for cofounding the web 2.0 news blog The Huffington Post, where he learned a thing or two about viral content.

Peretti coined the term, the Bored at Work network, which he considered to be a vast untapped demographic made up of millions of cube farm drones, already sitting at computers, looking for quick bits of distraction while their bosses attend meetings. And not only looking for viral content, but also already on Gchat, Twitter, or Facebook too, ready to forward content to their buddies. The key to tapping this far-reaching market, according to Peretti, is letting them decide what's popular.

Buzzfeed, launched in 2006, is powered by an algorithm that monitors over 120 million unique pages across hundreds of media portals like Time, Aol News, and TMZ, taking into account social sharing on platforms like Facebook, Twitter, and Stumbleupon. When the algorithm determines that a piece of content is going viral, it sends a red flag to Buzzfeed's editorial team. Buzzfeed also opens up its site to direct submissions from Buzzfeed users, who have the ability to tag and vote on pieces of content.

Buzzfeed Senior Editor Scott Lamb started out at an alternative weekly in San Francisco after graduating, and was immediately drawn to working on the website rather than the paper. He first recognized viral content as something new and interesting when he was introduced to the All Your Base Are Belong to Us phenomenon.

> They say you can't force a meme. And that's true. What you can do, though, is create the right environment for one to take off. And memes, most of them, have some element of social imperative, something inherent in them that makes you want to share. We're at this cool point where we all have access to easy social sharing, which I think mimics a lot of the roots of meme culture in boards, where people could easily and quickly read and respond to one another.

Buzzfeed also employs an in-house editorial team of meme-meisters, all with keen eyes for what could go viral. The editors monitor places like Reddit and Tumblr, spotting content that their robot might miss. They also create their own custom content, such as a list of pop starlets with chiseled male chests, and approve submissions from the algorithm and the users. Of course, everything is integrated into major social networks so users can easily share content and spot what's already trending where. Each piece of content submitted to the site has the potential to earn badges that say things like LOL, OMG, or Fail, which give the site a colorful, fun vibe.

And so every day, editors, users, and machines team up to create a steady drip of simple, shareable, and sticky content that's easy to consume in bite-sized chunks. They are constantly trying new things, tweaking the algorithm, and killing what doesn't work.

Though Lamb recognizes the influence of 4chan, he's quick to concede that *Good Morning America*–type mainstream content still pulls tremendous weight on the Internet. But those big media entities are increasingly waiting for content to percolate on the web so they can pounce on buzz-worthy content.

I also asked Lamb the obligatory "future of journalism" question. While he recognizes the power of Buzzfeed's model, he reminds me that Buzzfeed does not do any actual reportage—no interviews, no articles, nothing. They're curators, and we'll always need people doing the journalistic legwork, even if serious news sites trend toward a Buzzfeed-like model.

Know Your Meme

Google any meme. Chances are, within the first page of results, there's an entry for it on Know Your Meme. That's because it's the best place to figure out the who, what, when, where, and why of memetic culture.

Kenyatta Cheese, Jamie Wilkinson, and Elspeth Jane Roun-tree were working at Rocketboom, a web video company that produces a daily web news show. They were on 4chan every day, spending a lot of time on Encyclopedia Dramatica, and talking about the weird little subculture. Over time they started to no-tice that a lot of the stuff in that world was showing up in the mainstream. They'd notice an Adult Swim ad here, or a com-mercial there, that referenced somewhat obscure memes that in most cases weren't being credited to the original creator.

Thus was born the Rocketboom Institute for Internet Studies, a tongue-in-cheek laboratory conceit wherein the institute ana-lyzed memetic culture as video segments under the Rocketboom brand. Meanwhile, Jamie Wilkinson built a database platform in order to store information that would supplement the existing Know Your Meme video series. The database's popularity would eventually outstrip not only the Know Your Meme videos, but the Rocketboom series as well. It's a wiki site like Encyclopedia Dramatica, but generally safe for work, approachable for noobs, and with an added layer of straight-faced analysis and editorial control provided by a staff of Internet culture experts.

The typical KYM entry begins with a short introduction to the meme, along with a video or image representation. Then it sources the meme as best it can, along with charts representing Google search trends and social media stats. A description of why the meme is funny or interesting within the context of the memesphere usually follows. Finally, a few dozen examples of derivatives and mashups, followed by a place for commenters to discuss.

KYM is driven by user submissions, but on most entries at least one staff member is listed as one of the editors. Cheese believes the ease of use for the random user is integral to the site's value.

> There's the person who comes to us and says 'I saw this one image macro appear on a thread on such and such a forum back in 2003, and here's the link.' Sometimes that bit of information is more important than the high-level analysis from someone who's an expert in cultural theory.

According to Cheese, you have to be somewhat familiar with 4chan to be able to wrap your head around meme culture.

> Most of the real rules of 4chan are not explicit. They're things that you only understand after being a part of the culture. You have to hang around lurking for months before you get a handle on what's acceptable, or what will be successful. And you can only be a part of the culture if you're willing to be infected by it. You can't go in as a journalist or a marketer hoping to figure them out. You won't.

Of course, that doesn't stop social media "rock stars" from trying. Cheese says that about a quarter of the submissions at KYM are suspected of coming directly from content producers and creative agencies hoping to make their stuff go viral, but weeding out these forced memes is easy if you know anything about how Internet culture works.

There has been some tension between Know Your Meme and 4chan for a few reasons. /b/tards don't like it when anyone explains their subculture to NORPs (or normal ordinary respectable person; shorthand for someone whose mind hasn't been warped by the horrors of 4chan). And while /b/tards are happy to contribute to the memesphere anonymously and for no pay, when someone else starts selling T-shirts, people can get nasty.

> 4chan thought KYM wanted to commoditize, but we loved this stuff. Most of us had artist backgrounds, who were hyper-aware of the market commoditization of culture. That's not what we wanted for web culture.

Of course, it's not like Know Your Meme was ever hugely profitable (but it was acquired in March 2011 by Ben Huh's Cheezburger network, so that's probably going to change). Cheese sees KYM almost as a public service that sustained itself in order to properly archive and analyze stuff that no one in academia seemed willing or able to preserve properly.

> We think of the Internet as being this place for information to live permanently, but if there's no market value in keeping something online, it could be lost forever.

Tumblr

I started a Tumblr blog three years ago, when it was being positioned as a place for creative types to easily upload and share their stuff. At the time there was a little corner of the social network made up of New York media types who used their Tumblr blogs to post writing they couldn't sell. These bloggers were witty, insightful, and happy to engage with people (like me) who didn't have impressive media credentials, as long as they had something interesting to say.

Tumblr is a simple, streamlined blogging platform that allows users to follow one another, like on Twitter. The posts from the people you follow are collected in a feed, viewable in the Dashboard. Integral to the site's design is the Reblog function, which is used in lieu of comments. It copies someone's post to your blog, allowing you to add your comments. Then the original poster can re-reblog your post, if she wants. This creates a conversation, and allows people to riff on each other's creative work. It's a perfect platform for meme creation.

Tumblr was founded in 2007 by David Karp, a high school dropout who taught himself to code, and a small group of developers in New York. One member of the team, Christopher Price, is tasked with managing the community of communities and facilitating its growth. No easy task, considering that people use Tumblr for as many different purposes as you can imagine. Price's enthusiasm and knack for creating things that people wanted to share caught the attention of the Tumblr team, and they hired him. His personal Tumblr blog reads, "I work at Tumblr. I live in Manhattan. Dinosaurs are awesome," underneath a googly-eyed close-up photo of his face. His goofy online persona has become something of a Tumblr mascot.

Price tells me that the democratizing effect of the Internet excites him the most about the present age. Everyone now has the ability to find a huge audience for their work, whereas just a few decades ago the reach was limited to those who could buy the biggest radio towers.

Most of the Tumblr employees post a few times a day, but Price, going by "Topherchris," outpaces them all by far. This is a man who unabashedly loves memes, and he spends a sizable portion of his workday experimenting with them—seeing what works and what doesn't, tapping the community to create interesting new things. Unlike his coworkers, Price's online persona is silly, reflective of his childlike love for his medium of choice.

I asked him why he's so interested in memes.

There's a spot in Argentina called *Cueva de las Manos*, or Cave of the Hands. About 9,000 years ago, humans started painting images of their favorite food there, the guanaco. It's like a llama. It's no lolcat, but they're cute. Then, about 7,000 years ago, something happened. People started putting up hand stencils. You'd put one hand up on the wall, hold your bone-made pipe in your other hand, and blow paint through it towards the wall and your hand.

Why did people do this? Maybe it was an adolescent rite of passage. Maybe there are religious implications. Maybe they just thought it looked cool. What we do know is that somebody did it first. And then it was copied. And so on. Scattered amongst all these negative relief stencils of hands are a few paintings of *positive relief hands*. (That is, instead of a painting of the outline of a hand, it's a painting of a hand itself.) Think about that. Somebody approached this wall of stencils and said, "Here's another way to do that." That right there was the apex of meme technology at the time. Today we open things in Photoshop and hit "invert." Memes are our culture. Memes are our language. Memes use whatever technology is available.

Price lives and breathes Tumblr. He says it "pokes a spot in my brain that feels good," because it's so rewarding to share something he's made with others, to know they've appreciated it and to watch them share it with their friends.

With over 3 million users, it's safe to say that Tumblr is mainstream, though pockets of the Tumblrverse are still as bizarre as

179

can be. Consider Summer of Megadeth, a collective of NYC media malcontents who started a group blog (or *glog*) with no clear editorial mission other than to crack vaguely heavy metal–related jokes, mainly at the expense of New York media fameballs and random celebrities/pop personalities. Other times it's a place to complain about Tumblr. Or talk feminism. Or post twenty images of Warren Zevon in a row. The Calvinball concept is truly at play at SoM.

One member is the editor of a prominent music site. Another is an art director at an LA ad agency. Some are unemployed. A favorite meme is to uphold contrarian ideals that are typically seen as wimpy or "not very metal" and proclaim them as "so fucking metal" (Steely Dan being the example that comes to mind). The group's appreciation for schlocky heavy metal music is not dissimilar from 4chan's obsession with cute cats. SoM is actively antagonistic to outsiders, telling any confused onlookers to "delete your Tumblr." It relies heavily on an impenetrable, multilayered network of metal slang, ever-changing puns and recurring meme gags that ward off most people who wander onto the blog wondering what it's all about. It's said that if you're following SoM, you're missing the point. More recently members have taken to switching up the URL of the site so the casually interested have difficulty finding it. According to insiders, all the real action is happening in the back channel, a legendary email thread only accessible to the blog's mysterious contributors.

One contributor named Rendit described the site's aesthetic:

> It's really quite simple. Someone dumb (me) comes up with an almost-funny joke and represents it in the basest, most simplistic, and talentless way. Then! Someone smart does it again much bet-

ter, making actual reference to the source of the comedy and his or her work. After that, one of our members . . . will apply the image to an incongruous situation, perhaps making a comment on the tumblrtroversy of the moment. Hours later, [the aforementioned member] will show us all up with something like what you see above [a clever photoshop], but by then we've all forgotten what the joke was in the first place. And yet it lives on!

Like 4chan, it takes effort to appreciate Summer of Megadeth's nuances. You have to possess both a deep cultural understanding (and a knack for looking things up quickly when you don't get the joke) in order to make sense of any of it. Wordplay stacked on wordplay. Jokes are twisted, rearranged, recontextualized, self-referenced, connected to ancient, obscure callbacks. But when the meme du jour hits, and you really *get it*, there are few things more rewarding. They are drawing on a rich tapestry of rapidly evolving cultural tradition. If Tumblr has a /b/, it's right here.

There is a meme that states that 4chan users aren't supposed to like Tumblr users, because they're a bunch of artfag hipsters who steal 4chan's memes. This antagonism peaked with a "war" in November 2010, when /b/tards launched Operation Overlord, perhaps the dumbest and most ineffectual among the raids that were able to grab press. They planned to set up a bunch of dummy Tumblr accounts, build huge follower bases, and then flood users' dashboards with festish porn and gore, ultimately hoping to take Tumblr down with a DDoS (distributed denial of service) attack. Some Tumblr users retaliated even more ineffectually by spamming 4chan with references to Tumblr, *Twilight*, Harry Potter, and other cutesy imagery they knew would annoy /b/. But as one /b/tard put it, "Raiding /b/ is like pissing in an ocean of piss."

ROFLCon

For the last two years, hundreds have gathered at MIT to attend a very silly conference called ROFLCon (ROFL, which means rolling on the floor laughing, is a stronger variant of LOL). Reputable academics mingle with cosplayers. Internet nerds meet the stars of memes gone by. The conference attempts to host careful analysis of memetic culture and promotes the collection and preservation of Internet ephemera. Most of all, it's a lighthearted celebration of all things webby.

The primary organizer of the event is Tim Hwang, a researcher for the Barbarian Group, the meme-friendly digital agency. He's also part of the Web Ecology Project, an organization dedicated to the preservation of digital culture and folklore. The Web Ecology Project's latest project is a complete, downloadable archive of Encyclopedia Dramatica.

The germ of ROFLCon began when Hwang attended an event built around the popular nerdy webcomic *xkcd* in nearby Somerville, Massachusetts. *xkcd* is drawn and authored by Randall Munroe, who, before he was able to make a living from his stick-figure doodles, worked for NASA as a roboticist. *xkcd* is a powerhouse in the memesphere (for example, Munroe once created a site called http://www.wetriffs.com after bemoaning a lack of "guitar-in-shower" pornography on the web—a nod to Rule #34), and nearly all of Munroe's comics get the kind of hits most newspapers would kill for. The event was a simple meet-up based on nerd culture, but way too many people showed up.

So in 2008, Hwang and his friends decided to put on a legit convention for Internet nerdery. They brought in academics to

182

comment on Internet culture and invited meme stars to hang out too. It was a big success, garnering glowing press. Even Tron Guy showed up!

Tron Guy, aka Jay Maynard, was a flabby programmer whose spandex costume inspired by Disney's *Tron* went viral in 2004 via Slashdot and Fark, reaching a peak with appearances on *Jimmy Kimmel Live*. Tron Guy can be seen as a representative for people who display their unassuming quirkiness on the web. There's Peter Pan impersonator Randy Constan, Michael Blount of "Hello My Future Girlfriend," Ginger Kid, and countless more, but Tron Guy was one of the first. Like many meme celebrities, his appearance on the web was initially met with derision. But his appearance at ROFLCon was met with rapturous applause. Here was a guy who was doing his thing and simply could not give a damn what anyone else thought. Welcome to the Internet, where nerds are free to self-actualize to their hearts' content.

ROFLCon had a panel that included the guy who designed the Three Wolf Moon shirt, along with the first Amazon reviewer, drilling down to deep levels of what Hwang calls "micro-micro-microfame." The Three Wolf Moon is a kitschy t-shirt that would not look out of place on your stereotypical basement dweller or, these days, worn ironically on a hipster bass player. The shirt got thousands of reviews on Amazon, far outpacing sales. Reviewing the thing became a lightly competitive game. The goal was to come up with funny, creative ways to describe the Three Wolf Moon shirt. The top-rated review begins:

> This item has wolves on it which makes it intrinsically sweet and worth 5 stars by itself, but once I tried it on, that's when the

magic happened. After checking to ensure that the shirt would properly cover my girth, I walked from my trailer to Wal-mart with the shirt on and was immediately approached by women.

The shirt became a meme, parodied by CollegeHumor and covered by several major papers. This is the sort of phenomenon that the ROFLCon folks love to pick apart, analyze and commemorate.

Hwang's fascination with meme-dom began with early memes like Hamster Dance, Zombocom, and other single-destination sites. He recalls that Hamster Dance, like many sites of the day, had a stats ticker at the bottom of the page, so you could watch how big the thing was getting, and how quickly. He first recognized that Internet culture had bled into the mainstream when he saw Rick Astley perform "Never Gonna Give You Up" at the Macy's Thanksgiving Day Parade in 2008.

Hwang first encountered 4chan in middle school. He claims that at the time, a big part of the attraction to the Internet was finding nasty things to send to his friends. At the time he and his buddies were passing around a lot of Rotten and Stile Project links. At some point, this gave way to 4chan content.

As an informal meme historian, Hwang recognizes the cultural import of 4chan.

The content 4chan produces is so powerful. We are increasingly moving away from the Internet as it existed in the mid-90s. There was no one trying to commercialize or police it. We are also moving towards non-anonymization. On 4chan, you have to shape who you are by what you're doing. It also brings it back demographically to the way things were when I was first discovering the web.

According to Hwang, 4chan matters for two reasons. First, its users are "white blood cells" of the Internet, because they perform vigilante justice—against people who harm animals, for instance. He points to the increasing role that 4chan users have in geopolitics, as they have successfully brought down the sites of massive multinational corporations. Second, Hwang claims that although 4chan exists as this "other" state outside of the rest of life online, it is an important part of the web's cultural production.

Hwang laughs at the raw visual power of the Xzibit meme, which 4chan kick-started in 2007. You may know Xzibit as a rapper and host of the MTV show *Pimp My Ride*. But on the Internet, he's become so closely linked with his meme that the usual words used to caption image macros are no longer necessary; his smiling face says it all.

Pimp My Ride featured Xzibit and his gearhead crew retrofitting jalopies with outlandish accoutrements like flat-screen TVs or fish tanks. Xzibit would often say something along the lines of, "Yo/Sup dawg, I heard you like Xbox so we put an Xbox in your car so you can play Xbox on the road." A clever Photoshopper recognized this recurring line and made an image macro featuring a grimacing Xzibit captioned with, "Yo dawg, I herd u like cars so we put a car in yo car so you can drive while u drive."

The meme was a massive hit straight out of the gate. It's gotten to the point where just the picture of Xzibit's smiling face sans caption suggests recursion. The meme culminated two years later with a fuming Twitter response from an understandably frustrated Xzibit (I mean, the guy was a respected gangsta rapper at one point):

Everybody with the "sup dawg" shit can find the highest place in your house and jump on something sharp to kill yourselves.it's fucking old.

No matter how trivial memes like this may seem, millions of people participate in them every day. Tim Hwang's trying to figure out why. This kind of humor is just a sliver in the wider world of meme culture that he hopes to explore through ROFLCon and the Web Ecology Project. Naysayers look at something like the Xzibit meme and see a corny joke at best, but folks like Hwang see nothing less than tiny revolutions in entertainment, media, and human social interaction. Even moot showed up at the last ROFLCon after giving a TED Talk.

In his book *Cognitive Surplus*, Clay Shirky argues that the web is making us smarter, collectively. Humanity is working together like never before, each individual contributing something so minute as a single correction to an obscure Wikipedia entry or a photograph uploaded to Flickr. Even our Google queries help the search giant perfect its algorithms. Whether we realize it or not, we are behaving as a hive mind, and those tiny trivial inputs add up to monumental social change.

Reddit

4chan's influence in the memesphere isn't going anywhere soon, but Reddit is definitely catching up. Reddit is currently the biggest social content aggregator, recently taking the reins from Digg after that site's troubled redesign. Reddit users post pieces of content and "upvote" ones they like or "downvote" ones they don't. Even comments can be upvoted or downvoted, which makes browsing comment threads sorted by vote count half the fun.

For our purposes, the Condé Nast–owned but still very nerdy Reddit is interesting for three reasons. First, it acts as a gateway between 4chan and the rest of the Internet. Second, it's a place where the mainstream media has recently gone to routinely scrape through content for news. Third, it facilitates meme creation that rewards users in a way that 4chan doesn't.

Reddit is a good gatekeeper for 4chan because its users are immersed in a meme-saturated environment—but it's not anonymous and everything is archived, so its users don't act like sociopaths. There's also an incentive to be nice, or at least comprehensible, since everything that's said can be rated by fellow Redditors.

What truly sets Reddit apart is subreddits, which are tiny communities for infinitely granular subject areas. Where most sites would create tags for topics like "Tech," "Gaming," "News," and "Sports," Reddit allows its users to create their own tags, which quickly turn into tiny little communities that in many ways have replaced special interest blogs. For instance, I'm not into video games so much anymore, but I still play Starcraft, so I follow the Starcraft subreddit. It's very specific Starcraft news, all the time. I follow several dozen other subreddits, each pulling content from hundreds of blogs across the web, each sorted for the most interesting and funny content, and each appended with scintillating conversation. It's a fantastic platform that combines a high-level overview of the web with magnified looks at only the things I find interesting. I typically check Reddit every few hours to see what's going on in my world.

Reddit has become nearly as adept at creating memes as 4chan. Consider the Inglip mythos. Inglip is a RageToon-based series of comics built on the random pairings of words spit out by reCAPTCHA, a Google-owned user authentication service that forces users to type out squiggly words in order to let web pages know that they're not SPAM robots. It all started when one Redditor found the words "inglip summoned" in a reCAPT-CHA. He made a comic alluding to an ancient Lovecraftian deity ("Inglip has been summoned. It has begun"). Then another user followed up with the reCAPTCHA result "called gropagas," which he preceded with a question:

> I hope our dedication to your lordship has been satisfactory. Tell me, oh great Inglip, what should your followers call themselves?
> "called gropagas"
> "As you wish, my lord. We are the gropagas and united, we will take the world in your name!"

Hundreds of responses followed, fleshing out the Inglip mythos. And it's all based on randomly generated words. A few years ago, this sort of collaborative metahumor would have been found only on 4chan (or maybe Something Awful), but the rest of the Internet, with Reddit leading the charge, has caught up.

Reddit has also reappropriated 4chan's Ask Me Anything, or AMA threads, which have attracted some major celebrities in addition to nerd icons like moot.

The all-time top verified AMA threads include those of 74-time *Jeopardy!* champion Ken Jennings, actor Bruce Campbell, Columbine shooting survivor Brooks Brown, and a former Marine One crew chief. Unverified AMA threads, which are often even more interesting, include a military whistleblower, a girl who spent 16 months as a full-time BDSM slave, a person who was caught and tortured during recent rioting in Egypt, a man who only answers questions using MS Paint, a brain cancer victim with 2–6 months to live, and a four-year-old girl (with help from her dad). After a few controversies in which AMA posters were revealed to be trolls, Reddit has taken steps to integrate a verification process.

Canvas

When moot gave an AMA on Reddit on March 29th, 2011, most of the questions about Canvas, his new startup, dealt with his team's decision to integrate Facebook Connect into the site's private beta-testing period. Basically, if you wanted to be a part of Canvas, you had to reveal your identity. 4chan diehards felt betrayed. Their patron saint of anonymity had given up the good fight in order to cash in.

The top comment, which received over thirteen hundred votes, read, "How do you justify rallying against the lack of anonymity that Facebook provides and then requiring it for your next project?"

moot replied:

I think it's important to understand the difference between advocating for anonymous contribution, and a pro-anonymity-is-the-only-way!!!!! zealot. (I'm the former!)

I want the public to understand the importance of having the option to contribute anonymously. At SXSW, I focused on anonymous authenticity, and the creativity that anonymity allows for. The ability to fail quietly without having that failure associated with your name/identity allows for more experimentation and limit pushing. People also contribute in a totally raw, unfiltered way, that I'd argue is more authentic than real-ID [An ID authentication measure taken by game developer Blizzard to link players' in-game and forum identities with their real names].

He went on to outline some times when identity is preferable, such as places that experience lots of low-quality comments, like YouTube and TechCrunch. One detractor replied:

His worldview is balanced, if that's what you mean, but he answered nothing at all. Nothing proves to me that he won't use information from my account, just as nothing proves to me that Facebook itself won't. And we know they do. So his answer was the same as saying "please trust me". Well I won't.

But most respondents were OK with it. Of course, this was Reddit, not 4chan.

4chan uses basically the same software that it did when it started out, which itself was antiquated by the standards of the day. moot's vision for Canvas is a web community that takes advantage of faster browsing capability as well as the lessons he's learned from eight years of running 4chan. To fill that community with users who are going to push the platform forward, he's going to have to weed out trolls. The Facebook Connect integration is probably a good start. Canvas isn't 4chan 2.0.

It's basically a user-friendly, browser-based image-editing tool connected to an imageboard with light social networking features. It's simple for people who don't have editing ability or don't have a copy of Photoshop, and because it's hosted online you don't have to upload and download and reformat and resize in order to move content from your computer to the web. Ninety-nine percent of the people remixing images on Facebook (or 4chan, for that matter) don't need tools as robust as Photoshop because they're mostly only adding text or slapping a layer over an existing image. Canvas's remixing tool allows users to do these things. What's more, it's all archived, so users can post an image and watch their friends create genuinely clever remixes over time, without having to worry that it's going to fall off the edge in a few hours. Everything is shareable on Facebook, Tumblr, and Twitter. Surely they're working on integration with Reddit.

I'm looking at Canvas as I write, in May 2011. Someone has posted a blank page with the words "What is Canvas?" written on it. It was posted five days ago in the #drawing thread, so it's encouraging other users to draw response images. The first reply has written "a website" in the blank space and earned 9 stickers. The stickers represent basic emotional responses (happy face, sad face, heart, question mark, etc.). This response has earned some of each, but it looks like the smarty face, represented by a smiley with a distinguished mustache and monocle, is winning out.

Another has written a small essay within the image.

I begin by scrolling around, learning my way navigating throughout the site. It is interesting to see the amount of stuff I have already seen, and very quickly I realize, this is SFW. I get excited. I continue to look around and discover the 'remix' button. So I try it out and post a relatively funny picture (in my opinion). Nothing happens. I go to bed, thinking I am very unfunny.

I wake up in the morning with a cookie and two lol stickers and it's such a relief. I mean, I hardly got to sleep last night. So I find another popular thread, and post another idea I have. It immediately gets a #1 and a smiley and I get very excited and tell my friend. Then I go to bed.

I wake up the next morning to find that I have received over 50 #1 stickers. I am ecstatic and I go through the rest of my day overjoyed. I continue to read and post and come up with funny pictures, and even show my girlfriend the webpage because of how excited I am. Then my picture appears on the 'best' tab and I'm like FUCK YEA.

What is canv.as you ask me?

The greatest thing ever.

The post has 16 stickers and one comment: "dude your post rocks. long live canv.as!" The next post remixes the essay with a giant "TL;DR" plastered on top. (Too long; didn't read, a common 4chan dismissal for anything longer than a few sentences.) The next remixer answers the question, "What is canvas?" with a picture of actual canvas, the kind painters use.

I think this thing's going to be huge.

The News Media

Today there is a tremendous pressure on journalists to "create" viral content. When I was writing about memes for an Internet culture blog called Urlesque, I spent a lot of time tracking how the mainstream media picked up on memes, and over the course of 2010 I noticed that reporters were increasingly relying on Reddit to find news.

In January 2011, a Cleveland man took a video of a local homeless guy named Ted Williams, who happened to have a trained "golden radio voice," and posted the footage on YouTube. The video eventually found its way to Reddit, with the poster hoping that maybe a fellow user might be able to offer Williams some voice work. The footage of this down-on-his-luck, scraggly homeless guy juxtaposed with his sonorous voice shocked the community, and dozens came forward to help out. One offered to buy Williams a phone, another a suit, another studio time, and still more offered producing and editing services. Over a dozen Redditors specifically offered work in the Cleveland area. This outpouring of generosity is par for the course on Reddit, a mirror image of 4chan's collaborative destruction.

Within a day, Williams started getting coverage and interviews at every major news outlet. One particular story caught my eye. Indianapolis's Fox affiliate wanted a piece of that "homeless person with an unexpected talent" pie, so they sent a reporter out in the dead of winter and asked various homeless people if they had any special talents. The reporter asked them if they'd seen the footage of Ted Williams (what?) and told them that he was given a new house and job for his talents. One woman's eyes lit up with the realization that this could be her ticket out of destitution and she sang a soulful gospel tune. It was an unsettling display of the worst kind of bandwagon journalism, showing just how desperate the media is to be a part of the meme of the day. The video has since been taken down.

The Entertainment Industry

The relationship between show business and the web is strained. Only very recently have entertainment execs come to view the web as a unique platform for interactive content rather than just another channel to cram their existing products into. The influence of the memesphere can be seen moving in both directions. Cable TV shows like Tosh.0 and Best Week Ever focus heavily on the viral content of the moment. Late-night TV hosts joke about viral sensations. Morning talk shows bring on victims of trolling and YouTube microcelebrities.

Stephen Colbert gave a nod to Anonymous in February 2011, having previously flirted with Reddit on his show. For a split second, a Guy Fawkes mask (the Anonymous calling card) was superimposed over Colbert's face, leading many to believe that Anonymous had hacked into the broadcast and was sending a subliminal message to viewers. Others speculated that it was a winking recognition of the hacktivist group, expressing solidarity with their aims. It turned out to be a joke coming from inside the Colbert camp, which was used as a setup for a segment later that week.

On the other side, we see mainstream entertainment dipping its toes into the web. Celebrities now interact directly with their fan bases through Twitter. Conan O'Brien harnesses his vast network of Facebook fans with Team Coco. Bands signed to mainstream labels, such as OK Go, court YouTube audiences with videos produced with clever gimmickry engineered for viral success. Rocker Andrew W.K. recently did a live Q&A with 4chan, the first of its kind.

In strict terms, not much has changed but the technology. Entertainers have always wanted to create memes. The Internet just allows them to do so much more rapidly, cheaply, and to greater effect.

The Advertising Industry

Advertisers are increasingly recognizing the power of Internet memes. For example, Jennifer Aniston recently did a spot for smartwater featuring a host of Internet microcelebrities and cute cats in an attempt to jokingly reference the advertising industry's recent obsession with memetic culture.

I talked to Rick Webb, co-founder of the Barbarian Group, a digital ad agency based in NYC, about a viral project he helped conceive back in 2001 for Crispin Porter + Bogusky client Burger King. Streaming video had only recently become available to a majority of households, and ad agencies were beginning to take notice. That year, BMW had unleashed *The Hire*, a short film series produced, directed, and starring Hollywood A-listers. It was hugely successful, and opened up streaming video as a viable advertising platform.

But the Internet isn't just another visual channel. It allows for interactive content, and BMW's films, while innovatively placed, did little to take advantage of the Internet's core competencies.

Rick Webb was drawn to the web at an early age, when he discovered Usenet, a good way to connect with like-minded folks from outside his native Alaska. Webb's interests ran toward the countercultural, and the Internet fed his passions. Rick eventually found his way to Manhattan, where he now manages digital campaigns for global clients.

Before the blog era, a grassroots marketing strategy was, in Webb's words, "horrible and no fun."

It generally involved commenting on message boards, IM and email spamming, astroturfing [drumming up interest in a product or service by creating the illusion of an extant grassroots movement], and the like. We didn't do it. We focused on making great things and using what tools we had at the time—email, IM, traditional PR and maybe a little LiveJournal—to get it in front of people and get it to spread. But for those who wanted to pay to catalyze a meme, it was generally pretty sketchy. Lots of pretending to be enthusiasts on message boards.

Webb spends a lot of time coming up with memes for clients. Today he doesn't have to start from square one every time because the social web allows the Barbarian Group to maintain a constant identity on Twitter, Facebook, and the blogs of its employees. And they don't just blog about marketing stuff. Webb himself maintains a Tumblr blog dedicated mostly to the indie rock of his youth. His followers recognize that he represents an ad agency, but he's also a real human being. People who have no interest in "the biz" follow him because he's interesting, and he doesn't use his various platforms to jam marketing messaging down their throats.

When we did the chicken, the meme was initially propagated almost exclusively via email and some IM. Now we have all these tools and technologies that foster meme propagation. Twitter, Facebook Like, Tumblr, StumbleUpon and Buzzfeed are the big ones. None of those existed before.

When Webb wants to launch a viral campaign, he knows he can get it in front of ten or twenty thousand people (some of whom are journalists and powerful tastemakers) without spending a single media dollar.

So what's this "chicken" all about? Burger King had a long-time tagline, "Have it Your Way," and was trying to promote a new chicken sandwich. CP+B partnered with the Barbarian Group to create the Subservient Chicken, a campaign that would almost immediately go down as a classic advertising case study in every college marketing textbook.

Here's how it worked. If you went to Burger King's website and clicked on the appropriate link, you'd see a loading screen that read, "Contacting Chicken." Then a small Flash window appeared featuring a man in a chicken suit and a text field reading, "Get chicken just the way you like it. Type in your command here."

The first thing I typed back in 2001 was *fight*. To my delight, the chicken adopted a sword-fighting stance and began to parry and thrust at the camera. I typed in a naughty word. The chicken put his hands on his hips, walked to the camera, and shook his head disapprovingly.

Wait, what? Did they actually hire a guy to stand there all day performing commands?

Of course they didn't. They polled their agencies internally, asking, "What would you tell the chicken to do?" They pared thousands of responses down to the four hundred most common commands, and filmed responses for them all.

Trying to create an Internet meme was new territory for ad agencies. How were they able to convince the burger giant to run with such a wacky idea?

Luck. Small budget. Couldn't hurt. Amazing sales on the part of CP + B. Marketers were also learning about the concept of viral marketing at that time via think pieces in AdAge and were willing to experiment with very small amounts of their budgets.

Webb says that smart marketing departments have experimental budgets that they devote to playing with emerging trends. The Barbarian Group subsisted on those small experimental budgets until the chicken changed everything. The campaign was a raging success, one of the earliest examples of an agency harnessing the power of viral content. It cost almost nothing, and generated loads of traffic for the client. It was the first of its kind, establishing proof that viral marketing could work. "After that," says Webb, "the floodgates opened."

Advertisers have been trying to replicate the success of Subservient Chicken ever since. Webb says that brands are now more willing to be authentic and honest than they were before the rise of the Internet. In order to achieve success in the meme-sphere, they have to be able to create something that's interesting enough to watch or experience, but also something people will want to share.

When I showed Webb the Jennifer Aniston video, he had to laugh.

> What you see here, is that the divide between paid media and viral is blurring. This is not, technically, a viral video in the old sense, because a lot of money was spent getting the initial word out (never mind the budget that allowed them to pay for Jennifer Aniston).

It might be smarter, but compared to Subservient Chicken, the costs-to-results ratio is way higher. They paid a bundle to use Aniston. It guaranteed them a million views, but was it worth it? Not necessarily. A good idea is a lot cheaper than a celeb tacked onto some ad exec's idea of what memes are.

Just ask Portland's Wieden + Kennedy, who produced the legendary "The Man Your Man Could Smell Like" campaign for Old Spice, which, like the Subservient Chicken, holds up the industry press as being a game-changing campaign that took advantage of the Internet's core competencies in a way that hadn't been done before.

The original spot was simple. A hunky guy addressing the camera with a suave "Hello Ladies," followed by a goofy spiel about how showering with Old Spice body wash would turn the viewer's man into the kind of dreamboat that would buy you tickets "to that thing you love." The hunk, played by former NFL wide receiver Isaiah Mustafa, moved seamlessly from his bathroom shower to a beach in a single take, with the camera zooming out to reveal that Mustafa was, inexplicably, riding bareback on a mighty steed. The spot ended with a hilarious absurdism, "I'm on a horse," that became a mini-meme in its own right.

The ad would have been huge had W+K left it at that, but they followed up the TV spots with an interactive YouTube and Twitter experience that left many ad execs smacking their foreheads, wondering why they hadn't thought of something so simple (and cost-effective) years ago. They filmed Mustafa answering questions that came in from Twitter and YouTube, focusing on tech-savvy celebrities like Ashton Kutcher, Twitter's Biz Stone, Alyssa Milano, and Digg founder Kevin Rose. But the Old Spice Guy also responded to everyday people, like a random teenage girl named Lindsey.

The thirty-second responses were simply shot in the Old Spice Guy's bathroom, complete with props. All two hundred responses felt carefully crafted. Especially the response to anonymous.

Hello anonymous. I'm glad at least some of most of you are liking my new Old Spice commercial.

Random crown [holds up crown].

And that means a lot.

Large book [holds up book].

Because you're important to me.

Jewel-encrusted scepter [holds up scepter].

And I want to make you proud.

Freshwater fish [holds up fish].

So I always try my best.

Delicious cake [holds up cake].

Because you deserve the best.

The fish again [holds up fish].

So that's what I give you.

Thank you friends, you're my everything.

Expensive magnifying glass [holds up magnifying glass].

If you haven't guessed, the random objects are of course clever references to 4chan's random /b/ board. And delicious cake is a more direct reference to the aforementioned "get the cake" game. As you can imagine, /b/ freaked out and fell in love with Mustafa, which is interesting, because any less witty message would likely have been met with a massive trolling effort. The video response was smart, and seemed more like a friendly wink than a shallow attempt at generating buzz. This campaign marks the first time any corporate entity has actively courted 4chan, and I suspect it won't be the last. Old Spice was able to garner social media points by courting Digg and Reddit simultaneously, exploiting their longtime rivalry. Sales of Old Spice went up more than 100 percent.

Rick Webb says that paying for content in the memesphere can help, but only up to a point.

Buzzfeed and Stumbleupon, especially, are INSANELY good at helping juice your memes in the beginning. Amazingly good. Their ad offerings are *par excellence* for cheaply getting your first million views. The name of the game is to spend a little money and kick it off then it goes viral and millions of more see it for free.

Webb says that agencies have to recognize their strengths, because today everyone has the tools to make a Subservient Chicken. He argues that brands have to step up their games in order to outshine the rest of the Internet's fantastic amateur content. Just as Hollywood is competing with indie filmmakers by producing ever more expensive summer blockbusters like *Avatar* and *Inception*, agencies have to use their budgets to make simple ideas look fantastic. The Barbarian Group was able to do this with a campaign called Beer Cannon, in which they shot cans of Milwaukee's Best out of a cannon into various objects, filmed with an expensive slow-motion camera. That's a basic idea, but something your average teenager can't replicate.

Webb tells me that most ad people are aware of 4chan and poke around there, though the Barbarian Group has never executed any formal campaigns on the site. Generally clients don't want to have anything to do with 4chan, but agencies are happy to browse the site to keep an eye on memes bubbling up.

The Barbarian Group has been giant 4chan fans since the beginning. I still go on there constantly to poke around, reset my brain, learn about the psyche of certain types of people. There's definitely a window into the soul going on there, though you gotta temper it by going to some deep Christian websites and remember not everyone is pure id.

201

In Japan, Dentsu, the world's biggest ad agency, has a buzz research division that constantly monitors the activity of 2channel, hoping to spot memes and trends before they become mainstream. I'd bet that we'll see this more formal research happen in the West too—if not with 4chan specifically, with the surrounding host of sites that make up the memesphere.

The speed of appropriation on 4chan has certainly affected the rest of the web. The public has an insatiable appetite for new memes, so thousands are created every day. Ad agencies are no longer just competing with other agencies for your attention, they're competing with every teenage slacker packing a copy of Photoshop (or Final Cut, or ProTools).

Marci Ikeler is Director of Digital Strategy at Grey Group, a global marketing communications agency. She gave a presentation at South by Southwest Interactive this year, right after Christopher Poole's keynote, called "Haters Gonna Hate: Lessons for Advertisers from 4chan." She describes herself as a nerd first and strategist second, having taught herself to code at an early age.

Marci tells me she's been keeping an eye on 4chan for the last few years, and says that 4chan users have managed to get mass media attention by understanding what people are intrinsically interested in, something advertisers are sometimes not very good at.

Ikeler defines five properties of 4chan that she thinks advertisers can learn from.

First, "Bump." This refers to how communities self-select what kind of information is important to them, and furthermore what kind of information sticks around. According to Ikeler, a lot of old-school ad men hate to see chatter about their brands on social networks because it's not under their control. But it's in advertisers' best interests to view even the most antagonistic comments as valuable opinions coming from an honest forum. This kind of feedback can be tremendously valuable compared to the focus groups of yore. The key is to transition from a perspective of wanting to control the conversation to engaging the audience on the same level and allowing them to define what works about a brand and what doesn't.

Second, "Moar" (*more* in chan-speak, which often mocks bad spellers). This refers to the need for advertisers to hit the marketplace hard with many iterations of a brand concept, not just a single big piece like a Super Bowl ad. You want your audience to be hungry for more. According to Ikeler, the best way to meet that demand is with microcontent like tweets and Facebook replies.

Third, "Mods are asleep" (mods are forum moderators). On 4chan, users whisper this during off-peak hours in the hopes that someone will post content that would otherwise get them banned. Marci encourages advertisers to lay off a bit when moderating social media presence. A good example of a brand that failed to do this is Smirnoff Ice, who put the kibosh on an incredibly viral phenomenon called "Bros Icing Bros." The game had guys pranking their friends by leaving bottles of warm Smirnoff Ice around, which, according to the game's rules, had be drunk on sight. While Smirnoff was right in assuming that the subtext of the game was that Smirnoff Ice tastes terrible, the company lost an opportunity when it didn't embrace the prank and capitalize on its virality.

Fourth, Ikeler raises how trollish behavior can cause tiny PR crises and also disrupt community managers from dealing with legitimate concerns by drawing their attention toward triviality.

Fifth, "Not your personal army." This is a common 4chan response to any call to action deemed unworthy of anons' attention. Ikeler interprets this as a warning not to expect too much of audiences. They need to be given the motivation to participate in branding efforts. It's not enough to throw a bunch of social media tools online and expect people to show up and start creating buzz. In other words, "What's in it for me?"

My conversation with Ikeler ends on a note that would surely send chills down the spine of every creative director in the industry.

> Content is no longer valuable. We simply have too much content. There's more content being produced in a day than we could consume in our entire lives. Advertisers are in the business of creating content that's no longer valuable. We should be focusing more on curation and engagement.

She's right. And it's not just advertising. Publishing, show business, media, art and design too. 4chan shows us that there are enough creative people out there doing for free, and for zero recognition, what professionals have been paid to do for centuries. Furthermore, we have learned that what separated professional creatives from the amateurs wasn't so much a level of talent, but access to distribution channels. Now that the social web has provided so many amateurs with a way to reach millions, they're outshining the pros everwhere.

Chapter 7

The Meme Life Cycle

THROUGHOUT 2010 I wrote for an Internet culture blog called Urlesque. Our stated goal was to "uncover bits of the web." We reported most memes that came along, but for me the most interesting assignments allowed me to cover the way memes spread. How exactly does a no-name tween become an overnight celebrity, sharing iTunes chart space with global pop superstars like Ke$ha and Rihanna? How are people able to find out about memes? Why does one girl's tearful reaction to the *Twilight* trailer beat out a professionally produced viral campaign with a budget of millions? At this point we know what memes are, but where do they come from? How do they spread? The first step in answering these questions is an understanding of the Meme Life Cycle.

The following cycle is loosely defined. Memes don't always follow this pattern in this order, nor does their rise to mainstream exposure always include all eight of these steps, but it's a useful template.

Birth

Internet memes are born when the original source material is initially uploaded anywhere on the Internet. Fertile meme territory can be found all over the web, especially on community sites that encourage content uploading like YouTube, DeviantArt, or Facebook, but also on remote locations like personal webpages.

It could be a video of a guy riding a dirt bike into a railing, a hilariously comprehensive treatise on an obscure cartoon, a clever Photoshopped image, or video of a tween girl having a public emotional breakdown. Once a potential meme is on the web, it may sit idle for months or even years until it is discovered, likely by the meme curators at 4chan.

Discovery

Someone posts the item to 4chan, usually accompanied by a comment like, "Holy crap, you guys," or "WTF" (or OMG or LOL or rage or any number of strong emotions). If it's a good meme, the conversation thread explodes. Hundreds of people add their commentary. The meme spreads to other threads.

If it's an image, we'll see parodic Photoshops and image macros. If it's video, we'll likely encounter mashups and You-Tube Poop, a game in which users deconstruct and piece together video footage for psychedelic or absurdist effect. If it's audio, memes are remixed, chopped, screwed, mashed up. Even simple text memes, like creepy stories or hilarious personal experiences, will be retrofitted into a series of copypasta templates.

Before long, we can't scroll through /b/ without being inundated by the meme.

Aggregation

At some point, the meme jumps from 4chan to the broader Internet. This usually happens when someone posts the meme to a content aggregator like Reddit or Digg. These sites allow memes to flourish beyond the niche world of 4chan. They collect news stories, photos, videos—any piece of content—by allowing their communities of users to post whatever they want. When someone posts content to an aggregator, other users have the ability to upvote or digg it. As users promote content by the simple power of their approval, the most widely approved content rises to the top, or rather the front page, exposing it to a much wider audience.

Word of Mouth

Once memes reach the front page of an aggregator like Reddit, it takes no more than a few hours for people to start tweeting and blogging about the meme. Internet savvy types send links to their friends via instant message. The meme may begin to trend on Twitter or pop up on Google Trends, a list of frequently googled search terms.

Blog Pickup

This is typically when the Internet culture blogs discover the story. Sites like Buzzfeed, Know Your Meme, The Daily What,

Videogum, or any members of the Cheezburger Network, will pick up the meme and attempt to add context. Where did it come from? Why is it funny? Can we get an interview with any involved parties? These are the sorts of "value-add" propositions that blogs will try to score before their competitors. It's a race to get the most information before the meme explodes into the mainstream. The most comprehensive overview will often get the most links from mainstream media.

By this time the meme is being rehashed, as everyone wants to get in on the thing before it goes stale. Self-referential jokes and clever mutations of the meme abound on places like 4chan and Tumblr. Everyone on the Internet is able to enjoy the meme until . . .

Mainstream Exposure

There are two ways mainstream media tends to approach memes. If the meme contains anything negative or shocking, as memes often do, we see breathless nightly news exposés and daytime talk-show hosts bemoaning the State of Things.

If the meme skews toward the lighthearted or quirky, we see late-night talk-show bits or stars of popular memes guesting on morning radio shows. "Look at this wacky thing from the Internet," we hear. "What a world."

Commercialization

Only the biggest meme stars will ever see any money, whether it's through corporate sponsorship or by selling meme-related merchandise. Microsoft hired Paul Vasquez, star of the Double

Rainbow meme, to promote the Windows Live Photo Gallery software in a TV ad. Adah Bahner of Chocolate Rain fame shilled for Dr. Pepper, Firefox, Sony, Vizio, and more. Internet memes provide advertisers a roster of recognizable but reasonably priced spokespeople who are keen to translate their fifteen minutes of fame into some quick cash before their meme dies.

Death

Memes never truly die, but one could argue that it's time to move on when your hopelessly unhip mom or dad asks "Hey, did you see that thing on YouTube about that guy who punched out another guy on the subway?" No more remixes or Photoshops or fervent discussion threads. The meme is over, for now, as every bit of fascination is drained by unimaginative rehashes and abundant mainstream coverage. Particularly powerful memes are subsumed into the memesphere, to be resurrected as callbacks or mashed up with newer memes as comedic references.

A Tale of Two Memes

Let's chart the meme life cycle with two examples, both of which occurred in the summer of 2010. They weren't the biggest memes of the season, but they represent the two ways memes are generally consumed by the mainstream: hand-wringing sensationalism and lighthearted amusement.

Consequences Will Never Be The Same

In July 2010, an 11-year-old girl using the pseudonym Jessi Slaughter became embroiled in a microcontroversy on the streaming video site Stickam, where users accused her of engaging in a sexual relationship with a 20-something member of the scene band "Blood on the Dancefloor."

Birth: Jessi Slaughter Uploads Meme-worthy Content

Slaughter uploaded a response video to YouTube, in which she threatened those who taunted her online. Here's a taste of what she said:

> Hey YouTube it's Jessi Slaughter here and this is to all you fucking haters. OK guess what? You guys are bitches. You know what? You don't phase [sic] me. I'm just doing this just so you can tell I read the comments. I read the messages and I replied to them, but know what? I don't give a fuck. I'm happy with my life, OK? And if you can't like realize that and stop hating you know what I'll pop a glock in your mouth and make a brain slushie, OK? Cause you hater bitches—you're just, like, jealous of me. You're just saying that because you're jealous of me because I'm more pretty than you, I have more friends, more people like me, I have more fans . . . Um yeah, and all that shit.

The dialogue makes the girl sound like a hardened street urchin, but in the footage she comes off as a typically self-conscious little girl reeling off catchphrases she's picked up on TV.

Nonetheless, I couldn't conceive a video that would be more tailor-made to ignite the ire of 4chan. Here was an 11-year-old white girl taking on the thuggish bravado found between songs on gangsta rap albums. She was out of her element. On her Tumblr blog she claimed, "I can't be tamed." Plenty of people wanted to prove her wrong.

Discovery: 4chan Pounces

It wasn't long before the 4chan hivemind targeted Slaughter. Her unmitigated haughtiness and filthy mouth were perfect bait for /b/tards who would relish turning her life into a living hell for a while. Her video was posted in "You Rage You Lose" threads, which consist of people sharing how long they were able to last before they exploded into a rage while watching the video in question. The girl's complete lack of self-awareness drove 4chan into a frenzy. In their eyes, she needed to be put in her place. Since her parents clearly had no control over their daughter, it was time for Anonymous to carry out some vigilante justice.

They bombarded her social networking profiles with hateful comments, urging her to kill herself. They also sent pizza deliveries to her house and left threatening messages on her parents' answering machine.

A large measure of deindividuation—also known as mob mentality—occurs in many 4chan raids. Everything happens quickly, and the rush to be the guy that's able to score the dox (4chan slang for personal information like home address and phone number) is heady. When all was said and done, even some /b/tards claimed that they thought Anonymous had gone too far. At no point did the attackers stop to think, "Am I really antagonizing an 11-year-old girl? What kind of human garbage am I?"

Slaughter posted a follow-up video which rocketed the story

into meme history. Teary-eyed and hysterical, Jessi Slaughter begged her attackers to stop. While this would have been enough to solidify meme status, her father provided troll bait of an unparalleled variety.

> I'm gonna tell you right now. This is from her father! You're a bunch of lying, no good punks. And I know who it's coming from. Because I backtraced it. And I know who's emailing and who's doing it, and you've been reported to the cyber police and the state police. You better write one more thing or screw with my computer again, you'll be arrested! End of conversation! From her father! And if you come near my daughter, guess what? Consequences will never be the same. Ya lyin' bunch of pricks!

Slaughter's powerless father's empty threats, coupled with his obviously poor grasp on how the Internet works, gave 4chan trolls enough material to construct hundreds of image macros, video remixes, and more. The term "backtrace" has become a common ironic reference to one's inability to track the online activity of hackers and trolls. Similarly, "consequences will never be the same" has become a favorite closing for troll threats.

Due to the sordid nature of the controversy, this meme bypassed the **Aggregation** stage, as aggregation sites like Reddit and Digg tend to shy away from bullying like this. They're generally made up of friendly, positive folks, or at least people who play nice in order to maintain a reputation in the community. A lot of Redditors are also /b/tards. The community shapes the discourse.

Word of Mouth: "Check out this bratty little girl and her dumb redneck dad."

While it's difficult to document this sort of thing, one can easily imagine 4chan users instant messaging the video to their friends. I mean . . . I did!

Blog Pickup: Gawker and Urlesque Break The Story

Bloggers, on the other hand, had an opportunity to write hundreds of think pieces about the risks of cyberbullying and unsettling teenage Stickam subculture.

At Gawker, Adrian Chen wrote:

> Don't pick on 11 year-old girls. Seriously. No matter how dumb they seem—no matter how much they might seem to deserve it—they are, at the end of the day, 11 year-old girls. You wouldn't make an 11 year-old girl cry in real life; why do it on the Internet?

Cyberbullying is a constant. No amount of handwringing is going to change that, because it's nearly impossible to prosecute. Of course no one should be mean to 11-year-olds. But haters, as they say, gonna hate. The problem is more likely to be solved by empowering potential victims with knowledge of the realities of cyberbullying than by expecting anonymous sociopaths to be nice. Slaughter's parents gave the impression in multiple interviews that they had little understanding of what she was up to online, and furthermore seemed unable to enforce appropriate disciplinary measures.

I wrote as much in a blog post for Urlesque at the time. From there, the story was dissected by countless mainstream news sites.

Mainstream Exposure: Innocent Girl Cyberbullied, are Your Children Safe? Stay Tuned to Find Out.

It only took a few days before Slaughter and her parents were brought on morning shows to talk about their experience. Child safety experts descended onto the scene to dispense advice that ranged from "ban the computer forever" to "let your kid make mistakes."

This meme skipped the **Commercialization** stage, for obvious reasons.

Death: The Hivemind Moves On

For the most part, Jessi Slaughter has since stayed off the Internet (her father was later arrested for child abuse when he punched his daughter in the face), and as usual, trolls got bored and lost interest. While the jargon inspired by this meme will live forever, the Photoshops and remixes have mostly dried up.

Operation Birthday Boy

4chan may be well known for causing turmoil on and off the web, but deep down it has a heart. As much as /b/tards love to bring down the arrogant, they take pride in standing up for the little guy. Consider the story of William Lashua, a 90-year-old WWII vet from Massachusetts.

Birth: Look At This Poor Guy :(

In August 2010, someone posted an image to 4chan featuring a photo of a flyer found at a grocery store. The flyer featured an elderly man with kind eyes and a grumpy frown. It read, "Wanted: People for Birthday Party," and provided the time and location for the event.

Discovery: D'awww!

4chan's heart melted. They assumed that this poor guy was so lonely and friendless that he had to make signs advertising his own birthday party. Within hours, they decided to give him a birthday surprise. They tracked down his military record and contacted the VFW where the party was set to be held, not so they could harass him but to throw him the best party ever.

Aggregation: Reddit Starts Its Charity Engine

When someone posted the plan to the social news site Reddit, the thing exploded. As it turned out, William Lashua's grandson is a Reddit user. When he posted the following message to Reddit, it only fueled the effort to make Lashua's birthday special.

Kind folks of reddit, My family and I appreciate the outpouring of love and generosity. There has been a large misunderstanding. The poster which I'm told was found at the Gardner Stop & Shop was more a local notice for people that know him. It was in no way to indicate that he is alone. He has 7 children, many grandchildren, and even great grandchildren. In his younger years he was a foster parent to dozens of foster children.

215

He is well liked in the community, and will be fully supported on his 90th birthday

Thank you again for all the love and well wishes, we certainly never expected this.

Word of Mouth: "Check out this adorable old geezer."

The story spread to personal blogs and Twitter accounts. People posted photos of gifts and cards they planned to send. One guy who worked at a beef jerky company uploaded photos of his planned gift to the obviously toothless Lashua: a full case of dried meat. A Facebook group, which peaked at nearly seven thousand members, was created for people to share birthday wishes and collaborate on gift ideas. Lashua's image was Photoshopped and mashed up with dozens of other memes and meme templates.

Blog Pickup: The Daily What and Urlesque pick up the story

The heartwarming tale was an opportunity for small media outlets to feature the kinder side of the web's underbelly.

Mainstream Exposure: Internet Wishes Area Man Happy 90th Birthday

A local news station interviewed the Lashua family and the story ran on a few prominent news websites.

Death: 4chan Pats Itself on the Back

Reddit took images from the birthday party and 4chan users and subsequently shared with the community. According to one anonymous poster who contacted the American Legion, Lashua received fifty bouquets of flowers, twenty cakes, and five UPS trucks bearing cards.

Bottoms Up

Whether 4chan is an Internet Hate Machine or a place where people can collaborate on positive projects, no matter how misdirected, the exciting thing here is the way that information is now being discovered, disseminated, and consumed online. Creatives and tastemakers are no longer trying to shoehorn the web into their existing media channels, but are embracing it as a new source—*the* new source—of popular culture. People are creating their own fun, their own characters. They are engaged in a vibrant participatory culture with no rules or boundaries.

We've all heard statistics about how people are spending less time watching TV, listening to the radio, and going to the movies, and how that time is now spent on the Internet. This is why.

In the time it took you to read this chapter, thousands of new threads were started on 4chan. Hundreds of new posts went up on Reddit, Tumblr, and Twitter. Dozens of stories were picked up by culture blogs, and a few made it all the way to global news sites or even TV. A single photo, song, video, or story has gone viral, exposed to millions. Marketing agencies who under-

217

stand this process are among the few pioneers who recognize that they no longer possess the tools to drive culture—culture which no longer trickles down from above, but grows up and spreads laterally from below. This is why Stephen Colbert and Old Spice reach out directly to Reddit and even 4chan, respectively.

Welcome to the Memesphere

Once cultural artifacts go viral, they are subsumed into the lexicon to serve as the foundation for comedic callbacks, mash-ups, Photoshops, etc. The culture becomes so self-referential as to become virtually incomprehensible to those who do not live inside it. Think about your grandparents, and how your daily conversation about SMS texting and email wouldn't make much sense to them. That gap between those who are "in" and those who are "out" widens at a staggering acceleration, to the point where I might come back to the web from a short vacation and have trouble understanding what's going on. As the memesphere grows, it demands more of your attention.

This is largely because information isn't arranged linearly online. It's more like a complex network of rabbit holes which may or may not yield the information you're looking for. If you're looking for information, you do a Google search. But maybe you don't know what exactly to search for. So you try Wikipedia with a few different search terms.

You find that in order to gain a basic understanding of X, you must first learn about Y and Z. But then, in order to understand Z, you'll need to watch a YouTube video, check out a forum thread, and visit someone's Twitter account. You must probe many pathways, bouncing from one resource to the next and back, hunting for puzzle pieces. It's a skill that only today's younger generation is equipped to grasp, because we've grown up with the acceleration of consumer technology. It's an active, participatory quest for understanding. It's becoming second nature.

Today, this is the way humans learn, laugh, build, argue, discover, share, and live.

Surviving and Thriving in the Memesphere

One question I get more than almost any other in my line of work is, "How do you make something popular online?" The wording of this question belies a fundamental misunderstanding of how the web works, especially considering that it's usually asked by people who spend a lot of time online.

What made Rick Astley's "Never Gonna Give You Up" go viral, two decades after its release? This question is impossible to answer, because the song's viral success was based on several serendipitous events. Advertisers in particular want to be able to buy this kind of success, but there's no way a social media marketer would be able to mastermind a coup like this. It could only have happened by chance. Sometimes it just comes down to blind luck: slow news day, bad weather, a randomly placed 4chan thread.

Like pop songs, memes that behave like empty vessels are often the most successful. I've seen some memes plastered with several different languages. But sometimes the most obscure, unapproachable memes win out in the end because of increased enthusiasm from a small group of fans.

If there's anything 4chan users hate (along with the rest of the Internet), it's a forced meme, which someone, whether a wannabe Photoshop artiste or a grassroots marketing consultant, is desperately trying to make viral. While some companies have managed to pull off viral success, forced memes are most often met with yawns, if not outright contempt.

A Meme is Born: The Story of Keyboard Cat

Imagine creating some bit of entertainment and putting it up on YouTube for your friends, only to watch it become a massive global sensation. That's what happened to Brad O'Farrell when he posted footage of a cat playing a keyboard.

O'Farrell has spent time on Internet forums for years, originally going online so he could talk about video games. This was way before people "just got online to make social media profiles." O'Farrell says that his early Internet experiences gave him thick skin. But he still gives anonymous a wide berth:

> I'm actually kind of terrified of the Internet because of my tragic past on message boards, I'm always afraid doing an interview about keyboard cat will make me sound like a douche and make me a target of 4chan.

O'Farrell had a group of online pals that all followed each other's YouTube channels. The *vloggers* would make jokey little videos, but O'Farrell didn't seem to find his voice on camera, so he began using his channel to make mashups and other meme-ish creations.

At that time, O'Farrell's network of vlogger friends were making parody videos, sometimes of popular YouTube or Hollywood stars, or of one another. O'Farrell wanted to create content that would give his buddies something to parody, but he had no intention of creating a meme.

O'Farrell stumbled on a 30-year-old video of a cat "playing" a short tune on a keyboard (the cat was being manipulated by its owner, Charlie Schmidt). He thought it was funny in itself, but he came up with the idea of pasting the video at the end of fail videos, e.g., videos of people falling down or messing up or otherwise making an ass of themselves. He titled it, "Play Him Off, Keyboard Cat," referring to the vaudevillian practice of a musician starting to play to cue a flailing performer that it was time to exit the stage.

> The original title, "Play Him Off, Keyboard Cat" is sort of like mad libs. I renamed the cat "Keyboard Cat" (it was originally "Cool Cat") because it was more specific and evoked a character like "Pedobear," whereas Cool Cat could be referring to any cat. The "Him" part is an easily changeable template, for whoever the subject is of the parody. I was intending to make more follow up videos myself, so I was mostly just setting up a naming convention for a series of videos, but other people made them before I got around to it.

First he noticed that people were using his template to "play off" other videos. Then he noticed they were being posted on various forums, and realized that YouTube commenters were referencing other memes. That's when he knew that the sort of people who spend time playing around with memes were beginning to appreciate the video. At the time, O'Farrell was working for a web video company, who tasked him with promoting their content on YouTube. He often pitched YouTube directly at editor@youtube.com. This time he sent in Keyboard Cat with his usual suggestions, and the video was granted feature placement. From there it took off, spreading to 4chan and other meme-oriented sites.

> I thought maybe it would be a blip on the radar, one of those things like "hey look someone made the Mona Lisa out of Legos and it was on Boing Boing for a day", but the fact keyboard cat became elevated into the 'meme canon' surprised me. Even though a keyboard cat video alone isn't enough to make it onto big blogs these days, the character of Keyboard Cat itself is sort of permanently in the Internet consciousness. It's like how a satellite is launched into space with a rocket and then it detaches and is self-sustaining, the "Play him off" part was the rocket that got the "Keyboard Cat" character into the zeitgeist.

At this point, the video was getting enough attention that O'Farrell decided to attach ads. But he was worried that Charlie Schmidt might come out of the woodwork and want a piece of the pie or throw a DMCA (Digital Millennium Copyright Act) takedown notice at him. So O'Farrell tracked down Schmidt and explained the benefit of keeping the parodies online. Schmidt agreed, and now he's selling T-shirts, an iPhone app, and even a collection of Keyboard Cat's Greatest Hits—not to mention the TV commercials (Wonderful Pistachios used Keyboard Cat alongside Snooki, Chad Ocho Cinco, Rod Blagojevich, and characters from *Peanuts*, among other pop-culture heavyweights).

Currently, more than four thousand different YouTube videos feature Keyboard Cat.

O'Farrell agrees there's no way to guarantee that something will go viral, but there are ways to help it along, like putting it in a familiar format; making it easy to parody with basic software; and pitching well to editors and bloggers—but only if the content has legs and clear legal rights.

So this is 4chan's lighter side that has bled out into the rest of the web. Participatory culture, meme creation, viral media: whatever you want to call it, we're experiencing something new and exciting, and 4chan is at its forefront.

And yet 4chan is not just creativity. It's also creative destruction. We've already seen how anonymous trolls tried to ruin Jessi Slaughter's life. What would happen if they went after global corporations or political candidates of the highest order?

What happens when a toddler gets bored building sandcastles? He totters over to the next kid's creation and obliterates it with one unexpected kick.

Chapter 8

Merry Pranksters, Freedom Fighters, or Sadistic Bullies?

IN 2008 I was living in England, writing for a travel company. I remember returning from a trip to Spain, exhausted and dirty after a weekend of no sleep and near-missed departures. I transferred from the Eurostar train as the sun rose over London when I spotted a portly fellow in a Guy Fawkes mask wobbling toward me. We ended up sitting together on the train.

"Kind of early for a raid, don't you think?" I asked.

He pulled up the mask and grinned. "Never too early for lulz," he chortled. "You coming?"

"No. I had no idea there was something happening today."

I explained I'd never participated in any raids, but was generally aware of Anonymous's activity.

"Ah. A lurker then?"

"You might say that."

He flashed another grin, slouched into his seat, and started fiddling with a Nintendo DS.

This interaction freaked me out. It was the first time I'd witnessed someone acknowledge Anonymous in the "real" world. It was almost as if Indiana Jones or some other cinematic character had boarded my train. To me, Anonymous was part of the Internet, and this was real life. A bemasked Anon seemed as out of place on my train as Darth Vader.

It was a jarring moment. The lines between the Internet and real life weren't just blurry. They weren't even there anymore. Facebook brought everyone and their mom (literally) onto the Internet, and everyday people were living out their lives on the web like it was no big deal. And now, even the antisocial denizens of the web's pale, pulsating underbelly were drinking coffee on my train at five o'clock in the morning.

Troll Community

The trolling of the Usenet era can largely be seen as lighthearted, almost gentlemanly fun that actually had some social value in that it inoculated noobs to online life and encouraged them to absorb the social mores of the online community.

Journalist Julian Dibbell became aware of trolls when researching online gaming for an essay called "A Rape in Cyberspace" that he wrote for the *Village Voice* in 1993. The story chronicled a lone troll named Mr. Bungle who "raped" fellow players' avatars, forcing them to commit bizarre sex acts on each other via a "voodoo doll," a bit of code that allowed Bungle to take control of others' characters. The spectacle drove at least one victim to tears.

Back then, this kind of malicious trolling was mostly a solitary proposition. According to Dibbell, the attitude of the man behind Mr. Bungle was, "This is all just make believe, so let's just play around and see what happens when you poke this community with a stick." But for the victims it wasn't just a game. They felt violated. The essay was an early glimpse into the ways that online life and real life would bleed together in the coming decades.

Dibbell continued to track trollish behavior in online games, writing another landmark article about *griefers* (trolls who terrorize others within online games) for *Wired* in 2008. During that time, technology made it easier for people with trollish inclinations to find one another and engage in collective mischief. Trolls would set up sites and create FAQs dedicated to griefing tips. They congregated in anonymous IRC channels to plan coordinated attacks. Trolling became a more explicitly subcultural, even communal, behavior, as they realized they could cause a lot more damage—and generate a lot more lulz—working together.

The Habbo Hotel Raids & The Patriotic Nigras

Habbo is a global social networking site for teenagers that allows users to create cartoonish avatars that interact with each other in a Lego-like environment. The hub of the Habbo universe is the Habbo Hotel. It's where users access chat rooms and games. It gets 18 million unique visitors each month.

Because Habbo is populated mostly by kids, it became an easy target for trolls. First they came from Something Awful. The goons created a fake cult of nonconfrontational characters who wore gray hoods. They would chant mystical babble like "the path is gray" in an effort to convert other players, whom they called prismatics because of the colors in their costumes. They didn't disrupt the other players, but mostly just aimed to confuse. At one point they staged an "ascension," where the goons reenacted the Jonestown Massacre, complete with gray Kool-Aid. The prank climaxed when the goons disconnected simultaneously, vanishing into the ether after having consumed their gray beverage. Other goons posing as concerned friends and family went into hysterics, and those who weren't in on the joke were spooked.

4chan users, many of whom had also migrated from Something Awful, saw delicious opportunity in July 2006. In what came to be known as The Great Habbo Raid, hundreds of /b/tards joined Habbo, creating black, suit-wearing avatars with giant Afros. The avatars disrupted conversations, flooded chat rooms with racist spam, and generally annoyed people. In particular, they blocked access to the hotel's swimming pools, repeating, "Pool's closed due to AIDS." When moderators banned the trolls, the /b/tards accused them of racism.

Meanwhile, over in Second Life, a game world that attracts tens of thousands of players at any given moment, a group of /b/tards calling themselves the Patriotic Nigras spent their days messing with some of the community's denizens, especially the furries. Furries have long been a favorite target of 4chan for many reasons, but mostly because they take themselves so seriously. The furries flock to Second Life, where they are able to live out their "fursonas" in peace and mutual appreciation.

So the Nigras created Tacowood, a parody of the Furry utopia Luskwood, but instead of a beautiful forest populated by cuddly anthropomorphic critters, Tacowood comprised a "defurrested" wasteland strewn with the corpses of dead furries.

For my money, the best thing the Patriotic Nigras ever pulled off was their griefing of an in-game CNET interview with Second Life virtual real estate magnate Anshe Chung's avatar. The interview was interrupted when the Nigras conjured a parade of giant pink penises out of thin air, which danced across the stage, horrifying everyone involved.

In Julian Dibbell's aforementioned write-up of troll culture, one Something Awful goon who was part of a troll group within the game EVE Online said, "The way that you win in EVE is you basically make life so miserable for someone else that they actually quit the game and don't come back."

The Nigras and goons aren't really playing Habbo Hotel, Second Life, or EVE. They're playing the 4chan metagame. These kinds of trolls were purely "for the lulz," and they defined Anonymous's behavior in its early days. It was relatively mischievous fun at someone else's expense, and it didn't cross the line into the real world.

Mitchell Henderson Memorial Raid

On a spring afternoon in 2006, a seventh grader named Mitchell Henderson fatally shot himself in the head. His friends created a virtual memorial page on MySpace, leaving condolences for family members, prayers, and cherished memories.

One mourner's MySpace comment became a meme.

> He was such an hero, to take it all away. We miss him so, That you should know, And we honor him this day. He was an hero, to take that shot, to leave us all behind. God do we wish we could

take it back, And now he's on our minds. Mitchell was an hero, to leave us feeling like this, Our minds are rubber, our joints don't work, Our tears fall into abyss. He was an hero, to take that shot, In life it wasn't his task, He shouldn't have had to go that way, before an decade'd past.

The phrase *an hero* struck /b/tards as hilarious. On its face, the garbled grammar brought the lulz, but more importantly it was the idea that killing oneself is inherently heroic. On 4chan, an hero is now synonymous with suicide. When someone asks for advice on the /adv/ board, some smartass will inevitably suggest, "an hero?"

The way /b/ saw it, some emo wimp killed himself over a toy, and a bunch of whiners were turning the spoiled little shit into a hero. Something had to be done. In the midst of the tragedy, the page caught the attention of /b/, who spammed the page mercilessly with insensitive messages. They eventually found out his parents' home address and began prank-calling them, saying "Hi, this is Mitchell. I'm at the cemetery," or "Hi, I've got Mitchell Henderson's iPod." (For reasons I'm unable to determine, /b/ became convinced that Mitchell killed himself over a lost iPod, which probably contributed to their sense of the situation's lulziness.)

There is a cartoon of a 4chan troll euphorically licking the tears from the cheek of his victim. This harassment represents a nastier bent to Anonymous's trolling.

Tom Green LIVE! Raids

Remember Tom Green, the gonzo comedian who, like Andy Kaufman, made a career out of confusing and enraging NORPs? Green's cable access show was picked up by MTV in 1999, and for a few years he was among the most well-known comedians. After a few box office flops, he launched *Tom Green LIVE!*, a web show that continued in the spirit of his earlier show, which had featured unscreened prank callers.

In August of 2006, /b/tards flooded his phone lines with prank calls blurting out as many obscure 4chan memes as possible before Tom cut them off. There are videos on YouTube of an increasingly frustrated and unhinged Green putting up with abuse from /b/tards. Here was a man who was used to be in control of the situation. But the troller had become the trolled. Green eventually got wise and began to address 4chan directly, but this was perceived by Anonymous as further desperation. This represents the first time Anonymous went after a specific person on a large scale.

Hal Turner Raid

The trolling of white supremacist radio host Hal Turner represents a meaningful shift in Anonymous's behavior. It wasn't just for the lulz; it was, in chan-speak, "for great justice" (a line from the aforementioned *Zero Wing*). In their eyes, this guy was a villain who needed to be taken down. In lulzy fashion, of course.

231

In December 2006, Anonymous members flooded Turner's show with prank calls and brought down his website, provoking him to post all the prank callers' phone numbers, encouraging his true fans to retaliate.

In response, Anonymous dug up Hal Turner's criminal record along with his current residence and contact information. Hundreds of prank calls ensued. In the following months, Hal threatened 4chan and Anonymous, and they continued to prank his show and website. This conflict culminated with Turner filing a lawsuit against 4chan and several other sites for copyright infringement. The suit was dismissed.

Hal was convinced that he would be able to get the jerks that caused him so much pain, but he, like many others who wander into Anonymous's crosshairs, didn't recognize the collective's knack for asymmetrical warfare.

During the American Revolution, colonial forces were able to take out huge swathes of enemy combatants because, technically, they didn't play by the rules. They hid in the woods, sniped from a distance, and behaved in otherwise dishonorable fashion. The British forces were still operating under the old rules, and in some cases they got slaughtered. Those dishonorable tactics would become the strategies of future conflict. In today's War on Terror, insurgents use similar methods. They hide among civilians and employ other kinds of trickery. Military strategists call it asymmetrical warfare. It's why the US's magnificently powerful armed forces are still fighting a war after a decade of conflict. Hal Turner tried to fight 4chan with legal means and lost. Like the clumsy British forces, he was playing by old rules.

In a weary post, Turner eventually admitted defeat.

I am not certain where to go from here. My entire existence—short of my physical presence on this planet—has been utterly wrecked, by people I never met from places I've never been.

Anonymous: 1
Evil: 0

Anon Gets Cocky

In October 2006, Jake Brahm posted bomb threats to 4chan, and was subsequently investigated by the FBI, sentenced to six months in prison and six months under house arrest, and ordered to pay $26,750 in fines.

The following year, a teenager in Pflugerville, Texas, posted photos depicting pipe bombs (they were fake), threatening to blow up his school. A few other Anons tracked him down using Exif data (data that is embedded into photographs by digital cameras that details the geographic location of the photo, the make and model of the phone, the time the photo was taken, and more) and reported him to the police. He was arrested.

Several similar cases have followed in the years since. Anonymous loves to mess with people, but they seem to draw the line at indiscriminate killing. They are adept at finding and punishing Anons who step out of line.

Pedobaiting

We've all seen pedobaiting, though you may not recognize it as such. From 2004 to 2007, Dateline NBC's "To Catch a Predator" segment glamorized the police's use of undercover sting operations that were used to catch real-world child predators. The show follows a general format. The tech-savvy volunteers at Perverted Justice, an organization devoted to the prevention of child abuse, pose as children in chat rooms until they get the attention of a potential predator. They then entice the target to meet with the hypothetical child. They hire a child actor, put him in a house, and wait for the target to show up, at which point he's confronted by host Chris Hansen (whose oft-repeated line "Why don't you have a seat over there," is repeated constantly on 4chan) and eventually jumped by the cops.

Pedobaiting is a popular pastime for Anonymous members. The motivation is a mix of heroic do-goodery and naked schadenfreude. It's exciting to talk to a sicko, and the payoff is an intoxicating moralistic thrill. With a simple Google search one can find guides to pedobaiting that detail the most effective ways to entrap and report potential predators.

In late 2007, Anonymous laid their sights on 53-year-old Chris Forcand. They posed as underage girls under the name "serious," inciting conversations like the following:

> forcandchris: i adopt you
> serious: Mmm then we could play everday
> forcandchris: for sure
> forcandchris: andsleep together every night
> serious says: if we sleep that is ;)

forcandchris: true
forcandchris: cause we would have sex every night

Forcand was arrested by the end of the year, and the event was reported by several news outlets as the first time a suspected child predator was exposed by anonymous Internet vigilantes.

Just how prevalent is child pornography (aka CP, as well as Cheese Pizza, Captain Picard, and Christopher Poole) on 4chan? From my personal experience I can say "not very." But it's there. So why hasn't the site been shut down? First, the moderators are pretty vigilant about removing child porn as soon as it appears. And when they catch it, they report the offending IP addresses to the proper authorities, which is really all any photo upload site can do. The "4chan Party Van" is a jokey name for the FBI van that might appear outside your home if the moderators report you for posting CP. moot claims that child pornography is automatically reported to the National Center for Missing & Exploited Children's CyberTipline, which acts as a clearinghouse, forwarding the content to appropriate law enforcement.

But it still happens. On February 14, 2011, a Navy man admitted to acquiring child porn at 4chan. On May 18th, 2011, a man arrested for child pornography told the feds during a home raid that he obtained child porn there as well.

There probably aren't that many genuine pedophiles on 4chan in the same way there aren't very many genuine white supremacists on 4chan, or in society at large. People who behave outside the range of social norms tend to attract the most attention. Furthermore, trolls like to break the rules, and one of the only rules on /b/ is "No CP." Like the rampant racism, homophobia, and sexism seen on 4chan, the site's obsession with child pornography is rooted in irony, for the most part.

Enter Pedobear, a cartoon bear that is the closest thing /b/ has to a mascot. He's the most infamous 4chan meme, and was originally depicted as ASCII art.

Pedobear originally comes from 2channel. In Japan he is called Kuma, which is Japanese for *bear*, and has no association with pedophila. In 4chan's early days, there was a lot of memetic overlap between 2channel and 4chan, and Kuma made his way to English-speaking message boards. Now he often appears in 4chan threads in the Pedobear Seal of Approval, or its converse, a depiction of the bear muttering "Too old" at images of anyone over 16. "Is dat sum CP?" he asks, peeking his head into any thread with pics of kids. His arch-nemesis is Chris Hansen of "To Catch a Predator."

Pedobear's appearance in a thread can be used to signal that someone is looking for child pornography. He might appear

when someone posts a non-pornographic image of a kid. It's usually used as shorthand to say, "Dude, you're a pedophile." The
cuddly representation of such repugnant behavior encapsulates
the cutesy and sinister dichotomy present on 4chan. Although
meant to characterize pedophilia, Pedobear is also a mockery of
pedophilia, which many Anons have successfully fought against
in the real world.

But why would *anyone* joke about child pornography and
child predation, two of the most universally reviled behaviors in
human history? On 4chan, it's precisely because they're the most
universally reviled behaviors in human history. /b/tards love
nothing more than shocking NORPs with behavior that takes on
the appearance of deviance.

The media and even police have sensationalized Pedobear.
The San Louis Obispo County Sheriff's Department released a
Public Safety Information Bulletin entitled "A Seemingly Innocent Menace: An Introduction to 'Pedo Bear,'" which detailed the
perceived threat of the character.

> His cute face and nonthreatening appearance negate the truth
> of his sinister, much darker side.
>
> In fact, one of the things that make PedoBear popular is the
> controversy surrounding his licentious love of little girls. Pedo-
> Bear is and should be associated with the Internet and pedo-
> philes/sexually-preferential offenders who reportedly use him to
> communicate their interests in young children to each other.
>
> At the San Diego Comic Con 2010 in July of this year, law
> enforcement discovered an individual dressed in a PedoBear cos-
> tume, handing out candy and being photographed in contact with
> attendees, including multiple children. Once identified, the
> young man and his costume were excluded from the family-
> friendly event . . . Disguised as innocence, this underground

community that would make victims of our children, teasingly reaches out into the light of day.

The bulletin failed to mention that 99 percent of the time, Pedobear is used in jest. Real pedophiles aren't on 4chan for the lulz.

Project Chanology

Project Chanology is Anonymous's anti-Scientology effort. It changed everything, bringing the collective, along with 4chan, into the limelight, and gave Anonymous's efforts a pseudopolitical bent that would come to dominate the group's future endeavors. That masked man I saw on the train in Europe? He was part of Project Chanology.

Of course, the broader going anti-Scientology movement goes all the way back to Usenet days. Before delving into the early anti-Scientology movement, it's important to understand something about the ideals of hackers and even general Internet users from that era, all of whom today would be considered extremely tech-savvy given the structural barriers to entry that the Internet imposed.

Tech heads were, and still are, drawn to the Internet in part because it promises a level playing field, where all-important information is out in the open. As the WELL's Stewart Brand famously declared, "Information wants to be free." Enthusiasts in those days saw the Internet as a utopian future, where one could be taken at his or her word.

Usenet was home to a fervent discussion at alt.religion

.scientology, started in 1991 by Scott Goehring, a regular guy who wished to expose the hypocrisies and deceptions of the Church of Scientology. It soon became frequented by ex-church members, free speech enthusiasts, and other critics who found the church's suppression of information to fly in the face of geek principles. Among these geeks was Dennis Erlich, who joined the newsgroup in July 1994. Erlich was a former high-ranking member of the church who had been affiliated with none other than the founder of Scientology, L. Ron Hubbard. The newsgroup, which was already known for controversy and flame wars, exploded in size.

On December 24, 1994, previously secret documents dealing with mysterious concepts like "Thetan Levels" were leaked to the newsgroup, and the church wasn't happy. It hired lawyers to contact participants and demanded that the documents be removed. Subsequently the church attempted to shut down the newsgroup entirely, claiming copyright infringement.

On February 13th, 1995, church attorney Thomas Small, along with seven others, raided Dennis Erlich's home and spent six hours seizing files from his computer. Dennis complained about the raid that night, kicking off massive outrage. Several other raids occurred throughout the year. On August 12, 1995, Usenet poster and former Scientologist Arnaldo Lerma's home was raided by ten people from the FBI (two federal marshals, two computer techies, and several attorneys). They took his computer, backups, disks, modem, and scanner. Ten days later, two more raids took place. Even newsgroup users in the Netherlands and Sweden were investigated.

These raids infuriated the geeks, for whom technology is not so much a tool as an ideal in itself. The Church of Scientology, on the other hand, is shrouded in secrecy, and uses technology as a means to achieve an end: KSW, or Keeping Scientology Working. KSW is a church edict that declares the role of technology to be a primary tool for furthering the interests of Scientology.

Over the next few years the church spammed newsgroups with propaganda. In the early days of search engines, the church also employed web designers to build thousands of dummy web pages to flood search engines with Scientology-related information so criticisms of the church would be hard to find. The anti-Scientology movement became less about unmasking a pseudoreligion and more about upholding truth, transparency, freedom of information, and other lofty ideological goals.

Remember You're the Man Now Dog? In 2006, Scientology lawyers threatened that site's founder Max Goldberg, resulting in a flare of anti-Scientology sentiment among a younger, more lulz-seeking audience on the heels of a *South Park* episode that mocked Scientology.

Soon, the church became perhaps the first victim of what has come to be known as the Streisand Effect. The term was coined in 2003 by Mike Masnick of Techdirt, when actress and singer Barbra Streisand attempted to suppress the online dissemination of photos of her home, an effort which only drew more attention to the photos. Streisand unsuccessfully sued the photographer, which brought even more publicity.

Anti-Scientology sentiment continued to simmer throughout the early '00s. Even after the threats to Max Goldberg, geeks lost interest until January 15th, 2008, when the fight against Scientology took a decidedly lulzy turn. Gossip blog Radar ran a leaked church video of normally ultrasuave Scientology member Tom Cruise looking and sounding like a brainwashed pod person. The *Mission Impossible* theme music plays in the background as Cruise gushes about the power of Scientology. The whole thing was begging to be parodied thousands of times over, and it eventually was.

Gawker founder Nick Denton smartly hosted the video himself, racking up over three million page views. In the post, Denton called Cruise a "complete fanatic," teasing visitors with, "If Tom Cruise jumping on Oprah's couch was an eight on the scale of scary, this is a ten."

Cruise, for many people at the time, was the celebrity face of Scientology. Naturally, the church immediately attempted to suppress the distribution of the video, but the damage had been done. If deleting a few Usenet discussion threads was difficult in the early '90s, suppressing a video in 2008 was impossible. Nothing short of a federal decree could accomplish that, and even then illicit videos could be distributed through bit torrent and other file-sharing services. Stewart Brand's maxim about information wanting to be free had materialized on an Internet that never forgives . . . or forgets.

Why did it take so long for the anti-Scientology movement to pick up steam? Why was 2008 the year that the world took notice? Why anti-Scientology, rather than the hundreds of other causes one could rally around?

Lulz. The Tom Cruise video brought a lulzy angle to the anti-Scientology movement. Tom Cruise, and by extension his church, was seen as a buffoon who needed to be brought down a peg or two. Second, 4chan provided a platform around which thousands of activists could be quickly mobilized to take part in DDoS attacks, which required little effort from individual participants and could cause devastating damage in the aggregate.

DDoS attacks are often initiated by a piece of software affectionately called the Low Orbit Ion Cannon (LOIC), named after a fictional weapon from the *Command & Conquer* PC real-time strategy game. The LOIC allows someone who has zero technical ability to participate in collective attacks. You just push a button, point the "cannon" at a particular URL or IP address, and the software does the rest. The LOIC will flood the target address with "garbage requests." A website's server can only handle so much traffic at a given time. When thousands of users are all using the software simultaneously, pinging the site with garbage requests, the attacks can be devastating. And here's the best part—when they succeed, the individual attackers are virtually untraceable.

But that was just the beginning. Anonymous inundated the Church of Scientology with prank calls and black faxes. (Imagine pulling an entirely black sheet of paper out of your fax machine, soaking wet with wasted, expensive ink.) Anonymous spread the word far and wide on social networks and message boards.

On January 21, 2008, the following manifesto, entitled "Message to Scientology," was uploaded to YouTube, narrated by a digitized text-to-speech voice:

> Hello, leaders of Scientology. We are Anonymous.
>
> Over the years, we have been watching you. Your campaigns of misinformation; your suppression of dissent; your litigious nature, all of these things have caught our eye. With the leakage of your latest propaganda video into mainstream circulation, the extent of your malign influence over those who have come to trust you as leaders, has been made clear to us. Anonymous has therefore decided that your organization should be destroyed. For the good of your followers, for the good of mankind—and for our

own enjoyment—we shall proceed to expel you from the Internet and systematically dismantle the Church of Scientology in its present form. We recognize you as a serious opponent, and we are prepared for a long, long campaign. You will not prevail forever against the angry masses of the body politic. Your methods, hypocrisy, and the artlessness of your organization have sounded its death knell.

You have nowhere to hide because we are everywhere. We cannot die; we are forever. We're getting bigger every day—and solely by the force of our ideas, malicious and hostile as they often are. If you want another name for your opponent, then call us Legion, for we are many.

Knowledge is free. We are Anonymous. We are Legion. We do not forgive. We do not forget. Expect us.

Thus began Project Chanology, kick-started by anonymous users of 4chan and other chan-style boards where anti-Scientology discussions were held following the release of the Tom Cruise video.

I got in touch with "c0s," an Anon who claims to be the guy who created and uploaded the "Message to Scientology" video, in AnonOps, an anonymous IRC channel devoted to Anonymous's operations. I was immediately struck by how polite he was, and how willing he was to chat. Previously I'd only dealt with random /b/tards, who are a particularly different breed than those who are interested in the hacktivist strain of Anonymous found at AnonOps.

After chatting with c0s for a bit I got the impression I was dealing with someone who'd spoken with the press before. He eventually revealed his name, Gregg Housh, a guy who has appeared on countless radio and TV shows, often positioned by producers as a "spokesman" for Anonymous. Housh is quick to

243

clarify that he doesn't speak for the collective, and that he has no personal role in any of Anonymous's illegal activities, but he was heavily involved in their anti-Scientology efforts.

Housh started off our conversation by reiterating that the political efforts of Anonymous should be distinguished from the earlier trolls conducted by anons (lowercase *a*), who have even attacked Housh personally for his "justicefaggotry." When Housh went public with his identity, these "armchair assholes" doxed him, digging up his social security number, his bank account information, home address, and more. Housh suspects the /b/tards got hold of his information by looking up property records and going from there.

Housh claims that he and a small group of Anons basically started Project Chanology. He had hung around 4chan before, taking part in the Hal Turner and Habbo raids, before pursuing great justice.

I asked Housh to name a few things that the press consistently gets wrong regarding Anonymous.

> #1 talking about moot in any way for the last 4 years, since he has had nothing to do with it since then, and has actively avoided everything Anonymous has done (yet reaped the benefits with VC and jobs.)
> #2 is of course the use of the words group and member. ugh.
> #3 would probably be any attempt made to paint them as politically one way or another, since it is quite obviously apolitical

Housh recently gave a speech on the steps of New York's City Hall with a handful of other Anons, journalists whom he feels are responsible for the media climate marked by lazy and fear-mongering characterizations of Anonymous.

Housh is hardly the angst-ridden teenager that many journalists would like you to believe makes up Anonymous. He's in his mid-30s, and he's been online since '93, when he used a text browser. He remembers Usenet's eternal September, which he, perhaps jokingly, calls "the worst thing that ever happened to the Internet."

> Usenet before eternal september? Very few stupid questions, mostly just good chat and sharing interesting files. it was quite a good community of pretty intelligent people

Like the folks I spoke with at the WELL, Housh insists that in the early days the web wasn't a chaotic Wild West. The low number of active users prevented people from being "lost in the numbers," so antisocial behavior was more easily pinpointed and punished.

Anonymous released a second message, in similar style to the letter aimed at the Church of Scientology, a week after Housh's initial video. This time, Anonymous lashed out at the media.

> Dear News Organizations.
> We have been watching your reporting of Anonymous's conflict with The Church of Scientology.
> As you said, the so called Church of Scientology have actively misused copyright and trademark law in pursuit of its own agenda. They attempt, not only to subvert free speech, but to recklessly pervert justice to silence those who speak out against them.
> We find it interesting that you did not mention the other objections in your news reporting. The stifling and punishment of dissent within the totalitarian organization of Scientology. The numerous alleged human rights violations, such as the treatment

and events that led to the deaths of victims of the cult such as Lisa McPherson.

This cult is nothing but a psychotically driven pyramid scheme. Why are you, the news media, afraid of discussing these matters? It is your duty to report on these matters. You are failing in your duty. Their activities make them an affront to freedom. Remember, all that is necessary for the triumph of evil is that good men do nothing. This information is everywhere. It is your duty to expose it. It is easy to find. Google is your friend.

This is not Religious Persecution, but the suppression of a powerful, criminal, fascist regime. It is left to Anonymous. The Church has been declared fair game. It will be dismantled and destroyed.

We are Anonymous. We are Legion. We do not Forgive. We do not Forget. This is only the beginning. Expect us.

Anonymous continued harassing the Church of Scientology websites through the spring. They also engaged in Google Bombing techniques. A Google Bomb occurs when Google search results are successfully manipulated by spamming the search engine with specific keywords. For example, 4chan once bombarded Google with the key phrase "Justin Bieber syphilis." Within hours, Gawker and even the *San Francisco Chronicle* had run stories about the pop star's alleged STD. In the Scientology Google Bombing, Anons manipulated the church's search engine rankings so that certain keywords such as "dangerous cult" linked to the Church of Scientology website.

In February 2008, the anti-Scientology movement jumped off the flickering screen. Another video appeared, encouraging Anons to participate in physical protests at church headquarters around the globe. The protests were small, maxing out at a few hundred participants in English-speaking cities, but they occurred.

The protestors often wear Guy Fawkes masks—now the international symbol of Anonymous. The mask had previously become a vague symbol of faceless rebellion, popularized in 2005 in the film adaptation of Alan Moore's *V for Vendetta*, in which a masked anonymous figure incites a massive anarchic rebellion against an oppressive police state. The masks allow Scientology protestors to remain anonymous during real-life protests, and also grant them a perceived heroic flair.

By the summer of 2008, Anonymous had grown beyond the confines of 4chan. Gabriella Coleman, an anthropologist and leading scholar specializing in the documentation of hacker culture, emphasizes the diversity of the group. She tells me that although there are many young people involved in Anonymous, the perspective of "angst-ridden teenagers with no lives is a misconception."

> I think there's a kind of hypersociality among these people. A lot of them have very interesting lives. Some are PhD students, some are Dutch squatters, some are system administrators. Some are landscape artists. Some are very sophisticated political activists.

Nonetheless, the protests have uniformly taken a lulzy tone. Rick Astley's "Never Gonna Give You Up" blares from boomboxes. Protestors dress up like meme characters and wear outlandish costumes. In one photo, four protestors stand behind a sign reading "Truth is Free." Among them they wear a skeleton mask, a hockey mask, a *Star Wars* stormtrooper mask, and a nondescript alien mask. This motley crew is here for a cause, but more importantly it's here to have fun. The aesthetic isn't only for fun, however. The masks and costumery afford a distinct tac-

247

tical advantage: they allow Anonymous to attack the church, and when the church retaliates it just makes them look silly. Protestors have mostly steered clear of the law, but a few were detained here and there. By 2010, Chanology protests took place in over one hundred cities across the globe.

The lulzy nature of the protests is best illustrated by Operation Slickpubes. On January 8, 2009, a teenage protestor covered his body with Vaseline and pubic hair, presumably gathered from several friends. He ran into the New York Scientology building and rubbed his body on as much church property as he could. The entire affair is documented on YouTube.

Coleman says that Project Chanology is still active, even though it no longer gets any press.

> It doesn't have the kind of same support it used to, but there's definitely a core group of people who are dedicated, and in some odd way they've achieved some of their major goals. Prior to Chanology, I was very scared of being public about my work on the Church of Scientology. Now I've given 25 talks on Chanology and geeky protests against Chanology, so in many ways it was very effective.

Old time anti-Scientology activists from the Usenet days are mostly unimpressed by the activities of Project Chanology. They see the effort as counterproductive. Andreas Heldal-Lund, founder of the anti-Scientology website Operation Clambake, says, "Attacking Scientology like that will just make them play the religious persecution card. They will use it to defend their own counter actions when they try to shatter criticism and crush critics without mercy." However, some critics have formed alliances with Anonymous when they agreed to stop DDoSing.

Gabriella Coleman argues that Anonymous's attacks have done some real good.

> Scientology has received so much negative attention that they've refrained from legal intimidation tactics. If I had released some of the papers I've released recently six years ago, I would have been embroiled in legal battles. Anonymous really changed the landscape.

Sarah Palin Email Hack

On September 16, 2008, 20-year-old /b/tard David Kernell, the son of a Democratic state representative of Tennessee, hacked into Republican vice-presidential candidate Sarah Palin's email account. The hack was as simple as pie. Most password-protected websites will ask users a security question like "What was the name of your first pet?" or "Where did you go to high school?" If a user can't remember his or her password, they can change their password by confirming their identity through correctly answering the security question.

Kernell got his hands on Palin's email address, then googled her widely available personal info in order to access her emails, which he then posted to /b/. Kernell had hoped to find incriminating information, but came up dry. He posted the account and password to /b/, and then another 4chan user changed the password and tried to alert a friend of Palin's. The account was eventually locked by Yahoo! when a bunch of /b/tards tried to access it at once. Epic fail, as far as 4chan was concerned, but Kernell faced graver consequences: a year in prison followed by three years of supervised release.

Kernell, going by the name "rubico," recounted the tale on /b/, which was then published at Gawker and elsewhere.

Hello, /b/ as many of you might already know, last night sarah palin's yahoo was "hacked" and caps were posted on /b/, i am the lurker who did it, and i would like to tell the story.

after the password recovery was reenabled, it took seriously 45 mins on wikipedia and google to find the info, Birthday? 15 seconds on wikipedia, zip code? well she had always been from wasilla, and it only has 2 zip codes (thanks online postal service!)

the second was somewhat harder, the question was "where did you meet your spouse?" did some research, and apparently she had eloped with mister palin after college.

I found out later though more research that they met at high school, so I did variations of that, high, high school, eventually hit on "Wasilla high" I promptly changed the password to popcorn and took a cold shower . . .

I read though the emails . . . ALL OF THEM . . . before I posted, and what I concluded was anticlimactic, there was nothing there, nothing incriminating, nothing that would derail her campaign as I had hoped, all I saw was personal stuff, some clerical stuff from when she was governor . . .

The event was reported widely, and the hackers on steroids were making headlines again. Palin released a press release comparing the event to Watergate.

Steve Jobs Heart Attack Hoax

In October 2008, a rumor that Apple CEO Steve Jobs had suffered a heart attack appeared on 4chan. After the story was submitted to a CNN-owned website, Apple's stock price fell by a massive 5 percent.

4chan, Friend of the Animal Kingdom

On the heels of recent successes in Project Chanology, Anonymous continued to move away from the lulz and toward great justice. On February 15, 2009, two videos appeared on YouTube featuring a 14-year-old kid from Oklahoma torturing a cat. 4chan, whose users see cats as kindred spirits, figured out where he lived and gave his information to local police. In August 2010, 4chan hunted down a woman caught on security camera footage chucking a cat into a trash bin in England. Later that month they pinpointed the location of a pretty blonde teenage girl who was depicted on YouTube gleefully tossing newborn puppies into a river.

These three cases represent 4chan's softer side. Animal abuse is recognized on 4chan as the most sinister form of human evil, perhaps more so than child porn. 4chan users rallied, piecing together information bit by bit. With their powers combined, the efforts resemble something beyond what could even be accomplished by professional detective work.

Let's take a closer look at the case of the puppy-throwing girl. The original YouTube video was taken down, but someone saved it and re-posted it to LiveLeak, a site that specializes in hosting video footage that no one else will host. The poster wrote:

> We can determine from the picture so few things.
> One, based on assumption, she probably has a facebook account, no matter what country they're in.

Two, she is 5ft 6in-5ft 8in, blond, eye color unknown, Caucasian
She has something written upside-down on her red sweater, barely legible, might be of assistance if it's the product of a local store.
Let's work together on exposing this sicko! Use the comments.

From there, 4chan got to work. Someone posted the video to /b/, commenting:

Find this dumb little bitch and throw her into a river.

Another wrote:

She's european. Sounds either Swedish or German, based on what she says at the very end. "Voit." If anyone speaks these languages, maybe they can decipher what she's saying.

The hunt continues:

Nope. Not German. Sounds slavic to me. Seriously, that makes me rage.

The conversation continues with cries for justice. Eventually someone provides a list of potential perpetrators' Facebook pages.

Youtube account owners name is Martin. They live in Bugojno, use googlemaps.
[link to a YouTube account] This faggot commented their youtube account and is a possible friend.
This is the Vrbas river, the one from the video.

The thread is peppered with criticisms from those who would decry moralfaggotry.

Despite the naysayers, this crowd-sourced detective work is one of the most exhilarating things about 4chan. They are able to accomplish much in the aggregate that they wouldn't alone. As philospher Pierre Lévy says, "No one knows everything. Everyone knows something."

All it takes is one person to translate a bit of dialogue, recognize a style of license plate, or pinpoint a specific mountain range in the background of a fuzzy YouTube video. These detectives use Google Maps, Flickr, Facebook, WhoIs, the Internet Archive, property records, and a host of other tools to dig up a wealth of information. The work would intimidate any single /b/tard, but together, hundreds or thousands of slackers can rival a small government's intelligence efforts.

Adam Goldstein Raid

In July 2009, a disgruntled customer posted an exchange he'd had with computer repair serviceman Adam Goldstein to Something Awful, hoping to incite the wrath of the SA goons. The customer had bought a computer monitor from Goldstein's eBay store, and it was never delivered. When the customer complained, he swore at Goldstein, who demanded an apology, claiming that he had three lawyers in the family, implying that a lawsuit could be on the way.

When Something Awful failed to build enough momentum around the kerfuffle, a goon brought the matter to /b/'s attention.

> Evening gents'
> We at Something Awful require your assistance. While goon-

dom and bee-ocity can accomplish much we have stumbled upon something so utterly delicious we couldn't keep it away from you raving lunatics.

The meat of the matter is that Adam L. Goldstein LLC who runs a crap company called ATECH computer services decided to be a king-sized douche. After poking and prodding we found that he is a raving lunatic! So, whilst we are under the reigns of our admins and thusly cannot do much beyond making fun of him on our forums . . . we give you the information to do whatever with.

When goons and /b/tards began to spam Goldstein's email, he discovered the Something Awful thread dedicated to his alleged poor customer service. He paid the SA membership fee in order to dispute the claims, and eventually started threatening lawsuits (or as 4chan calls frivolous legal action, "lolsuits").

That's when Anonymous's wrath descended on poor Goldstein. They brought down his website, figured out where he lived by scraping his MySpace page, and created an Encyclopedia Dramatica entry for him. They bombarded his home and office with mocking phone calls, porn mags, pizza deliveries, sex toy deliveries, death threats, and black faxes. They even scheduled visits from call girls and Jehovah's Witnesses and posted fake flyers warning the neighborhood of Goldstein's purported pedophilic past.

But perhaps most damaging was that Anonymous discovered Goldstein was charging exorbitant prices for things like spyware removal and wireless network configuration, and posted this information to Reddit and Digg, where it was discovered by the blogosphere, destroying Goldstein's online reputation.

Operation Payback

In mid-2010, several Bollywood producers hired a company called Aiplex Software to DDoS websites that ignored takedown notices, in an effort to mitigate the piracy that was increasingly eating up their revenue. In retaliation, Anonymous, who I doubt gives much of a crap about Bollywood films, but who seeks to fight antipiracy wherever they see it, launched Operation Payback. They targeted not only Aiplex Software, but also the Motion Picture Association of America, the Recording Industry Association of America, the British Phonographic Industry, and the International Federation of the Phonographic Industry, bringing down the sites for a combined thirty hours. These efforts then bled into attacks on related law firms, antipiracy organizations, and even KISS's Gene Simmons, who encouraged record industry execs to "Be litigious. Sue everybody. Take their homes, their cars."

They brought down Simmons's website for over a day, and redirected it to a popular torrent site, The Pirate Bay. He eventually was able to put his site back online, responding:

> Our legal team and the FBI have been on the case and we have found a few, shall we say "adventurous" young people, who feel they are above the law. And, as stated in my MIPCOM speech, we will sue their pants off.
>
> First, they will be punished. Second, they might find their little butts in jail, right next to someone who's been there for years and is looking for a new girl friend. We will soon be printing their names and pictures.
>
> We will find you. You cannot hide. Stay tuned.

His impotent threats, like so many of those Anonymous has targeted, were sheepishly removed a short time later after his site was brought down again. Then Anonymous went after the RIAA because it sought legal action against file sharing site Limewire.

In December 2010, Amazon, Paypal, Bank of America, Post-Finance, MasterCard, and Visa decided to stop processing donations for the global news leak network WikiLeaks, which had recently caused global controversy by posting sensitive internal documents. These payment-processing sites had bowed to political pressure, refusing to work with WikiLeaks. In retaliation, Anonymous launched DDoS attacks against several of these companies, successfully bringing down the websites for Master-Card and Visa. A 16-year-old boy from the Netherlands was arrested in relation to the attack, and the FBI is probably still investigating.

HBGary Federal Hack

In February 2011, Aaron Barr, the chief executive of the security firm HBGary Federal, announced that he'd infiltrated Anonymous and would reveal his findings in an upcoming conference.

Anonymous hacked into HBGary Federal's website and put up a mocking message. They acquired and published embarrassing emails tainted with the hubris of someone who thought he'd beaten Anonymous. This was a company that positioned itself to its clients as a leader in computer security. A company that had contracts with the NSA. And it had been bested by a bunch of amateur pranksters. Epic fail.

Up until then, Anonymous hadn't been able to do a ton of damage. So they brought down a few websites for a few hours. No big deal. But this was something different. They brought HBGary Federal to its knees by using basic, widely known hacking techniques that could have been stopped had HBGary Federal's employees taken a few 101-level password protection measures. Congress is now investigating the firm's relationship with the NSA.

Operation Sony

Anonymous's most recent effort is ongoing as of this writing: on January 11, 2001, Sony sued George Hotz and several others for "jailbreaking" (i.e., busting through intentionally placed limitations in a piece of hardware) and reverse-engineering a PlayStation 3 console. Sony accused Hotz of violating the Digital Millenium Copyright Act and committing computer fraud and copyright infringement. Hotz had fiddled with a PS3, and they wanted to prevent him from telling others how to pull it off. What's more, they acquired the IP addresses of visitors to Hotz's blog.

On April 17, Sony was attacked by an unknown entity, leading to the compromise of seventy-seven million accounts (along with personal information and credit card details), and a devastating twenty-four-day outage of Sony's PSN Network, where users play games against each other via the web. Some have speculated that Sony's reputation is so damaged that it will be forced to exit the "console wars."

Some representatives of Anonymous have denied involvement on behalf of the collective, but the coincidence is remarkable. The similarly silly and anonymous hacker group Lulz Security has claimed responsibility for the attack. On May 29, 2011, Lulz Security also successfully hacked PBS in retribution for an episode of *Frontline* that was perceived as unfair to WikiLeaks. Because they're operating anonymously and in a lulzy fashion (for example, posting news stories about Tupac Shakur's New Zealand whereabouts), they may as well be operating under the Anonymous banner. Their methods, motivations, and aesthetic are identical, however they don't seem to recruit or share Anonymous's populist ideals. And unlike Anonymous, they're a discreet group of skilled individuals which could conceivably be dismantled.

Gabriella Coleman guesses that it's impossible to know who is responsible for the Sony hack.

It's just impossible to verify, because there is a very well-organized cybercrime mafia that exists in Russia and Bulgaria and other places, and they can very much exploit what Anonymous is doing. There's a well-known security flaw at Sony, and the next thing you know they steal all the credit cards and then someone at Sony claims it's Anonymous. Or, maybe it really was Anonymous. No way of knowing.

From the beginning, Anonymous experienced lots of infighting because there is no clear managerial structure. Multiple groups claim to be the *real* Anonymous at any given moment. AnonOps itself was attacked by Anons who felt that the site's moderators were taking too much credit for Anonymous's victories, and attempting to establish hierarchies of control within the ranks. The rogue group was presumably led by a disgruntled

AnonOps admin named Ryan. Even worse, Ryan leaked the IP addresses of hundreds of registered AnonOps users. If the infighting has weakened Anonymous through wasted time and money spent getting servers back online, it has helped to solidify one of the group's most cherished principles: No one's in charge here.

I got in touch with another Anon, using the handle Anonymouse, who claims that he helped kick-start Operation Sony. Anonymouse immediately gave me a laundry list of misconceptions about 4chan and Anonymous. He too had been dealing with clueless reporters, and wanted to make sure I had a basic understanding of how his community works.

Anonymouse says he transitioned from observer to participant around August 2010. His role is PR, though he clarifies that nobody is assigned to a specific post within the ranks of Anonymous. It was just a need he felt equipped to meet. By the measure of most 4channers, Anonymouse is a newfag, having discovered 4chan after the "bincat" episode in 2010, when a woman was caught on security camera throwing a cat into a garbage bin. 4chan vigilantes harassed the woman, generating mainstream BBC news coverage about 4chan. Anonymouse's initial fascination with 4chan culture soon gave way to a greater passion for the political efforts of Anonymous.

Anonymouse claims that ops usually start off from chatter in anonymous IRC channels, coupled with recruiting on chan boards and Twitter. When enough people have gotten behind a particular endeavor, someone will create a unique IRC channel, which serves as a virtual base of operations. Recruitment for the legal elements (physical protests rather than hacks and DDoS attacks) continues to take place on various social networks.

It's important to remember that since anyone can claim to be Anonymous, and anyone can think of a cause to rally behind, not every operation announced by Anonymous represents anything close to an official, unified movement. The group is exceedingly amorphous, and operations live and die by the power of the word-of-mouth behind them. Movements are often announced with the distribution of poster-like images that detail the important elements of an operation, usually including a criticism of the offender, a description of the plan of attack, and a call to action, with links to appropriate IRC channels.

One poster passed around during Operation Sony reads:

Operation SONY
Do you really own your own property?

Should you go to jail for making your PS3 run your own programs?
iPhone jailbreaker George Hotz, or Geohot, altered the Sony Playstation 3 console to run homebrew applications. Sony then hit him with lawsuit after lawsuit.

Should you be sued for breaking an agreement you didn't make?
GeoHot never signed into the PlayStation network with his PS3 and never agreed to the terms of service (that changed AFTER he already purchased the system).

Should you have your personal information revealed for watching a YouTube video?
Sony demanded social media sites, including YouTube to hand over IP addresses of people who visited Geohot's social pages/ videos, as well as his PayPal Account.

Sony thinks so.
We don't.

Let's not allow Sony to commit this injustice. It's time to get
pissed OFF and not pissed ON.
On the 16th of April, go to your nearest Sony outlet and protest!
Bring your friends. Be pissed. Raise some noise.
Together, we shall make History.

Get in the IRC! Coordinate your protest!:
www.irc.lc/anonops/opsony
Join the Facebook Group: http://tinyurl.com/sonyprotest

Anonymouse tells me that Operation Sony began on the
AnonOps IRC channel, where we're chatting now, as an offshoot
of Operation Payback. He runs a channel called #recruit, where
he answers questions from curious /b/tards who wander over
from 4chan. moot and his mods try to ban users looking to recruit for raids under a policy likely put in place to disassociate
4chan with the illegal actions of Anonymous. Anonymouse and
his cohorts use dynamic IP addresses in order to evade the 4chan
"banhammer." According to Anonymouse, moot announced this
rule to prevent the Chan Wars, but he likely brought more attention to the ideological conflict between the chan admins, eventually igniting a chan war "of epic proportions, the likes of which
had never been seen."

Anonymouse, like many of the Anons I've spoken with, holds a
certain nostalgia for the pre-2007 4chan, claiming that it represents an Internet "before people started putting fences all over it."

The Internet is slowly becoming a closed system. You have to
register for almost everything and free registration sites are becoming paid ones. Couple that with government attempts to
exert control of what people can do or say online and you have
the attempted downfall of the biggest technological revolution

261

mankind has ever witnessed. The Internet has so much potential to make the world more free and enlightened.

Anonymouse is also quick to dispel the notion of the Dorito-munching neckbeard. He calls himself "an extremely social person" who feels that media misinformation is among the biggest threats to Anonymous.

> They screw up specifically because they don't get the concept of a "group" with no hierarchy, social structure, pecking order, or organization. The press are always looking for a "boss", but there isn't one. The FBI are the same.

Gabriella Coleman says that there must be a hierarchy, but it's flat. Certain people have to run IRC channels, for instance.

> Anons are creating propaganda, even the ones who aren't tech savvy. There's different groups of people who have authority and power but it's fragmented. That fragmented nature helps to distribute the power. There are some who are very powerful on one operation but not others. There are some that are powerful across the network, but only technically and not politically. It's kind of complicated, but what's clear is that there are some groups of people that carry a lot of authority. With the big operations, where they're DDoS'ing, there are technically people who are coordinating it.

I asked Anonymouse about a recent bit of coverage from Gawker regarding the HBGary Federal hack. Their reporter claimed that Anonymous really is a handful of legit hackers. (Incidentally, Gawker was hacked a few months prior by a group called Gnosis, exposing 1.2 million passwords. The attack allegedly had nothing to do with Anonymous.)

Anonymouse thinks that the press is asking the wrong questions, claiming that they tend to focus on the illegal hacks rather than the illegal acts that the hackers are able to expose. He says that most of the media coverage belies a "sick" acceptance of HBGary's activities, using government power to spy on its citizens. He draws parallels to the freedom-fighting actions of Anonymous and those of Bradley Manning and Julian Assange, who have also experienced a fair amount of negative press.

> How about prosecuting the soldiers named in one of the Afghan war diaries as having shot a bunch of unarmed teenagers? The number one response I've noticed when I argue about this is "Well this is the real world, corruption happens, deal with it." I'm left gaping. Sure it happens. Murder and rape happen too, does that mean we should just say "Oh sure we'll just leave the murderers alone, it happens. I don't understand it to be honest. "White collar crime" is somehow regarded as something which we should ignore.

HBGary Federal was developing software to influence public opinion polls by creating thousands of fake social networking profiles. From Anonymouse's perspective, this is about as antidemocratic as it gets, and Anonymous should be praised as heroes.

> Here's the really frightening part in my view. HBGary were a small, obscure security company. We only went after them because they tried to dox a bunch of us. It was an act of personal revenge at first, rather than actively hoping to expose crime. But look what happened. The can of worms we opened was millions of times bigger than anyone ever expected. Same kind of situation with Operation Payback. [A leak of fifty-three hundred IP

addresses collected by a UK firm because they were associated with pirating porn.] When the emails were leaked nobody expected the sheer amount of black ops which would be exposed. I guess you dream of a day when technology has empowered enough common people that it will be nearly impossible for any government entity or corporation to pull this kind of shit.

Now I put this question: Is the entire corporate world rotten to its core? If two tiny, obscure companies are involved in that level of corruption, what does it say about the bigger players?

About an hour into our conversation, Anonymouse claims that he's the guy who "created" Operation Sony, explaining how the movement evolved out of Operation Payback. He argues that the effort is essential because Sony was attempting to acquire private information about people who had merely viewed an online jailbreaking guide.

The idea that merely reading a piece of information could make you a legal target is terrifying. Here's an analogy: Making a bomb is illegal. But should you be arrested just for looking up the fact that gunpowder is made of Potassium nitrate, sulphur and charcoal in a rough 75/10/15 ratio?

When one looks at what Anonymous and WikiLeaks have been able to achieve, it almost seems possible that the utopian future of Anonymouse's dreams is attainable. He foresees a perhaps stateless world in which large organizations behave because they have no other choice. When information moves freely, corporations and civic leaders will be relentlessly held accountable by an informed public. Anonymouse is optimistic that the efforts of Anons will contribute to the breaking down of cultural and national barriers. It's pretty pie-in-the-sky stuff, but I can't help but feel energized about the future when talking to him.

Middle East Activism

Most recently, some Anons have been fighting for freedom of information in the Middle East, in what is perhaps the collective's most noble and important mission yet. In 2011, Amnesty International, the human rights NGO, focused its annual report on what could be called the "information economy." It recognized the Orwellian truism that he who controls information controls the world. Today's networking technology has placed new power in the hands of the people, which has enabled them to keep their governments more accountable. For one, information is more freely available. Also, social networking platforms give people an opportunity to initiate activism. Because freedom of information is an ideal all Anons seem to share, they are happy to fight censorship and promote truth across the globe, even if it doesn't generaste much lulz.

In January 2011, Anons (some Tunisian, some not) launched Operation Tunisia long before most Western media outlets had even reported the widespread unrest there. Anonymous initially became interested in Tunisia originally because of the country's censorship of WikiLeaks, but the protest took on a life of its own.

Anonymous accused Tunisian authorities of phishing operations (i.e., tricking users into giving away their passwords to obtain sensitive information and potentially remove criticism from blogs and social networking sites). Some journalists known for their criticism of the Tunisian government were targeted; in some cases their Facebook and Gmail accounts were hacked, and their blogs were shut down. Anonymous retaliated, successfully DDoS-ing eight websites, including those representing the Tunisian president, prime minister, the ministry of industry, the ministry of foreign affairs, and the stock exchange. Beyond the DDoSs, Anonymous created informational materials to guide dissidents on concealing their identities on the web. A few Anons developed a Firefox extension to protect Tunisians from phishing.

Anonymous also participated in the revolution in Egypt. They helped mirror sites that had been censored by the Egyptian government, brought down President Hosni Mubarak's website, and, in typical lulzy fashion, sent pizza deliveries to the country's embassies.

Go Go Go!

Anonymous has grown beyond 4chan, to the point where the media no longer mentions 4chan in reports on Anonymous. But according to Gabriella Coleman, the collective still uses 4chan as a recruiting tool. She says that there is an Anonymous that's very much still into trolling and raiding, and is sometimes upset with Anon's new moral dimension. But the Anons who are more politically minded, while still somewhat unpredictable, want to work with academics and journalists to get their message out.

Interestingly, Anonymous seems to care more about online offenses than, say, actual genocide. The attitude seems to be, "No way. Not on *our* Internet." Although Anonymous's inability to effect change off-line probably has something to do with their webby focus.

I've profiled just a few of Anonymous's biggest efforts. They've also attacked furries, pro-anorexia support groups, bestiality enthusiasts, the Westboro Baptist Church, and countless others lolcows. Whether the target be a random tween or a multinational corporation, all of these attacks lie somewhere on the spectrum between "for the lulz" and "for great justice." But of course, one Anon's justice is another's lulz.

Targeted by Trolls—The Spaghettios Girl Speaks

In 2010, an art piece performed by Natacha Stolz, a student at the Art Institute of Chicago, appeared on YouTube. The piece, called "Interior Semiotics," is daring, even among art house fare. In the video, a young woman opens a can of alphabet soup, which she'd previously filled with dirt. She mixes the dirt with water, creating mud, while reciting an obscenity-laced poem:

> Dirt is all around us, everything is shit. We apply meaning, value, and worth to the shit surrounding us. We live by this meaning, and by our words, we live by worth, and apply value, but, everything is shit.

She then smears the mud onto her shirt as the poem descends into monosyllabic babbling akin to glossolalia. She then puts down the can, pulls out some safety scissors, cuts a hole in her jeans. What happens next was the subject of some commenter controversy. Some thought she was masturbating and urinating. It turns out she was releasing tomato soup from her vagina, allowing it to spill forth onto a platform below. She then calmly wipes clean the platform and walks offstage as a few dozen art students applaud.

I asked Stolz to explain the piece in her words.

> The piece is about language and our relation to objects and value that they obtain. I used the structure of Schneeman's piece interior scroll and re-structured to talk about commodification. That's at least where I was thinking but all that doesn't come across in the video as parts of it are focused on the audience. The poem is suppose to be simple, repetitive and casual. When referring to shit I'm using the word since it has other meaning . . . not suppose to be just referring to feces but that's also an interesting layer.

Natacha says the piece was well received by the audience at the time, even by some students' parents. If this performance had been limited to those in attendance, it probably would have passed into the ether. Art students (and boy do these kids look like art students) are accustomed to seeing provocative performances. YouTube exposed Middle America to the video, and the righteous indignation that followed rung through the halls of the Internet. As one commenter put it, "Pretentious hipster bullshit."

Most of the attention came from 4chan, in a "You Rage You Lose" thread, where the motivation for trolling was driven not just by the usual lulz, but an undercurrent of class warfare. In Anon's eyes, here were a bunch of trust-fund hipsters smelling their own farts and calling it art. Spaghettios girl must be destroyed.

Stolz quickly traced the attention back to 4chan due to the memey language used in the hateful comments. When she started getting random friend requests on Facebook, she switched the name in the video description to a Facebook alias that she'd been using for another art project. As the video peaked five hundred views, the threatening phone calls and voice mail messages started coming in. Some asked if she could perform in private. Others propositioned her for sex. What could she do?

I wasn't sure what to do exactly, I reached out to some teachers but no one could get back to me. I wasn't so worried about someone confronting me in person, but I was really nervous about what it would mean as it soon was everywhere. When googling my name, it's almost the only thing that comes up. I was in class in September, and this girl I was sitting next to started watching the video during break. I was charging my computer in the back of the room and I heard the two students behind her mention Spaghettio's, then I was there standing behind all of them watching them watch the video and talk about it without them knowing it was me.

Stolz wisely retreated from the spotlight and did not engage with 4chan in a public way, though she did have some fun "messing with people" on /b/, a process she defines as trolling the trolls. As of this writing, the Interior Semiotics video has received over a million views. Stolz plans to integrate the experience into future work.

Chapter 9

The Anti-Social Network

Facebook in particular is the most appalling spying machine that has ever been invented. Here we have the world's most comprehensive database about people, their relationships, their names, their addresses, their locations and the communications with each other, their relatives, all sitting within the United States, all accessible to US intelligence. Facebook, Google, Yahoo—all these major US organizations have built-in interfaces for US intelligence. It's not a matter of serving a subpoena. They have an interface that they have developed for US intelligence to use.

Now, is it the case that Facebook is actually run by US intelligence? No, it's not like that. It's simply that US intelligence is able to bring to bear legal and political pressure on them. And it's costly for them to hand out records one by one, so they have automated the process. Everyone should understand that when they add their friends to Facebook, they are doing free work for United States intelligence agencies in building this database for them.

So declared WikiLeaks founder Julian Assange in May 2011 during an interview with Russian news site RT. A spokesman for Facebook responded to CNET:

> We don't respond to pressure, we respond to compulsory legal process . . . There has never been a time we have been pressured to turn over data [and] we fight every time we believe the legal process is insufficient. The legal standards for compelling a company to turn over data are determined by the laws of the country, and we respect that standard.

Facebook provides an increasingly invaluable service to its users, allowing them to connect and self-actualize in exciting new ways. But with convenience comes tension. Do we really want any single entity to possess so much of our private information? Many net-savvy types who don't have turned to anonymous IRC channels, message boards, and open-source alternative social networks like Diaspora to interact with friends, especially when engaging in activities of questionable legality.

Not surprisingly, 4chan is one of these places. The site's radical approach to online community (relative to other communities of its day) has shaped the tenor of the discussion on the site. Some have called it the Anti-Facebook, due to its refusal to track even bare-bones data on its users. The two sites were launched within a few years of one another. Both were built on shoestring budgets by young, hungry introverts who ganked the basic idea from someone else and made it work. Both are wildly successful, but in very different ways.

Facebook, with five hundred million users, dwarfs 4chan. Facebook emphasizes the cultivation of a robust identity. It maintains a closed system with a lot of rules. It made its founder billions of dollars, brought generations of people online and furthermore made them active. Facebook has redefined how humans communicate. Speaking purely in terms of scale, 4chan is a tiny playground for bored geeks in comparison.

In David Kirkpatrick's *The Facebook Effect*, Facebook founder Mark Zuckerberg famously declared:

> The days of you having a different image for your work friends or co-workers and for the other people you know are probably coming to an end pretty quickly . . . Having two identities for yourself is an example of a lack of integrity.

Facebook has struggled over the last few years to define its stance on privacy as it relates to the site's sometimes shockingly targeted advertising platform. And even the best privacy policy is rendered null when a massive security breach occurs. Zuckerberg wants to encourage what he calls radical transparency—which certainly sounds nice, but is it really best for you?

Facebook was originally a niche community of like-minded college kids, who turned to the site because they were unsatisfied with other services that did not offer exclusivity. Now that Facebook is full of moms, where do we turn to express ourselves the way we want?

In 2010, journalist Jeff Jarvis elucidated the public's increasing concern about Facebook's privacy policy.

> They conflate the public sphere with the making of a public. That is, when I blog something, I am publishing it to the world for anyone and everyone to see: the more the better, is the assumption. But when I put something on Facebook my assumption had been that I was sharing it just with the public I created

and control there. That public is private. Therein lies the confusion. Making that public public is what disturbs people. It robs them of their sense of control—and their actual control—of what they were sharing and with whom (no matter how many preferences we can set). On top of that, collecting our actions elsewhere on the net—our browsing and our likes—and making that public, too, through Facebook, disturbed people even more. Where does it end?

4chan offers a place where people are completely in control of their identity, allowing for expressions of opinions without repercussions. In a 2010 TED Talk, Christopher Poole explained his view on anonymity:

> The greater good is being served here by allowing people—there are very few places now where you can go and be completely anonymous and say whatever you like. Saying whatever you like is powerful. Doing whatever you like is now crossing the line, but I think it's important to have a place [like 4chan].

Poole outlined 4chan's core competencies and further explained his devotion to privacy in a spring 2011 South by Southwest keynote speech. He described a "loss of the innocence of youth," using the example of a child who moved to a new city and could reinvent himself in his new town. Or even an adult who got a new job and wanted to change the way he was perceived by coworkers. When you have a social network tracking your identity wherever you go, online and off, that sticks with you. "You can't really make mistakes in the same way you used to be able to," says Poole. "The cost of failure is really high when you're contributing as yourself."

When you're anonymous, it allows people to be more flexible and creative, and poke and prod and try a lot of things that they might not were they to have a little picture of their face next to all their contributions.

I think anonymity is authenticity. It allows you to share in a completely unvarnished, unfiltered, raw way. I think that's something that's extremely valuable. In the case of content creation, it just allows you to play in ways that you may not have otherwise. We believe in content over creator.

So where's the future? Will the Internet move inexorably toward proprietary networks that require identification, or will the open-source movement provide popular alternatives that cater to a public that, given the rise of Anonymous, seems to be growing more averse to a strong cross-platform identity? Some doomsayers have prophesied the end of the Internet as we know it, with companies like Facebook becoming so integral to the web experience that the open Internet will be seen as a Wild West–like blip in Internet history. Others believe the future lies with the freaks, the hackers, the Anons.

Hyperbole aside, it will probably be a mixture of both. Clay Shirky draws a metaphor from an old 1986 computer game created by LucasFilm called *Habitat*, considered to be the godfather of massively multiplayer online games like *World of Warcraft*. In the infancy of multiplayer gaming, software engineers' programming knowledge outstripped their understanding of social behavior, and their user experience decisions were not based on previous knowledge. One contentious game play element in *Habitat* was "Player vs. Player" or "PvP" killing. Experienced players were able to handily murder noobs, which made the game less fun for everyone but those who'd been there the longest. In addition, the very concept of virtual murder was controversial. It didn't take long for trolls to start randomly killing other players as they wandered around the virtual town. But if the engineers were to disallow PvP killing entirely, they would rob players of the thrill of danger and the joys of conquest. The moderators held a poll, asking if killing should be allowed in *Habitat*. The results were split 50/50. So they compromised. Killing would be disallowed inside the carefully manicured urban areas, but the moment you left town and headed out into the frontier, you were announcing to other players that you were down to scrap, if need be. This clever solution pleased most players, and continues to be the standard for many massively multiplayer games.

So will the Internet continue to look. Those who value safety over freedom will hang out on Facebook and other proprietary communities and mobile apps walled off with identity authentication. And those willing to brave the jungles of the open Internet will continue to spend time in anonymous IRC channels and message boards like 4chan.

Poole's keynote speech also spoke to 4chan's focus on meritocracy. Other communities that focus on identity, and on rewarding people with points, badges, and other accolades, develop strong hierarchies. Sometimes this is good. You want the smart people who continue producing compelling content to be rewarded.

But there are two ways this can go wrong. The first is encouraging self-promotion at the expense of quality content. You don't see social media gurus trying to game 4chan in the same way that they do Twitter and Facebook. The second is that it can put the focus on strong personalities rather than on strong content.

Longtime veterans of communities are organically given more respect and their words sometimes given more weight than they deserve. On 4chan, you're only as respected as your latest post. Its users are happy to let the hivemind take credit for their creative work for nothing in return but the private satisfaction of entertaining or informing one's /b/rothers and the sense of belonging that goes with it.

The success of 4chan as a meme generator has challenged everything we thought we knew about the way people behave on the web. People are willing to spend shocking amounts of time creating, collaborating, documenting—and all with no recognition. The implications are staggering. Give people a place that facilitates creation and sharing, and they will conjure entire civilizations (witness the overwhelming amount of lore preserved at Encyclopedia Dramatica).

While much of 4chan's content is pure wankery, there's something special at work there. 4chan allows its users to be jerks, but more importantly it provides a platform of social networking that focuses on what one is saying rather than who is saying it. For all you know, the guy who started a thread about particle physics on /b/ is Stephen Hawking. It's meritocracy in its purest form. The smartest, funniest, fastest, strongest content wins, regardless of how popular, good-looking, or renowned the post's author is. Anonymous neither accepts nor grants acclaim.

There are essentially twin themes that make 4chan what it is: the participatory creative culture and the spontaneous social activism. They can be seen as two manifestations of a process that social media researcher danah boyd calls "hacking the attention economy." Whether through creativity or creative destruction, 4chan's /b/tards (or lowercase *a* anonymous) and the politically oriented trolls (or capital *A* Anonymous) are exceptionally skilled at getting people to take notice, without spending a single dollar to promote their work. Neither of these capabilities could exist on Facebook at the same scale because they are only made possible by 4chan's emphasis on anonymity and ephemerality.

Many have speculated that if Christopher Poole had played his cards right, he could have made bank with a community as big and as dynamic as 4chan. I'm skeptical. The moment one tries to monetize something like 4chan is the moment it stops being 4chan. Poole would have had to place content restrictions in place in order to draw advertisers and sponsors. And without restrictions, no company in its right mind (aside from the lowest level of pornographers) would want to advertise on 4chan as is. Furthermore, turning 4chan into a profitable business would likely agitate the userbase to the point where it would revolt against 4chan. 4chan users have turned against the site in the past, and I'm sure that any attempt to make much more revenue than what's required to pay server bills would result in not just a mass exodus, but raids and trolls of epic proportions.

Poole recognized that. He rode the 4chan wave, gradually building a personal brand in order to generate interest from investors so he could finance Canvas. Many people in his place would have attempted to cash in a lot earlier, only to be met with failure. moot played it cool, managing the fringe elements of 4chan as best he could, learning through trial and error how online community works. I believe he was only able to pull it off because, like many start-uppers of his generation, he doesn't seem to be in it for the money. He wears the same plain hoodie and t-shirt at parties that he wears when speaking in front of thousands. He's a true nerd who was able to feed his passions through web community as a teen, and now he wants to give that experience to as many others as possible.

In its infancy, 4chan acted like a swirling tornado, traversing the geography of the Internet, picking up properties of the different web communities that came before it: the collaborative creativity of the Something Awful goons, the penchant for grossout content from Rotten, the anonymity of the Far East boards, the gleeful trolling of Usenet, and so on. 4chan collected all those characteristics and mashed them up into a unique slurry of content and community.

Throughout the past eight years, 4chan has grown large enough to get attention, and other communities have formed in its wake. Know Your Meme was created to analyze memes, Buzzfeed to report them, the Cheezburger Network to monetize them. Reddit was born, which built small fences around content creation and communication that corralled the creative culture of 4chan, with fantastic results.

But as 4chan has scattered pieces of itself throughout the web, it approaches mainstream. Does this mean the golden age of 4chan is over? Will it cease to be what it once was, when millions of people buy this book and learn all of its secrets?

"I'm not ready to say that 4chan's over," says Know Your Meme's Kenyatta Cheese. "If anything, 4chan will just go back to being the place it was a few years ago."

I'm with Cheese. As those twin themes of 4chan become increasingly embedded in the mainstream, 4chan will go back to what it was before it started getting write-ups in *The New York Times:* a place for bored teens to shoot the breeze. When I asked danah boyd if she thought 4chan had jumped the shark, she pointed out that a lot of 4chan users who were there from the beginning have become *literal* oldfags. If you were 15 when 4chan started, you're now 23, and most likely looking for something very different in your browsing experience. When I first discovered 4chan, I was captivated, but it's certainly not part of my daily routine. I have to imagine that the turnover rate for /b/ tards, at least (the enthusiast boards probably hold onto people's attention for much longer) is very high, in the same way that hanging out down by the railroad tracks is only interesting for a summer or two. But aren't those summers still supremely formative, even if it's just killing time? Even if 4chan has handed off its twin characteristics to the broader web, it still contains something inimitable that is now a part of the psyche of an entire generation, and, I predict, of generations to come. Pretty epic.

Epilogue

"Keep your money we do it for the lulz."

IN THE WEEKS since I finished writing this book, Anonymous has become a household name. The media still doesn't quite know what to make of it, and straight society is trying to figure out what it's all about. Are these individuals really a bunch of leaderless teenage geniuses? A cabal of trained anti-American terrorists? Do they represent the future of civil disobedience, or are we experiencing a brief burst of web-based pranksterism that will come to an end as soon as the rest of the Internet is able to adapt to their methods?

On June 12, the group attacked the websites of the Spanish Police in solidarity with three people who'd been arrested for their involvement with Anonymous (authorities have also arrested Anons in Britain, Australia, Spain and Turkey over the last few weeks). Three days later Anonymous attacked ninety-one Malaysian government sites in retaliation to their web censorship. The following week, Anon brought down several local government websites in Florida in response to the arrests of several members of a nonprofit who'd been feeding homeless people against Orlando city ordinance. Meanwhile, Anonymous dug up contact info for 2,500 employees of biotech giant Monsanto due to the company's business practices that, according to Anonymous, are marked by environmental unfriendliness.

The latest attack was widely reported on July 11. Anonymous leaked 90,000 emails taken from the servers of military intelligence contractor Booz Allen Hamilton. These sensitive documents contained correspondence between the company and members of various military branches, the Department of Homeland Security, the State Department, and others. Anonymous laid out their charges against Booz Allen Hamilton in a press release:

> Anonymous has been investigating them for some time, and has uncovered all sorts of other shady practices by the company, including potentially illegal surveillance systems, corruption between company and government officials, warrantless wiretapping, and several other questionable surveillance projects.

Furthermore, Anonymous has fractured into conflicting subgroups. The most important splinter group claims no affiliation with Anonymous: Lulz Security, or LulzSec, has snottily targeted several major corporations, claiming ownership of attacks and pranks on Fox, PBS, Sony, the CIA, and the FBI. Their motto: "The world's leaders in high-quality entertainment at your expense."

Throughout May and June of 2011, LulzSec alerted the public to a new high-profile hack every few days via the LulzSec Twitter account, which has amassed over 283,000 followers as of this writing. Rather than operating within the vast, anarchic Anonymous, LulzSec carved out a niche—a small cadre of hilarious trolls who all clearly know their stuff. They didn't recruit, but their ideology was similarly populist in nature. The group initially distanced themselves from the Anons, but banded with them during Operation Anti-Security, or AntiSec, an ongoing effort marked by vague anti-government sentiment. LulzSec released a maritime-themed press release calling all "lulz lizards" to action:

> We encourage any vessel, large or small, to open fire on any government or agency that crosses their path. We fully endorse the flaunting of the word "AntiSec" on any government website defacement or physical graffiti art . . . To increase efforts, we are now teaming up with the Anonymous collective and all affiliated battleships . . . Top priority is to steal and leak any classified government information, including email spools and documentation . . . If they try to censor our progress, we will obliterate the censor with cannonfire anointed with lizard blood.

In early June, cybersecurity firm Black & Berg issued a challenge, "Change this website's homepage picture and win $10K and a position working with Senior Cybersecurity Advisor, Joe Black." LulzSec hacked into the site, emblazoning the homepage image with their mascot, a monocled, wine-swilling stick figure, and to add insult to injury wrote "DONE, THAT WAS EASY. KEEP YOUR MONEY WE DO IT FOR THE LULZ" across the page. It wasn't even close to being LulzSec's biggest attack, but it so perfectly crystallized their mentality and exemplified their ethos of trolling for trolling's sake, with any political outcome perceived as a pleasant side benefit.

Rival factions with names like Team Poison, The A-Team, Web Ninjas, and a guy calling himself th3 j35t3r (leetspeak for "the jester") leaked the usernames of LulzSec's core members. After fifty days of mayhem, LulzSec abruptly called it quits, though it's likely many of the group's major players will continue to act under the banner of Anonymous or rebrand completely. Large organizations are likely scrambling to improve security measures, but they can only do so much to out-think a sprawling mass of devious computer geeks with anarchic inclinations. It's likely that Anonymous will exist for a long time, in one form or another, as long as there are a few people ready to exploit the missteps of the powerful, the corrupt, and the laughable.

Throughout my account of this curiously influential site, I traced the motivations that drive Anonymous, from the freedom-fighting proclivities of early hackers to the group's paradoxical obsessions with the revolting and the adorable. Closely linked with the rise of Anonymous is the story of "little-A anonymous," a phraseterm I've used to describe the broader movement of anonymous social interaction and content creation. There's no question that Anonymous has outgrown 4chan. Few pieces of media coverage even mention the site from which Anonymous spawned anymore. But I'm confident that when their hacktivism ceases to be a novelty, future historians will look back and recognize that the story of little-A anonymous is just as meaningful.

Acknowledgments

MANY THANKS TO everyone, from entrepreneurs and university professors all the way down to anonymous hackers, who took time away from more gainful pursuits to contribute interviews. To my wonderful agent Chelsea Lindman, for her faith in the project. To my editor Stephanie Gorton, for her insight and discernment, and to everyone at Overlook. To the team at Urlesque, for giving me a platform to expose the darker bits of the web. To Kelly Noonan, for her constant encouragement, to Chris Menning, for lending me his encyclopedic knowledge of memes, and to Nick Douglas, who contributed not only a keen understanding of web culture, but five years of unflagging enthusiasm for my creative work. Finally, to my parents, Clay and Glenda, and Uncle Bob, who surrounded me with love and books and a healthy appreciation for the peculiar.

Bibliography

4chan. "FAQ." http://www.4chan.org/faq.

4chan. "Rules." http://www.4chan.org/rules.

Aditham, Kiran. "SXSW Keynote: 4chan's Chris Poole Discusses Canvas, 'Fluid Identity.'" Mediabistro.com. Last modified March 13, 2011. http://www.mediabistro.com/agencyspy/sxsw-keynote-4chans-chris-poole-discusses-canvas-fluid-identity_b15564.

Anderson, Nate. "'Operation Payback' attacks to go on until 'we stop being angry.'" Ars Technica. Last modified September 30, 2010. http://arstechnica.com/tech-policy/news/2010/09/operation-payback-attacks-continue-until-we-stop-being-angry.ars.

Anonymous. "Anonymous:Response to The Media." Posted by Anon-Press. Last modified January 25, 2008. http://www.youtube.com/watch?v=pcr1trjtLaU.

Anonymous. "Message to Scientology." Posted by ChurchOfScientology. Last modified January 21, 2008. http://www.youtube.com/watch?v=JCbKv9yiLiQ.

Bibliography

"Anonymous member covered in pubes runs into scientology building." Posted by SDBSeth. Last modified January 10, 2009. http://www.youtube.com/watch?v=yrZk0C91mfg.

Anonymouse. Interview with the author. May 1, 2011.

Ashby, David. Interview with the author. March 30, 2011.

Ashby, Janet. "Hey Mr. Trainman." The *Japan Times* online. Last modified November 18, 2004. http://search.japantimes.co.jp/member/member.html?ek20041118br.htm.

Astley, Rick. "The 2009 TIME 100." Time.com. Last modified April 30, 2009. http://www.time.com/time/specials/packages/article/0,28804,1894410_1893837_1894180,00.html.

BBC. "Activists target recording industry websites." Last modified September 20, 2010. http://www.bbc.co.uk/news/technology-11371315.

Bernstein, Michael S., and Andrès Monroy-Hernández, Drew Harry, Paul Andrè, Katrina Panovich, and Greg Vargas. "4chan and /b/: An Analysis of Anonymity and Ephemerality in a Large Online Community." Massachusetts Institute of Technology & University of Southampton, 2011.

boyd, danah. "'for the lolz': 4chan is hacking the attention economy." Zephoria. Last modified June 12th, 2010. http://www.zephoria.org/thoughts/archives/2010/06/12/for-the-lolz-4chan-is-hacking-the-attention-economy.html.

boyd, danah. Interview with the author. May 28, 2011.

Brand, Stewart. Interview with the author. May 8, 2011.

Bright, Peter. "Anonymous speaks: the inside story of the HBGary hack." Ars Technica. Last modified February 15, 2011. http://arstechnica.com/tech-policy/news/2011/02/anonymous-speaks-the-inside-story-of-the-hbgary-hack.ars.

Brophy-Warren, Jamin. "Modest Web Site Is Behind a Bevy of Memes."

The *Wall Street Journal* online. Last modified July 9, 2008. http://online.wsj.com/article/SB121564928060441097.html.

Brown, Janelle. "The Internet's public enema No. 1." Salon. Last modified March 5, 2001. http://www.salon.com/technology/feature/2001/03/05/rotten/index.html.

c0s. Interview with the author. May 1, 2011.

Cheese, Kenyatta. Interview with the author. May 25, 2011.

Chen, Adrian. "How the Internet Beat Up an 11-Year-Old Girl." Gawker. Last modified July 16, 2010. http://gawker.com/5589103/how-the-internet-beat-up-an-11+year+old-girl.

Chen, Adrian. "Stupid California Police Warn Parents of Pedobear, the 'Pedophile Mascot.'" Gawker. Last modified September 12, 2010. http://gawker.com/5636011/stupid-california-police-warn-parents-of-pedobear-the-pedophile-mascot.

Coleman, Gabriella. "Phreaks, Hackers, and Trolls and the Politics of Transgression and Spectacle." In *The Social Media Reader*, ed. Michael Mandiberg. New York: NYU Press, forthcoming.

Coleman, Gabriella. Interview with the author. May 14, 2011.

Curtis, Drew. Interview with the author. May 4, 2011.

Dawkins, Richard. *The Selfish Gene*. Oxford: Oxford University Press, 1976.

Dawkins, Richard. Interview with the National Public Radio. August 30, 2010. http://www.npr.org/templates/transcript/transcript.php?storyId=129535048

DeGrippo, Sherrod. Interview with the author. April 22, 2011.

Denton, Nick. "The Cruise Indoctrination Video Scientology Tried To Suppress." Gawker. Last modified January 15, 2008. http://gawker.com/5002269/the-cruise-indoctrination-video-scientology-tried-to-suppress.

Dibbell, Julian. "A Rape in Cyberspace." *The Village Voice*. December 23, 1993.

Dibbell, Julian. Interview with the author. May 26, 2011.

Dibbell, Julian. "Mutilated Furries, Flying Phalluses: Put the Blame on Griefers, the Sociopaths of the Virtual World." *Wired*. Last modified January 18, 2008. http://www.wired.com/gaming/virtualworlds/magazine/16-02/mf_goons?currentPage=2.

Dolgins, Adam. *Rock Names*. Secaucus: Citadel Press, 1998.

Doane, Seth. "A Day with Golden-Voiced Ted Williams." CBS News. Last modified January 5, 2011. http://www.cbsnews.com/8301-500803_162-20027506-500803.html.

Doctorow, Cory. "Anonymous infighting: IRC servers compromised, IP addresses dumped, claims of coup and counter-coup." Boing Boing. Last modified May 10, 2011. http://boingboing.net/2011/05/10/anonymous-infighting.html.

Emmett, Laura. "WikiLeaks revelations only tip of iceberg – Assange." RT. Last modified May 3, 2011. http://rt.com/news/wikileaks-revelations-assange-interview/.

Encyclopedia Dramatica. "Hal Turner." http://encyclopediadramatica.ch/Hal_Turner.

Fark post. "Judge determines unsolicited finger in anus is crude, but not criminal." Last modified March 12, 2004. http://www.fark.com/cgi/comments.pl?IDLink=869740.

Fark post. "It's official. A two-mile stretch of Tennessee highway has been adopted by 'Drew Curtis' TotalFark UFIA.' Link goes to a photo of the sign." Last modified April 3, 2006. http://www.fark.com/cgi/comments.pl?IDLink=1993763.

Figallo, Cliff. Interview with the author. April 14, 2011.

Fox News. "Report: Steve Jobs Heart-Attack Hoax a Teen Prank."

Last modified October 24, 2008. http://www.foxnews.com/story/0,2933,443962,00.html.

Frank, Ted. Interview with the author. May 5, 2011.

Frommer, Dan. "Here's How BuzzFeed Works." *Business Insider*. Last modified June 11, 2010. http://www.businessinsider.com/heres-how-buzzfeed-works-2010-6.

Furukawa, Hideki. "Q&A With the Founder of Channel 2," in "Japan Media Review" via the Online Journalism Review. Last modified October 22, 2003. http://www.ojr.org/japan/internet/1061505583.php.

Greenberg, Andy. "Amid Digital Blackout, Anonymous Mass-Faxes WikiLeaks Cables To Egypt." *Forbes*. Last modified January 28, 2011. http://blogs.forbes.com/andygreenberg/2011/01/28/amid-digital-blackout-anonymous-mass-faxes-wikileaks-cables-to-egypt/.

Grossman, Wendy M. "alt.scientology.war." *Wired*. December 1995. http://www.wired.com/wired/archive/3.12/alt.scientology.war.html.

Harold C. "Hal" Turner v. 4chan.org et al. Filed January 19, 2007. http://dockets.justia.com/docket/new-jersey/njdce/2:2007cv00306/198438/.

Haughey, Matt. Interview with the author. May 24, 2011.

Heffernan, Virginia. "The Hitler Meme." *The New York Times* online. Last modified October 24, 2008. http://www.nytimes.com/2008/10/26/magazine/26wwln-medium-t.html?pagewanted=all.

Heilemann, John, and Mark Halperin. *Game Change: Obama and the Clintons, McCain and Palin, and the Race of a Lifetime.* New York: Harper, 2010.

Huh, Ben. Interview with the author. April 1, 2011.

Hwang, Tim. Interview with the author. March 29, 2011.

Iezzi, Teressa. *The Idea Writers*. Basingstoke, UK: Palgrave Macmillan, 2010. 55-61, 169-175.

Ikeler, Marci. Interview with the author. May 27, 2011.

Jarvis, Jeff. "Confusing *a* public with *the* public." Buzz Machine. Last modified May 8, 2010. http://www.buzzmachine.com/2010/05/08/confusing-a-public-with-the-public/.

Jenkins, Henry. "Critical Information Studies For a Participatory Culture (Part One)." Confessions of an Aca-fan. Last modified April 8, 2009. http://www.henryjenkins.org/2009/04/what_went_wrong_with_web_20_cr.html.

Johnson, Joel. "What Is LOIC?" Gizmodo. Last modified December 8, 2010. http://gizmodo.com/5709630/what-is-loic.

Katayama Lisa. "2-Channel Gives Japan's Famously Quiet People a Mighty Voice." *Wired*. Last modified April 19, 2007. http://www.wired.com/culture/lifestyle/news/2007/04/2channel.

Katayama Lisa. "Meet Hiroyuki Nishimura, the Bad Boy of the Japanese Internet." *Wired*. Last modified May 19, 2008. http://www.wired.com/techbiz/people/magazine/16-06/mf_hiroyuki?currentPage=all.

Kirkpatrick, David. *The Facebook Effect: The Inside Story of the Company That Is Connecting the World*. New York: Simon & Schuster, 2010.

Know Your Meme. "It's Over 9000 Penises." Last modified July 17, 2010. http://knowyourmeme.com/memes/its-over-9000-penises#.Tf JI10ea9xM.

Know Your Meme. "Tom Green Raids." Last modified June 07, 2009. http://knowyourmeme.com/memes/tom-green-raids#.TfJHF0 ea9xM.

KTTV. "Anonymous." KTTV Fox 11 Los Angeles. July 26, 2007.

Lamb, Scott. Interview with the author. May 24, 2011.

Lee, Chris. "Rebecca Black: 'I'm Being Cyberbullied.'" The Daily Beast. Last modified March 11, 2009. http://www.thedailybeast.com/blogs-and-stories/2011-03-17/rebecca-black-friday-and-cyberbullying/.

Liveleak. "Twisted Girl Throws Puppies in River." Last modified August 30, 2010. http://www.liveleak.com/view?i=bb4_1283184704.

LoseTheGame.com. "FAQ." http://www.losethegame.net/faq.

Lueg, Christopher, and Danyel Fisher. *From Usenet to CoWebs: Interacting with Social Information Spaces*. New York: Springer, 2003.

Macsai, Dan. "Cheezburger Network CEO: I Can Has Media Empire?" Fast Company. Last modified October 8, 2009. http://www.fastcompany.com/blog/dan-macsai/popwise/cheezburger-networks-ceo-i-can-has-media-empire.

Malda, Rob. "AC = Domestic Terrorists?" Slashdot. Last modified July 28, 2007. http://yro.slashdot.org/story/07/07/28/1145204/AC--Domestic-Terrorists.

Malda, Rob. Interview with the author. May 9, 2011.

Margulies, Lynne, and Joe Orr. *I'm From Hollywood* (documentary film). Directed by Lynne Margulies and Joe Orr. Joe Lynne Productions Inc., 1989.

Masnick, Mike. "Since When Is It Illegal To Just Mention A Trademark Online?" Techdirt. Last modified January 5, 2005. http://www.techdirt.com/articles/20050105/0132239.shtml.

McCarthy, Kieran. "Cat eating video causes mayhem." The Register. Last modified August 30, 2001. http://www.theregister.co.uk/2001/08/30/cat_eating_video_causes_mayhem/.

Nakamura, Lisa. Interview with the author. May 10, 2011.

Newman, Ron. "The Church of Scientology vs. Dennis Erlich, Tom Klemesrud and Netcom." Last modified March 23, 1997. http://www2.thecia.net/users/rnewman/scientology/erlich/home.html.

Bibliography

O'Farrell, Brad. Interview with the author. May 24, 2011.

OhInternet. "An Hero." http://ohinternet.com/An_hero.

OhInternet. "Boxxy." http://ohinternet.com/Boxxy.

OhInternet. "Chris Forcand." http://ohinternet.com/Chris_Forcand.

OhInternet. "Adam L. Goldstein." http://encyclopediadramatica.ch/Adam_L._Goldstein.

OhInternet. "Pedobear." http://ohinternet.com/Pedobear.

Okeh, Ndee. "The Protochannel and the First Channel—Ayashii World and Amezou World—The Grandparents of the Western Imageboard Culture." Last modified March 21, 2011. http://yotsubasociety.org/node/2.

Okeh, Ndee ("Jkid"). Interview with the author. June 3, 2011.

Paskin, Willa. "Antoine Dodson Gets a Reality Show." *New York Magazine*. Last modified January 21, 2011. http://nymag.com/daily/entertainment/2011/01/antoine_dodson_gets_a_reality.html.

Peretti, Jonah. "Mormons, Mullets and Maniacs." New York Viral Media Meetup. August 12, 2010.

Poole, Christopher ("moot"). "The case for anonymity online." Last modified February, 2010. http://www.ted.com/talks/christopher_m00t_poole_the_case_for_anonymity_online.html.

Poole, Christopher. "IAM Christopher Poole, aka 'moot,' founder of 4chan&Canvas." Originally posted March 29, 2011. http://www.reddit.com/r/IAmA/comments/gdzfi/iam_christopher_poole_aka_moot_founder_of_4chan/.

Price, Christopher. Interview with the author. June 1, 2011.

Raftery, Brian. " King of Cheez: The Internet's Meme Maestro Turns Junk Into Gold." *Wired*. Last modified January 25, 2010. http://www.wired.com/magazine/2010/01/mf_cheezking/2/.

Ragan, Steve. "Anonymous' Operation: Sony is a double-edged sword." The Tech Herald. Last modified April 5, 2011. http://www.thetech herald.com/article.php/201114/7017/Anonymous-Operation-Sony-is-a-double-edged-sword.

Raymond, Eric. "September That Never Ended." http://www.catb.org/jargon/html/S/September-that-never-ended.html.

Reddit. "I am William J Lashua's Grandson. Please read this." Last modified September 2, 2010. http://www.reddit.com/r/reddit.com/related/d8uyh/i_am_william_j_lashuas_grandson_please_read_this/.

Rendit. "Hello Discerning Consumer of Internet." Last modified December 28, 2010. http://rendit.tumblr.com/post/2498287662/summerofmegadeth-scenes-from-a-meatup-relative.

Reisinger, Don. "Assange: Facebook is an 'appalling spy machine.'" CNET. Last modified May 3, 2011. http://news.cnet.com/8301-13506_3-20059247-17.html#ixzz1LNaW3qw2.

Rheingold, Howard. Interview with the author. May 5, 2011.

Ross, Bryan. "Guilty Plea in NFL Dirty Bomb Hoax." ABC News. Last modified February 28, 2008. http://blogs.abcnews.com/theblotter/2008/02/guilty-plea-in.html.

Rotten. "Censorship @ Rotten Dot Com." Last modified May 1997. http://www.rotten.com/about/obscene.html.

Rutkoff, Aaron. "Sean Connery Delivers A Line That Eventually Sparks an Internet Fad." The *Wall Street Journal* online. Last modified November 7, 2005. http://online.wsj.com/article_email/SB112801537556955862-lMyQjAxMDE1MjA4NzAwMTc1Wj.html.

Ryan, Yasmine. "Tunisia's Bitter Cyberwar." Al Jazeera. Last modified January 6, 2011. http://english.aljazeera.net/indepth/features/2011/01/20111614145839362.html.

Sausage, Eddie Lee. "Some Notes Toward a History of Shut Up, Little Man!" Last modified 2008. http://shutuplittleman.com/history.php.

Schonfeld, Erick. "Time Magazine Throws Up Its Hands As It Gets Pwned By 4Chan." TechCrunch. Last modified April 27, 2009. http://techcrunch.com/2009/04/27/time-magazine-throws-up-its-hands-as-it-gets-pwned-by-4chan/.

Schwartz, Mattathias. "The Trolls Among Us." *The New York Times* online. Last modified August 3, 2008. http://www.nytimes.com/2008/08/03/magazine/03trolls-t.html.

Shii. Interview with the author. March 30, 2011.

Shirky, Clay. *Cognitive Surplus: Creativity and Generosity in a Connected Age*. New York: Penguin Press HC, 2010. 17-20.

Shirky, Clay. Interview with the author. May 24, 2011.

Shirky, Clay. "Tiny Slice, Big Market." *Wired*. Last modified November 2006. http://www.wired.com/wired/archive/14.11/meganiche.html?pg=2&topic=meganiche.

Slyck. "Gene Simmons Directly Threatens Anonymous With Legal Action, Jail Time." Last modified October 17, 2010. http://www.slyck.com/story2088_Gene_Simmons_Directly_Threatens_Anonymous_With_Legal_Action_Jail_Time.

Smith, Hortense. "New Viral Video Hero Comes With Complications." Jezebel. Last modified August 1, 2010. http://jezebel.com/5601835/the-new-viral-video-hero-comes-with-complications.

The Smoking Gun. "Another 4chan Fan Arrested On Federal Charges," Last modified February 14, 2011. http://www.thesmokinggun.com/documents/internet/another-4chan-fan-arrested-federal-charges.

The Smoking Gun. "Arrested Man Credits 4chan With Helping Him Grow His Child Porn Collection." Last modified May 18, 2011. http://www.thesmokinggun.com/buster/child-pornography/4chan-child-porn-bust-657210.

Stirland, Sarah Lai. "'Don't Tase Me, Bro!' Jolts the Web." *Wired*. Last modified September 19, 2007. http://www.wired.com/threat level/2007/09/dont-tase-me-br/.

Stolz, Natacha. "Interior Semiotics." Last modified March 27, 2010. http://www.youtube.com/watch?v=I9lmvX00TLY.

Stolz, Natacha. Interview with the author. May 24, 2011.

Sulake. "Habbo Hotel—Where else?" http://sulake.com/habbo/?navi=2.

Tate, Ryan. "Apple's Worst Security Breach: 114,000 iPad Owners Exposed." Gawker. Last modified June 9, 2010. http://gawker.com/5559346/apples-worst-security-breach-114000-ipad-owners-exposed.

Templeton, Brad. Interview with the author. May 9, 2011.

Thorpe, David. Interview with the author. May 5, 2011.

Walker, Rob. "When Funny Goes Viral." *The New York Times* online. Last modified July 16, 2010. http://www.nytimes.com/2010/07/18/magazine/18ROFL-t.html?_r=2&ref=magazine.

Webb, Rick. Interview with the author. May 3, 2011.

Wei, William. "Where Are They Now? The 'Star Wars Kid' Sued The People Who Made Him Famous." Business Insider. Last modified May 12, 2010. http://www.businessinsider.com/where-are-they-now-the-star-wars-kid-2010-5.

Wei, William. "Where Are They Now? 'Numa Numa Guy' Is Creating The Next CollegeHumor." Business Insider. Last modified June 18, 2010. http://www.businessinsider.com/where-are-they-now-the-star-wars-kid-2010-5.

Wikichan. "The Complete History of 4chan." http://wikichan.net/The_Complete_History_of_4chan#2003.

Wortham, Jenna. "Founder of a Provocative Web Site Forms a New Outlet." *The New York Times* online. Last modified March 13, 2011.

Bibliography

http://www.nytimes.com/2011/03/14/technology/internet/14poole
.html.

Zetter, Kim. "Palin E-Mail Hacker Says It Was Easy." *Wired*. Last
modified September 18, 2008, http://www.wired.com/threatlevel/
2008/09/palin-e-mail-ha/.

Index

298

Index

Index